GRIEF AND ENGLISH RENAISSANCE ELEGY

GRIEF AND ENGLISH RENAISSANCE ELEGY

G. W. PIGMAN III

California Institute of Technology

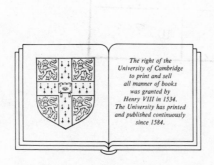

CAMBRIDGE UNIVERSITY PRESS

Cambridge

London   New York   New Rochelle

Melbourne   Sydney

Published by the Press Syndicate of the University of Cambridge
The Pitt Building, Trumpington Street, Cambridge CB2 1RP
32 East 57th Street, New York, NY 10022, USA
10 Stamford Road, Oakleigh, Victoria 3166, Australia

First published 1985

Printed in Great Britain at
the University Press, Cambridge

Library of Congress catalogue card number: 84–45450

British Library Cataloguing in Publication Data
Pigman, G. W.
Grief and English Renaissance elegy.
1. Elegiac poetry, English – History and criticism
2. English poetry – Early modern, 1500–1700 – History and criticism
I. Title
821′.009   PR539.E45

ISBN 0 521 26871 0

For Celeste

CONTENTS

vii

ACKNOWLEDGMENTS

I have incurred many debts while writing this book. An Arnold L. and Lois S. Graves Award and Caltech's Division of Humanities and Social Sciences gave me the time to begin my research. I would like to thank Roger Noll, then chairman of the division, for arranging a supplement to the Graves Award. The wonderful resources of the Huntington Library and the cooperation of its staff greatly facilitated my work. For permission to reprint the sections of chapters 2 and 6 which originally appeared in their pages I thank the editors of *English Literary Renaissance*. My editors at Cambridge University Press were very helpful; Andrew Brown offered me shrewd advice, and Eric Van Tassel meticulously and promptly edited the manuscript. Edith Huang of Caltech's Computer Support Services provided indispensable assistance while I was phototypesetting the book.

Thomas M. Greene encouraged me, at a time when I sorely needed encouragement, to stay with my first attempts at understanding Renaissance funeral poetry, and his careful reading of the first draft of the manuscript clarified the direction it was taking. I am deeply grateful to him for his support of all of my work since my days as a graduate student. Stephen Marmer helped me learn most of what I know about mourning. The advice, criticism, and friendship of Jerome McGann sustained me throughout the revision of the manuscript. I would also like to thank John Benton, Louis Breger, Ronald Bush, Margaret Ferguson, David Glidden, Daniel Javitch, W. T. Jones, and Annette Smith for their comments on various drafts. My wife, Celeste Moore, improved every draft, but that is not the only reason I dedicate the book to her.

INTRODUCTION

I began the research for this book in an effort to understand two
lines in one of the most famous poems in the language:

> And O ye *Dolphins*, waft the hapless youth.
> Weep no more, wofull shepherds weep no more....

This leap from plaintive helplessness to authoritative consolation
has troubled many readers of 'Lycidas'. How can the speaker's
voice change so abruptly and dramatically? Infusion of grace?
Intervention of Michael the archangel? Neither of these solutions
seemed persuasive to me, and although I had no explanation to
offer, I remained convinced of the unity of 'Lycidas'. My own
groping for an explanation led me to Milton's allusive criticisms
and revisions of pastoral elegy, particularly Virgil's *Eclogue* 10
and Theocritus' *Idyll* 1. It occurred to me that what gave the
poem its unity was Milton's insistence on the inability of pastoral to console for death; Milton was triumphantly opposing
Christian consolation to pagan mourning. I was rather pleased
with this interpretation – even though it did not explain the shift
of voice – until I asked myself what was Christian about consolation, what was pagan about mourning, and what were the attitudes of Milton and his contemporaries to consolation and
mourning?

When I began to investigate these questions, my understanding of mourning in Renaissance England was largely restricted to
the lines from *Twelfth Night* which I have prefixed to the second
chapter, and to Jonson's 'Of Death'.

> He that feares death, or mournes it, in the iust,
> Shewes of the resurrection little trust.

Here was confirmation of the notion that mourning was unchris-
tian. I had no suspicion that Jonson is far from representative
of the early seventeenth century: his attitude towards mourning
is a throwback to the 1550s. I did not realize that attitudes

1

towards mourning changed significantly during the English Renaissance, but I quickly learned that I was not alone because literary and cultural historians have paid little attention to mourning despite a number of studies on death and the *ars moriendi* tradition.

Attitudes to mourning begin to change towards the end of the sixteenth century. In the early part of the century Englishmen are acutely anxious about grief, which they regard as subversive of the rule of reason and domestic and social order. The bereaved are likely to feel – and be made to feel – that their grief reveals their irrationality, weakness, inadequate self-control, and impiety. The major purpose of consolation is to induce the bereaved to suppress grief, and authorities on the letter of consolation deploy a battery of reasons in their attack on the bereaved, oblivious to what George Eliot calls 'that insensibility to another's hardship which applies precept to soothe pain'. Some theologians condemn all mourning as evidence of lack of faith, and others allow a moderation in mourning which hardly differs from complete suppression of grief. By the first decades of the seventeenth century total condemnation of mourning entirely disappears from the moral and theological tracts, while increasingly more tolerant conceptions of moderation take its place. Sympathy for bereavement is more prominent than anxiety at exceeding the bounds of moderation. In the letter-writing formularies condolence ceases to be an opening gambit, a ploy to secure the bereaved's attention before marshalling reasons to give over grief; it becomes an integral part of the letter, occasionally its major purpose.

This historical sketch of the emergence of a more compassionate and less anxious attitude towards mourning requires a few qualifications and explanations. First, the more sympathetic attitude does not replace the more severe one, which is still held by a number of people today, and Jonson, to take the most extreme example, is a reminder that the emergence of sympathy is neither uniform nor unilateral. Second, the reasons for the shift in attitude are obscure, and it seems to me that it is too early to offer an explanation. Not enough is known about the history of the emotions and of the family, and more detailed studies are needed, not grand attempts at synthesis on the basis of inadequate information. Third, I am describing attitudes towards mourning more than actual feelings of bereavement:

what people believed they should feel and the reasons why they felt it necessary to control or suppress their feelings.[1] Attitudes towards feelings and the feelings themselves are, of course, intimately related, and one of the crucial factors which determine the course of mourning is the attitude which the bereaved hold towards the emotions in general and grief in particular. Fourth, the increasing tolerance of mourning does not mean that people felt less sorrow and distress at the deaths of their loved ones in the sixteenth century. The existence of so many instructions for letters of consolation and of so many religious and moral strictures suggests that mourning seriously disturbed large numbers of people. It is hard to believe that so much anxiety about mourning arises unless people *are* mourning. What changed was the ability to live with the process of mourning in oneself and in others.[2]

What does this change in attitude towards mourning have to do with elegy? For most of the sixteenth century poets are anxious about the mourning contained in their poems and often express sorrow only to turn upon themselves for indulging in it, but towards the end of the century defensiveness about mourning becomes less pressing and persistent, and this self-abusing reversal ceases to be so common. An ideal of personal expression of grief begins to replace critical self-restraint, and one occasionally finds simple and direct expressions of loss instead of wildly hyperbolic grief. The history of elegy from Surrey to Milton reveals the same shift in attitude towards mourning as do the letter-writing treatises and the moral-theological tracts. In fact, some of the evidence from elegy is earlier and stronger, and the popularity of elegy as a form occurs at the very time that attitudes towards mourning are relaxing.[3]

Chapter 4, through an examination of several collections of elegies, both Latin and English, traces the shift in elegy from 1551 to 1638, the year of the first publication of 'Lycidas', but a characterization of the poems of the five major elegists treated in chapters 5 to 7 will provide a more dramatic sketch of the development of elegy. My interpretations of these poets focus on expression of grief, from the conflicts arising from Jonson's blocked mourning to the simple, uninhibited sorrow of King's 'Exequy'. I focus on the ways that poets express or avoid expressing grief in full awareness that many of them are not personally grieving. Scores of poets who have little or no personal attachment to the subjects of their elegies choose to write as if personally grieving instead of restricting themselves to encomium, an option which remains available throughout the period. Their grieving verse presents an image of what they consciously or unconsciously feel to be appropriate mourning and apppropriate funeral poetry and thus helps to chart the development of Renaissance elegy. Even though an ideal of sincerity in elegy arises towards the end of the sixteenth century, as one can see from the frequent attacks on artificial grief, the issue of sincerity is not as important as what are perceived as the feelings a bereaved person should have and how these feelings are expressed in verse.

Surrey has considerable difficulty when he tries to express sorrow, and his elegy becomes awkward when he makes a transition from praise of the deceased to his own feelings. He circumvents this difficulty in his most successful elegy, 'So crewell prison', by allowing lament for his dead friend to emerge almost spontaneously in a meditation on two different periods of residence in Windsor Castle. Spenser wrestles with the moral problem of grief which occupies the consolers and theologians examined in chapters 1 and 2. 'November', as becomes apparent from the imitation of Marot, centers on a major dilemma of Christian mourning, the coexistence of grief and joy. In *Dapnaida* Spenser offers an *exemplum* of excessive grief, but no explicit condemnation of it. Jonson's elegy cannot be properly understood without reference to the severest theological position on mourning, which is presented in chapter 2. His elegy contains almost no expression of sorrow that is not at once rejected; some of the poems, in particular 'On My First Sonne', are especially moving because of a tension between contradictory desires to express and suppress grief. King's 'Exequy' is shockingly different from anything written by Surrey, Spenser, or Jonson. King achieves an intimacy of address and a simple expression of affection and sorrow that is unmatched in the period, although approached by passages in Milton.

What about 'Lycidas' itself and the abrupt movement from lament to consolation? How does the poem fit into the development of elegy and the change in attitudes towards mourning? Once one examines earlier elegiac reversals which repudiate the mourning which precedes consolation, the change in voice turns out to be not as startling as the gentle tone in which the consolation is delivered. 'Lycidas' is an unusually defiant poem, which challenges God's ordering of the universe, but the consoling voice that delivers the 'Weep no more' speech does not rebuke the angry questions which precede. The mature, even serene, acceptance of the process of mourning at its most disturbing is a major part of the greatness of 'Lycidas', and the originality of this acceptance is all the more striking for the earlier condemnations of grief. As for the transition from lament to consolation itself, Milton's imitation of Virgilian and Theocritean pastoral proves to be important, but not because Milton feels that mourning is pagan. Milton adapts the precedent from *Eclogue* 10 and *Idyll* 1 that the subject of lament delivers the final speech after a procession of mourners and the tradition that a prosopopoeia of the dead is a fitting conclusion for consolation. Along with a crucial convention from ancient hymns these adaptations allow one to see that the most sympathetic consolation in English elegy is spoken by the spirit of Lycidas himself.

The Psychology of Mourning

There are two primary reasons for invoking contemporary psychological theory in a study of Renaissance elegy. First, a comprehensive theory of the process of mourning makes it possible to confirm the commonsense view that elegy represents a form of mourning. Currently, the dominant scholarly opinion runs that elegy is the poetry of praise, a branch of epideictic rhetoric. Although it is undeniable that many elegies are no more than encomia, it is hard to explain why, if lament is essentially an indirect kind of praise, the bereaved are so frequently urged to give over their grief or why poets so frequently rebuke themselves for expressing it. On the other hand, psychological theory has no difficulty explaining the presence of praise in laments or the displacement of lament by praise. Even poems which are pure encomia are part of the process of mourning because idealization of the dead is one of the commonest occurrences in bereavement.

Second, if one remains within Renaissance views of the motives and purpose of consolation – a desire to help the bereaved by curing their grief – one cannot account for the pervasive recognition of the inefficacy of consolation or for the consoler's hostile tone. Although preceptors of consolation realize that the bereaved usually reject the customary barrage of reasons not to grieve and rarely take comfort from consolation, they continue, until the early seventeenth century, to advocate the same sort of attack on grief rather than something else – for instance, sympathetic support for the painful work of mourning. Since the Renaissance account of consolation yields a disquieting paradox – why cause pain if you know it will not be effective – one has to look elsewhere for an explanation, and contemporary theories of mourning provide the clue: for the consoler, in prose or in verse, consolation is a defense against the breakdown of an ideal of rational self-sufficiency.

The major controversies in the psychological literature concern issues which are not crucial for this study.[4] To a nonspecialist, most of these disputes seem either terminological or ideological; agreement on matters of substance is profound. Mourning is the process set in motion by the death, or sometimes by the anticipation of the death, of a person to whom the bereaved is attached.[5] In everyday speech 'grief' is a synonym for 'mourning', and some theorists prefer it as the technical term, but there are advantages to distinguishing between the two.[6] I use 'mourning' to refer to a process and 'grief' to refer to an emotion, intense sorrow. This distinction makes it possible to realize that the condition first described by Helene Deutsch as 'absence of grief' is a form of mourning.[7]

The essential concept for understanding the process of mourning is denial.[8] Mourning, in the words of Martha Wolfenstein, is a 'painful and protracted struggle to acknowledge the reality of the loss'.[9] The stages of mourning represent the development of this acknowledgment at the expense of the desire to deny the loss. Unresolved mourning represents the triumph of denial; the bereaved clings to the dead to avoid conflicts of guilt and self-reproach or suppresses grief as if no loss had taken place.

Since the major types of unresolved mourning are exaggerations, prolongations, or delays of the stages of mourning, let us consider the stages first. They do not form a linear progression, but overlap to a certain extent, and an individual may oscillate from one to another. It is difficult to assign periods of time to any stages except the first, as so much depends on circumstances of bereavement such as the nature of the relationship with the deceased, the kind of death, the bereaved's age, personality, and attitude towards the emotions.

The first stage is numbing. It usually begins shortly after the bereaved learns that death has occurred, and may last as long as a week. Outright disbelief of the death is a common response. Normal behavior may continue automatically as if nothing had happened, or violent and sudden outbursts of distress and anger may interrupt the numbness. Numbing serves as a psychological buffer which allows the loss to be absorbed gradually.[10]

In numbing the loss is often explicitly denied or disputed; feeling freezes to avoid something which might overwhelm. In the second stage, yearning and searching, the loss is recognized intellectually and is beginning to be accepted emotionally, while at the same time the bereaved behaves as if the dead could be recovered. Yearning can last for months, sometimes years.

In this stage the bereaved intensely longs for and is preoccupied with the dead, relives in memory events leading up to the death, loses interest in people and things that used to be enjoyable, sobs, cries aloud, breaks into tears, wanders about restlessly, suffers from insomnia, or has fits of anger. This stage is characterized by outbursts of distress and anxiety and can be the most alarming to the bereaved because they may fear they are on the verge of breakdown. Many adults share the feelings of a nine-year-old boy who

vividly evoked the awful prospect of unstoppable grief that would overwhelm children if they were not able to 'forget' about a painful loss: 'They would cry and cry. They would cry for a month and not forget it. They would cry every night and dream about it, and the tears would roll down their eyes and they wouldn't know it.'[11]

Particularly alarming, both to the bereaved and to those who try to comfort them, are the strong, apparently unmotivated outbursts of anger which come from 'nowhere'.

Some anger after a death is usually directed at the deceased for abandoning the bereaved, even though many adults will not admit, either to themselves or to others, that they feel such an emotion.[12] Some anger results from the frustration of the search for the lost object. Anger is often directed at people held responsible for the death, and comforters are often greeted with anger, since even if the consoler is sympathetic, part of the bereaved wants to recover the lost person rather than be reminded of the death. One must insist upon anger as a reaction to death because this emotion is usually just as important in mourning as sorrow, although not nearly as widely recognized: various kinds of anger often occur in Renaissance elegy.

A certain amount of ambivalence characterizes all strong attachments. Since it is normal to be angry at the deceased for desertion, death tends to exacerbate ambivalent feelings. A common way to handle them is to split off the positive and negative components. The deceased is idealized, and anger is directed towards someone else or towards the self, in which case guilt is the result. The greater frequency and intensity of guilt in abnormal mourning often correspond to a greater degree of ambivalence, although the bereaved can feel guilty for surviving or for imaginary or real responsibility for the death.

Yearning is the emotional counterpart of searching for the lost object, and much of the behavior of the bereaved becomes comprehensible once one realizes the powerful wish to recover the dead and the searching which it initiates. The restless wandering of this stage is not aimless after all; its goal is to find the lost person. Searching explains the phenomenon of being mysteriously drawn to or consciously revisiting places frequented by the dead, as in Hardy's poems on the death of his first wife.

During the third stage of mourning, despair and disorganization, a decrease in yearning and anger indicates that acceptance of loss is increasing, as repeated frustrations of the search for the dead drive home the finality of loss.[13] As unconscious hope in the possibility of recovery dies away, memories which have been spurring the bereaved to search for the deceased tend to produce a passive sadness. In this stage a sense of the continuous presence of the dead may replace the wish for recovery. The bereaved may feel the lost person a perpetual companion or imagine him or her in an appropriate place such as the grave or a favorite chair. The bereaved may feel that he or she has become more like the dead or even that the dead is somehow within.

During the final stage of mourning, recovery and reorganization, emotional acceptance of the death is nearing completion. The bereaved may become free to form new attachments, although this depends greatly on circumstances. The old attachment, however, does not disappear. As Freud wrote to Ludwig Binswanger in 1929,

Although we know that after such a loss the acute state of mourning will subside, we also know we shall remain inconsolable and will never find a substitute. No matter what may fill the gap, even if it be filled completely, it nevertheless remains something else. And, actually, this is how it should be. It is the only way of perpetuating that love which we do not want to relinquish.[14]

All writers on the subject regard unresolved mourning as an exaggeration or abbreviation of aspects of normal mourning. The two major variants of abnormal mourning are extensions of different stages: absence of grief prolongs and exaggerates numbing, while chronic mourning extends the second and third stages, yearning and despair. These two variants sometimes combine. A long period of numbing may yield to a long and incapacitating period of chronic mourning. In both variants denial of the loss is hindering its acceptance.

In absence of grief the bereaved appear to be unaffected by the death, which does not greatly disrupt their life. People who suffer from this condition tend to be proud of their self-reliance and of their control over their emotions, which they often consider weaknesses. They will almost surely view tears as evidence of weakness and are probably afraid of emotional breakdown. They may already be incapable of feeling or become so if they cannot feel and understand their loss. Their condition is particularly unfortunate because it may easily escape the attention of others, who believe that recovery is taking place. In fact, others may encourage suppression of grief, because grief usually upsets those who witness it. The condition is usually unhealthy because suppressed grief disturbs the bereaved's life in some seemingly mysterious way: for example, compulsive caretaking of others, or hysterical symptoms of the illness which caused the death. More commonly the bereaved becomes depressed without knowing why or feels that relations with others are hollow and unsatisfying.

Chronic mourning is much easier to identify than absence of grief because the characteristics of normal grief are prolonged and exaggerated. Anger, often accompanied by self-reproach and guilt, persists intensely. Despair gives no sign of ending, and the bereaved's life does not become reorganized. Thoughts of suicide are common; some successful attempts occur. Wishing to win back the dead, the sufferer may preserve everything the way it was before the death or may unconsciously recreate relations with another that try to duplicate those with the deceased in an effort to undo the death.

Any attempt to understand why one person is able to work through the stages of mourning to recovery and why another is not must take into consideration a wide range of factors. Besides the nature of the relationship with the deceased and the kind of death, the most important factor is the bereaved's personality and the experiences which have molded it. People likely to suffer from disordered mourning usually have personalities disposed to form anxious and ambivalent relations, to take compulsive care of others, or to assert independence of emotional ties. The second two types of personality try to deny the importance of their own emotions. They submerge their own needs and feelings in the care they bestow on others or do not let themselves become attached. These people are not in touch with their feelings, which they are likely to view with suspicion, and hold to an inflexible standard of self-control. In short, one of the most important factors determining the course of a bereavement is the attitude which the bereaved has towards the emotions in general and in particular towards grief and the process of mourning itself. A clear conception of the attitudes towards grief in Renaissance England is important for understanding the feelings which bereaved individuals were likely to experience and the expression of those feelings in the elegy of the period.

Chapter 1

THE ANGRY CONSOLER

But truly, you deal with me like a physician that, seeing his patient in a pestilent fever, should chide him instead of ministering help, and bid him be sick no more. (Sidney, *The Countess of Pembroke's Arcadia*)

Consolations for death are as old as anything in literature, and the commonplaces of consolation are remarkably tenacious, as if those who use them are bent on proving there is nothing new under the sun.[1] Nevertheless the modern reader of sixteenth-century literature is likely to be struck by the harsh tone of its consolations. The consoler often sounds angry, chides, and gives reasons why the bereaved should not mourn. By the beginning of the seventeenth century a shift in feeling has occurred, and some of the letter-writing formularies, the foremost repository of precepts for consolation, prescribe a gentler, less domineering type of consolation. The change in attitude is clearest in the different role assigned to expression of sympathy. The letter of consolation is becoming the letter of condolence.

The sixteenth century inherits some important assumptions from ancient consolation. First, man is distinguised from the beasts by his possession of reason, a higher faculty than the 'passions';[2] man is most human when most rational. Second, the pain of bereavement stems from mistaken ideas about death, not from the rupture of an emotional bond. Third, it is shameful and egotistical to feel sorrow for one's own loss. The traditional consoler considers himself a physician waging war against diseases of the mind. His major instrument or weapon is reason; his purpose, to extirpate grief by proving that it is irrational to be sad. He thinks of grief as Massinger's Welborne does of love: 'Wounds of this nature are not to be cur'd / With balms, but corrosives.'

11

Shaming the Bereaved: Erasmus

Erasmus' extraordinarily popular and influential *De conscribendis epistolis* (1522) neglects none of the important arguments against grief and contains the shrewdest discussion of the consoler's psychological strategies of any ancient or Renaissance text.[3] Although Erasmus devises his precepts with close attention to ancient practice and does not create a category for which one cannot find an earlier example, he is the first to elaborate a system and make its psychological foundations explicit. Guided by his sure sense of decorum, the accomodation of speech to the circumstances of its utterance, Erasmus presents three types of personality and their reactions to bereavement.

The first case allows a direct approach, and Erasmus pays little attention to it.

una simplex et aperta, per quam argumentis declaramus non esse causam dolendi: quum viro sapienti nihil accidere possit triste praeter turpitudinem, neque a quoquam laedi possit nisi a seipso. Huiusmodi validis pharmacis utemur, quoties nobis cum philosopho aut alioqui viro cordato res est. (pp. 432–33)

One method is simple and straightforward; we prove with reasons that there is no cause for grief because nothing miserable can befall the wise man besides dishonor, and because he cannot be harmed by anything but himself. We will use robust drugs of this type whenever we are dealing with a philosopher or some other judicious man.

Erasmus can pass over this case so quickly – he says nothing else about it and gives no example – because he appears to share Cicero's conviction that this Stoic argument only works with those wise men who do not need consolation (*Tusculanae disputationes* 3.77).

In most cases the consoler must proceed by indirection. Some people have firmer spirits, suppress their grief, and do not wish to seem in need of consolation; they resemble those who regard illness as disgraceful, hide their pain, and refuse to summon a doctor.

His hac arte erit obrependum, ut negemus nos consolandi gratia scribere, quum multis modis perspectam habeamus illius eximiam sapientiam, tum infractam animi magnitudinem omnibus fortunae procellis maiorem, tametsi fatebimur casum esse eiusmodi ut alium quemlibet facile possit deiicere, tamen non dubitare nos quin homo a puero verae philosophiae praeceptis institutus, longo rerum usu doctus, ad haec invicto quodam animi robore praeditus, fortiter ferat quod ex communi mortalium lege vitari non potest; nos illius fortitudini gratulari velle potius quam dolori mederi. (p. 433)

We must sneak up on these people with this stratagem: we say we are not writing for the sake of consoling because we have seen in many ways his excellent wisdom and his unbroken greatness of mind superior to all the storms of fortune; even though we admit the accident to be of a kind to cast down easily anyone you will, nevertheless we do not doubt that a man raised from a boy on the precepts of true philosophy, taught by long experience, and furnished with a kind of unconquered strength of mind will bravely bear that which is inevitable because of the common law of humanity; we wish to rejoice in his fortitude rather than cure his grief.

This sentence shows quite clearly how the consoler tries to stifle grief, at least its expression, without appearing to console. By flattering the bereaved, the consoler simultaneously grants and takes away permission to grieve. Anyone might grieve at such a misfortune, but the bereaved would demean himself by falling to the level of anyone. The consoler attempts to imprison the bereaved in a cultural ideal, and this is an effective strategy, since the individual's self-esteem is intimately connected with living up to society's ideals.

Erasmus respects people of this kind, 'who from a kind of modesty of noble mind suppress and conceal any great grief of the spirit' ('qui pudore quodam generosae mentis, quamlibet magnum dolorem animi premunt ac dissimulant', p. 433). He does not respect the other class which must be approached indirectly, people of infirmer spirit who are totally possessed by grief. They are to be treated like lunatics who imagine themselves to have horns, scales, or long noses, and who detest anyone who does not feel as they do, but love those who go along with them. Here, then, is the place for condolence; one simulates grief and proceeds as if one were consoling oneself. Expressions of sympathy serve the same function which T. S. Eliot ascribes to meaning in poetry: they are bits of meat which the burglar tosses to the watch-dog so that he can go about his business. Erasmus does not even consider the possibility that a consoler might really sympathize.

After these different introductory strategies, Erasmus recommends a common procedure: reasons why death is not the evil it appears to be, examples of famous men who have bravely borne misfortune, an exhortation to resume former virtues, and a concluding offer of assistance. He realizes that consolation can assume a hectoring tone. He cautions the consoler not to appear to lecture or command and advises the bereaved to reply to an imperious consoler with 'We easily give proper advice to the sick when we are healthy. If you were in my place, you'd feel differently' ('facile quum valemus recta consilia aegrotis damus. Tu si hic fies, aliter sentias', p. 464; Erasmus is quoting Terence, *Andria* 309–10). This awareness makes the severity of Erasmus' examples all the more striking. I am not referring to the brief 'Familiar Consolation with My Reprimand' ('Consolatio familiaris cum obiurgatione mea'), a series of sharp, chiding questions interspersed with exhortations. Nor to the briefer 'Jesting and Familiar Consolation' ('Consolatio iocosa et familiaris'), which ridicules a husband's grief at the death of his 77-year-old wife, and of which its most recent editor says, 'On imagine mal qu'une pareille lettre ait pu jamais être adressé à un correspondent' (p. 463). I have in mind the fictive letter to Antonius Suketus on the death of his son, originally the *Declamatio de morte*, which Erasmus intends to be humane and sensible, not domineering or rebuking.

The letter oscillates between seeking to moderate and condemning grief despite protestations of its legitimacy and of personal sympathy. It takes away with one hand what it gives with the other and places the bereaved in an emotional and intellectual bind. After exordial condolence, the letter alternates general reasons not to grieve with coercive *ad hominem* rhetoric, lists several examples of fortitude in enduring bereavement, quashes the father's complaint about the untimeliness of his son's death, imagines the son's stern speech from heaven, and concludes with a catechistical summary.

One does not know whether to be more impressed by the vehemence or by the brevity of Erasmus' sympathy. For three sentences he cannot control his tears, needs consolation himself, and would be inhuman and shameless if he tried to prohibit a father's grief. Yet after three more sentences he is urging Suketus to cast off all grief at once.

Quanquam enim hoc fortunae telum, paternum pectus altius ferire debuit, tamen illud tibi praestare solet singularis sapientia, ut omneis casus humanos, non solum forti et infracto, verumetiam alacri perferas animo. Proinde tibi constes oportet, ut animi dolorem, omnino iustissimum (quis enim neget?) si nondum potes abiicere, certe premas et modereris. Cur autem non etiam abiicias? (p. 442)

14

And all be it, that the ilke stroke of Fortune oughte deper to perce your fatherly breast: yet your great wysedome was wont so to rule you (in all your dedes) that ye nat onely with a stronge and a stoute mynde, but also with a glad and a mery chere, wolde suffre and passe ouer all suche chaunces as happe to mankynde. wherfore ye oughte so to settell your selfe, that if ye can nat as yet put awaye clene the sorowe of your harte (for no man can denye but that ye haue ryghte good cause to be heuy) yet at the least wyse some what suppresse and moderate the same dolour. And for what cause shulde ye nat clene forgette it? (sig. A2ʳᵛ)

In the very act of praising Erasmus insinuates that Suketus will lose his reputation for wisdom if he does not continue to live up to the standards he has maintained. By assuming that Suketus will moderate his grief, the ostensible goal of consolation, Erasmus can proceed to do what he has just said would be inhuman and shameless, prohibit all grieving. This is the last one hears of the justness of this grief or of Erasmus' own until the end of the letter.

Holding Suketus to the ideal of the Stoic wise man, Erasmus harps on the insanity and futility of grief. He slants his favorite argument – death is common to all – so that grief brands the bereaved as claiming self-indulgent exemption from the fate of humanity.[4] The self-control of his *exempla* is nearly absolute. Their usual reaction is not to be moved at all, and their fortitude of spirit is a challenge to Christians, who should be ashamed to be surpassed by pagans – and female pagans at that.

After cataloguing the miseries of this life, Erasmus allows the son, who may be laughing at and condemning 'our' grief, to strike the final blow from heaven. (One may well wonder whose grief, as Erasmus has not mentioned his own since the opening sentences.) The son asks whether they envy his felicity, since he has escaped all the miseries of the world, or whether he has deserved their hatred so much that they would recall him to earth. He demolishes their one defense – 'But ye say, that you on your part wepe and make lamentation' (sig. C3ʳ; 'At nostram ipsorum vicem ploramus, inquitis', p. 454) – by calling it an argument of the selfish and showing that he is of more use to them as an intercessor with God than he ever could have been on earth. Erasmus concludes the son's address by asking Suketus, 'If that your sonne (I saye) shulde saye these wordes to vs: myghte we nat well be ashamed thus to lament and mourne as we do?' (sig. C3ᵛ; 'Haec, inquam, si nobis loqueretur filius, nonne merito nostri luctus nos pudesceret?', p. 455). If Suketus does not feel ashamed of his grief by this point, it is through no fault of Erasmus.

Wilson and the Rule of Reason

The section on consolation in Thomas Wilson's *Arte of Rhetorique* (1553) is heavily indebted to Erasmus. Wilson, like Erasmus, hammers away against the folly and futility of grief, uses *sermocinatio* to dispose of the bereaved's complaints of untimely death, and believes that the universality of death is the most comforting reason not to grieve. Moreover, all but one of Wilson's classical *exempla* of restraint are in Erasmus. There are significant differences, however. Wilson has greater faith in straightforward appeals to reason and relies less on manipulations of the bereaved's self-image in the battle against grief. His greater faith in reason accompanies a greater anxiety about the emotions. He is more worried by the theological implications of mourning, which he apparently believes Christianity condemns as despair and faithlessness. The tone of his letter is not as angry, although it is bullying from time to time. In a word, Erasmus makes the bereaved feel ashamed of grief, while Wilson makes him or her feel guilty. Erasmus simultaneously condones moderate grief and argues that all grief is unworthy of a self-respecting man; Wilson allows a modicum of grief while suggesting that any grief reveals sinful weakness.

'Reason' echoes throughout the *Arte*; in the four-page preface alone the word appears fourteen times. This preface recounts the origins of man and society with the apparent purpose of exalting the importance of eloquence. What emerges is a frightening picture of anarchy when the rule of reason is not maintained. The Fall ended the domination of reason over the passions, and the Hobbesian state of nature was the result, until God 'stirred up his faythfull and elect, to perswade with reason, all men to societye'.[5] From Wilson's point of view, anything which might subvert reason threatens the dissolution of society and a return to bestiality. The stakes are thus very high for the consoler; he must restore the rule of reason lest chaos come again.

Wilson cannot make up his mind exactly how just a cause for sorrow death is. Before presenting his example of comfort, he asserts that death, as a 'harme' which must happen to everyone, should 'bee moderately borne' (p. 83), but towards the end of the letter he quotes 1 Thessalonians 4.13–14 as a condemnation of all mourning, not just immoderate mourning. The latter passage suggests that Wilson adheres to the Christian tradition which prohibits mourning as despair and faithlessness, a tradition we shall examine in the next chapter, but at other times Wilson only insists on moderation, the position of the majority of Christians since Ambrose.[6]

A sentence from Wilson's dedicatory letter to *Vita et obitus* captures his uncertainty about the status of mourning.

Caeterum ex omnibus maxime ingemiscendum est (si tamen est ingemiscendum) heroum Suffolciensium lamentabile desiderium: et optandum (si tamen est optandum) ut nulla talis aliquando calamitas nos omni dignissimos calamitate afflictaret. (sig. A2ᵛ)

Moreover, out of all [these deaths from the sweating sickness] we must especially groan over (if really we should groan over) the lamentable loss of the Suffolk heroes, and we must wish (if really we should wish) that no such calamity ever afflicts us who deserve every calamity.

Just as emotion takes charge, an intellectual reservation intrudes, not to forbid the emotion, but to call it into question. The overall impression which Wilson's uncertainty makes is that moderate mourning, although not forbidden, is a dangerous weakness that should be overcome as quickly as possible. His concession to mourning is guilt-ridden and anxiety-producing; the bereaved is left with the apprehension that mourning may be a sin and will certainly turn into one if not suppressed. And how long does one have to master grief? Wilson mentions a Bibulus, who lost both his sons at the same time and mourned for only one day.

And what coulde a man doe lesse than for two children to lament but one daie: and yet in my mynde he lamented enough and euen so muche as was reason for hym to do, whose doynges if all Christians woulde folowe, in my iudgement they shoulde not onely fulfill natures rule, but also please God highly. (p. 101)

Erasmus uses the same *exemplum* without drawing any such radical conclusion (p. 447), and Seneca, the ultimate source for the story, asks Wilson's question, but leaves the matter at that (*Consolatio ad Marciam* 14). Since this is what Wilson means by moderation, he is hardly more lenient than those who prohibit all grief.

Wilson's 'example of comforte' is the letter which he wrote Katherine Brandon, the mother of Henry and Charles, Dukes of

Suffolk, on their deaths in 1551. Wilson was tutor to Charles, the younger son,[7] and edited a volume of memorial poems in Latin and Greek, to which he prefixed a biographical sketch of the brothers. The *Arte* abounds with laudatory references to them, and the model encomium is in their honor. Wilson was surely trying to maintain the favor of Katherine Brandon by paying so many tributes to her children. Both admiration for the brothers and self-interest suggest that Wilson believes his letter of consolation an acceptable offering to their mother – in any event, not harsh or offensive – and he realizes the dangers to which a consoler exposes himself, 'For all extreme heauinesse, and vehement sorowes, cannot abyde comforte, but rather seeke a mourner that woulde take parte with theim' (p. 83).

Wilson, unlike Erasmus, is constantly raising the drama of mourning to the religious plane. He insists on viewing the Brandons' deaths as God's judgment on English sinfulness, particularly the 'vnsaciable couetousnesse' which oppresses the poor. Their deaths reward their virtuous lives by removing them from this wretched world and warn others to amend their own. Wilson does not even spare Katherine Brandon herself.

And I doubt not but your grace is thus affected, and vnfaynedlye confessinge youre owne offences, taketh this scourge to come from God as a iuste punishment of Sinne, for the amendemente not onelye of your owne selfe, but also for the amendemente of all other in generall. (p. 87)

A few sentences later Wilson assures her that she is not especially to blame: 'And yet I speake not this, as thoughe I knewe anye cryme to be more in you, then in anye other' (p. 88). These words insist on her guilt even while they are exonerating her from a larger share than anyone else. Wilson is encouraging her to feel guilty in the faith that guilt will redirect her sorrow away from her children towards the state of her soul. Wilson makes the point again and again: we should mourn our sins and amend our lives rather than lament the dead.

Wilson's harsh attitude towards mourning stems from his obsession with the rule of reason and correspondent suspicion, if not terror, of the emotions. This obsession is what draws him towards the sterner Christian position on mourning, not the other way round. His attitude towards mourning is part of a pattern of beliefs and behavior in his writings and life.

First, for Wilson, living is largely a question of willpower. In the commendation of justice Wilson declares his faith in the will.

The wise of all ages, inspired by God, have established just patterns of behavior.

Therefore, if we doe not well, we must blame our selues, that lacke a wil, and do not cal to God for grace. For though it appere hard to do wel, because no man can get perfection without continaunce: yet assuredly to an humble mynde that calleth to God, and to a willyng harte that faine would do his best, nothing can be hard. (p. 42)

Wilson's attitude towards the will is guilt-ridden and guilt-producing. Any failing is a sign of insufficient effort; any failure to suppress a passion or to act in accordance with virtue or the law is laid squarely on the head of the offender.

Second, along with this cult of the will goes great devotion to order, law, and punishment. In fact, the commendation of justice is really a paean to force and punishment: 'But thankes be to God, we hang theim a pace that offende a lawe, and therefore we put it to their choise, whether they will be idle and so fal to stealyng, or no: they knowe their rewarde, go to it, when they will' (p. 42). Wilson's passion for social order also appears in his obsession with male superiority; he is disturbed by the violation of hierarchy implicit in placing the mother first in the phrase 'My mother and my father' (p. 189; cf. pp. 26, 96). After his return from Italy, Wilson devoted his political career to law and order. In the words of A. J. Schmidt, 'He terrorized his queen's enemies until his name became a byword with them.'[8] In the autumn of 1571 Wilson conducted several examinations in connection with the Ridolfi conspiracy; he put two servants of the Duke of Norfolk to the rack, 'and so engrossing was this occupation that he took up his residence, and wrote letters "from prison in the Bloody Tower"'.[9] Doubtless Wilson's own imprisonment and torture at the hands of the Inquisition in Rome in 1558 did not mitigate his hatred of Catholicism. This hatred was returned by English Catholics in exile in the Netherlands, who threated to kill him because of his violent antipapist policy. In the parliament of 1571 Wilson argued for retaining the law which punished usury by death and for the imprisonment of sturdy beggars.[10] The following year he demanded before Parliament the death of Mary, Queen of Scots.[11] In all of these activities one can see Wilson fighting valiantly for what he considers the rule of reason, ruthlessly crushing all those who set themselves against it.

The English Formularies

Sixteenth- and seventeenth-century English authors produced a mass of formularies containing precepts and examples for letter writing. Most of the works written in English were intended for a middle-class or unlearned audience; Latin formularies continued to be used in the schools throughout the seventeenth century.[12] For many years the English formularies do not offer a version of consolation substantially different from Erasmus'.[13] In the seventeenth century, however, they do suggest a shift in sensibility, although not as strongly nor as early nor as consistently as the moral and theological tracts and funeral poetry. Moderation continues to be advised, but some model letters of consolation become less harsh and chiding and more tolerant of grief.

In the anonymous *Prompters Packet of Private and Familiar Letters* (1612) one begins to notice more concern with condolence than in earlier letter-writing formularies. Condolence is still reserved for the beginning of the letter and yields to forceful reasons to moderate grief, but no longer seems so transparently a form to be gone through before the real business of consolation. The consoler is learning how to convey sympathy more convincingly and spends more time in condolence. In the first letter, for example, the consoler declares he is afraid of stirring up tears, has waited until both his and the bereaved's grief have abated, and needs comfort himself because the deceased was bound to him by election instead of blood. He laments the early death which has moved so many people; the deceased left 'nothing behinde him but sorrow and teares, and a desire alwaies to bewaile him, alwaies to wish for him'. Nevertheless, condolence is still an opening gambit. The consoler cuts short his profession of grief, 'But what doe I meane to be carried away thus by griefe from my purposed end? Let vs leaue all sorrow, and rather enuious of his felicitie, then mooued with his losse, let vs reioice at his fortune' (sigs. E5^v–6^r).

Nowhere is a shift in sensibility more evident than in *A Speedie Post With certaine New Letters* (1625) by I. W., Gent.[14] Condolence carries the day.

The bitter newes of the death of P. Q. hath so throwne downe and mortified me, that being ioyned to the little health wherein I am, leaues me no sense to any thing, but to sorrow: and if my heart had beene of

20

yron, when I read your letter, it would haue beene a powerfull Adamant, to haue drawne from my eyes a riuer of teares. (sig. G2ᵛ)

This opening to 'Condoling the death of a friend' is not a ploy to win the bereaved's goodwill because no attempt is made to repress grief. There is only implicit consolation in the assurance that P. Q. is in heaven and that his fame on earth will never die. Another letter, simply called 'Condoling', also offers no consolation. I quote it in its entirety.

Our Reuered friend C. S. is passed to a better life. I rest comfortlesse, for so great a losse: and liue in a manner, that it well appeares I liue without ioy, and cannot tell whether I may take comfort, that, that happy soule loued mee much, or whether I may weepe, that he left me so soone: I will weepe, for to wretched and miserable men, nothing is more comfortable then teares. (sig. G3ʳ)

The personal focus of the letter is quite striking once one remembers the earlier condemnation of self-love in the bereaved. C. S. is removed to heaven, and this consideration does not check grief, but rather allows the condoler to dwell on his own loss. I. W. does not completely break with consolation, however. His brief 'Aduertisement and condoling of a friend vpon the death of his mother' is by no means severe, but does hold the son to an ideal of masculine self-restraint. Once again I quote the whole letter.

What is this life? but a short and cloudy winters day, wherein many are cut off in the morning; others at mid-day, and few see the euening: but your mother hath finished her course neere the last houre; with that puritie, and innocency of life, as she began the first: it is a great comfort, to all vs that are akin, and to you in particular, that is her sonne: who mee thinkes I see betweene the affection of zeale and loue to your mother, and the Decorum of manly fortitude, passe ouer this accident, with your wanted [sic] prudence. Whereby nothing remaines to tell you concerning this: but for your greater consolation; that in my armes shee yeelded vp her spirit. (sig. G3ᵛ)

The insistence upon self-restraint may be due to the great age of the deceased, but this insistence accompanies a consolation that soothes the feelings rather than strengthens the reason: the mother's death in the arms of a friend.

Cupids Messenger (1629) resembles *The Prompters Packet* more than *A Speedie Post*, but nevertheless shares the new emphasis on condolence.

The acquaintance I had with your vertuous wife (honest friend) makes me feele the sense of her loss, for hee that can be insensible of the losse

of a good woman, is an alien to nature, and a rebell to all morall vertues.... Giue me leaue to ask you why you mourne, I meane not why
you mourne outwardly; which is an old custome and a matter of for-
mality, but why doe you mourne inwardly, which is the true sorrow:
you will say (I say) for the losse of a companion.

The reader familiar with earlier letters of consolation expects the
consoler to proceed to prove that this loss is actually no loss
because the letter appears to be following the usual pattern of
condolence giving way to rebuke. The continuation is a
surprise.

Indeed you doe well, for as a man was solitary before God gaue him
one, so should he be after God takes her away: but there is a meane in
all things. To be hard hearted is beast like, to bee tender is effeminate,
to be sensible is manly. (p. 3)

The consoler, to be sure, does not let himself be carried away
justifying the bereaved, but sympathy is on the rise.

This brief survey of the English formularies shows that
assumptions about the purpose and method of consolation and
attitudes towards grief changed within a century after Erasmus'
seminal *De conscribendis epistolis*. After Erasmus, almost no
consolers consider a category of bereaved who scorn consolation
out of lofty self-sufficiency. Only Angel Day, who follows
Erasmus more closely than anyone, includes this category,
although several authors use the corresponding topos of apolo-
gizing for giving advice to the expert. Consequently, condolence
becomes the opening for almost every letter of consolation. In
the first decades of the seventeenth century the letter-writing formularies begin to devote more attention to expression of sympathy, which occasionally overshadows or even eliminates the
repression of grief by argument. Even when the letters use the
old tactics to make the bereaved ashamed of grief, they rarely
sound as angry as Erasmus. In 1640 one even finds a defense of
immoderate mourning, although almost all authors hold to a
conviction that moderation of grief is morally, socially, or reli-
giously necessary.[15] Thus, the formularies reveal a definite trend
towards greater tolerance of grief, and I take this as one sign that
this disturbing emotion is achieving more social acceptance and
is rousing less profound anxiety. As we shall see, moral and religious tracts and funeral poetry offer earlier and stronger evidence
for this change.

Fear of Breakdown and Defensive Anger

Why should consolers consider it their duty to assail their bereaved friends with reasons for stifling their grief? Why should consolers so often sound angry with the bereaved? Why should a culture sanction such coercive and cruel methods?

If confronted with these questions, a typically severe consoler would reply something as follows. Grief is a serious disease, physically, mentally, and spiritually; it causes unnecessary mental anguish, saps the strength of the body, and can even lead to death. Theologians warn us that immoderate mourning offends God and thus endangers our chances of salvation. It is foolish to indulge such an unnecessary passion, since it is simply the result of false opinion; nature exacts only moderate mourning, a temporary disturbance of body and soul. The relief or cure of such a dangerous and incapacitating disease requires stringent measures. What you take for anger is merely the firmness of the physician insisting on what is good for the patient. I am doing my friend a great service by helping him to master an unruly passion and am no more severe with him than I am with myself. I hope that someone will be just as 'angry' with me, should I give way to grief.

This answer accounts for the consoler's conscious motivation and is perfectly consistent with cultural assumptions about reason and emotion, self-control, and masculine and feminine identity, but overlooks one important factor – the widely recognized ineffectiveness of consolation. The whole strategy of insinuating condolence shows that consolers realize that they run the risk of alienating the recipients of their letters or even of making matters worse than they were before. Erasmus, Wilson, and Day are explicit about this. Erasmus, for example, advises timely consolation, 'But it is necessary that we do this [console] cleverly, lest like unskilled doctors, we aggravate rather than alleviate a recent and still raw wound' ('Verum scite id faciamus oportet, ne velut imperiti medici vulnus crudum adhuc et recens exulceremus potius quam mitigemus', p. 432).[16]

Erasmus, Day, and Buchler provide for the possibility that consolation will succeed in relieving grief, but they are considering all types of misfortune, not just bereavement, give no indication of the situations in which they think that consolation is effective, and, in any event, offer many more unconsoled responses. But at least they admit the possibility of relief; to judge from the responses which their seventeenth-century successors frame, everyone else agrees with Shakespeare's Leonato that it is impossible to 'patch grief with proverbs'.[17] Day allows that the consoler may give relief, but writes an example which admits a temporary mitigation before bursting out,

Follie were it for mee to thinke, or you to beleeue, that the pensiue imagination of a thing so neere, as wherupon concerned erst, the sum of all my ioyes, pleasures and happinesse, could with the vehemencie of a fewe speeches (more of zeale then equitie deliuered) bee suddenlie remooued. (p. 127)

Breton's bereaved is grateful for the friendly concern and apologetic about his inability to control himself (sig. B1^r). The respondent to the stern religious arguments in M. R.'s *A President for Young Pen-Men* offers thanks and asserts that he has received no little comfort before protesting, 'but let mee tell you that a collop cut out of the flesh puts neere home to the heart, and therefore as far as a man may not offend God, giue me leaue to be my selfe' (sig. G2^r). Markham's bereaved father angrily and passionately defends his grief, 'Haue I not iust cause, miserable old man, to languish and pine away, when he for whom I sought to liue is violently snatched from me?' (sig. K4^v).

Since consolation is ostensibly oriented towards the needs of the bereaved and seeks to cure or at least to relieve grief, this awareness of failure calls the consoler's altruism into question. Why add to the bereaved's pain if there is so little chance of comfort? Consolers do not consider what consolation does for them, and the vehemence with which they proceed suggests more direct emotional involvement than might appear at first. Since the bereaved are not being relieved, much less cured, by consolation, what does the consoler get out of it?

Almost all consolers call grief a disease; some, like the one in Macropedius, admit their fear it will prove an infectious menace to society. Several call grief, in the words of Erasmus, 'greuous and vnquiete to theyr frendes, acqueyntance, and company' (sig. A4^r; 'gravem ac molestum amicis ac familiaribus vitaeque sociis', p. 443). But it is much more than just troublesome; it is personally threatening because of the consoler's identification with the bereaved.

For the consoler acts as if bereaved himself, and I am not

merely referring to the fictive condolence which allows the consoler to offer his own successful struggle with grief as a model for his correspondent. First, the consoler's catalogue of the miseries of this world embodies the despairing view of life which the bereaved often embrace: 'In mourning it is the world which has become poor and empty.'[18] Second, it is quite common for a bereaved person to feel deserted or betrayed by someone who has died and thus be angry with that person. This anger is unconsciously redirected towards other people if ambivalence towards the dead is too painful to tolerate, in which case the dead may be idealized. This process occurs in numerous consolations (not to mention funeral elegies). In Erasmus' letter, for example, the dead son is assumed to be in heaven, while the father is angrily attacked and all but threatened with loss of esteem and friendship if he gives in to grief. Third, mourning is a protracted struggle to accept something which one wishes had not occurred or could be reversed. Throughout the process, part of the bereaved refuses to believe in the loss and tries to deny its reality. The consoler also tries to deny the reality of the loss by showing that what may appear to be loss is actually gain, and one of the strongest arguments against grief satisfies the longing to deny the loss. The consoler asserts the dead's continued interest in the life of the bereaved and promises reunion in heaven.[19]

These similarities suggest that the consoler identifies with the bereaved and is proving his mastery of past bereavements and strengthening himself against future ones in order to convince himself of his own firmness. Rational self-sufficiency is the ideal which the consoler strives to maintain; he tries to master the world and to insulate himself from all those calamities which he elaborates by controlling his feelings. Death represents a particularly severe challenge to someone who holds this ideal. Death threatens not only to mock his mastery of the world by ending his life, but also to expose his self-sufficiency by revealing his emotional attachment to and need for others by severing the attachment. For the consoler's ideal leaves no room for personal, emotional needs; they are swept away as egotistical self-indulgence. As Suketus' son says from heaven, to bewail one's own loss shows the mind of one who considers himself instead of the dead.

The consoler's intolerance of grief in others suggests a strong fear that it might overwhelm him, a fear of collapse. All grief must be suppressed to remove evidence of emotional vulnerability. The likelihood that someone else will abandon the ideal of rational self-control and fall victim to the passions provokes an angry, defensive effort to contain expressions of grief and thus assert control over it in the bereaved. Anger is an acceptable form of emotional release, as it testifies to firmness and strength of character rather than weakness and dependence.[20] By taking action against grief, the consoler acts out his own victory over it and guards against succumbing to it. He is seeking to prove in advance that the bereaved's retort does not apply to him – 'If you were in my place, you'd feel differently.'

Chapter 2

THE EMERGENCE OF
COMPASSIONATE MODERATION

Clown. Good madonna, why mourn'st thou?
Olivia. Good fool, for my brother's death.
Clown. I think his soul is in hell, madonna.
Olivia. I know his soul is in heaven, fool.
Clown. The more fool, madonna, to mourn for your brother's soul, be-
    ing in heaven. Take away the fool, gentlemen.
(Shakespeare, *Twelfth Night*)

In Renaissance England a consoler seeking support from Christianity in the battle against grief has three major options, although they are not equally available throughout the period because the theological discussions of mourning, like the letter-writing formularies, are more sympathetic towards grief by the early seventeenth century. The most common and familiar position is also the most flexible and confusing: grief is permissible but must be moderate. Conceptions of moderation differ dramatically, however, and moderation can be opposed to one of two excesses, immoderate mourning or inhuman insensibility. Some views of moderation are even more severe than total prohibition of grief, and moderate mourning can range from a day, as Wilson suggests, to much longer and more turbulent periods. Unrestricted mourning never finds a theological champion, but some advocates of moderation insist upon mourning as a necessary expression of humanity. This second position is really a matter of emphasis because the necessity of moderation is never lost sight of. The third position has not received much attention – it has never been considered by scholars of Renaissance literature – and is indeed held by only a minority, primarily in the middle of the sixteenth century. Rigorism, as I shall call this third position, prohibits and condemns all grief for those who have died virtuously and are in heaven. If a good Christian dies, one should rejoice at the soul's deliverance from this world and its translation to heaven. If one mourns, one either is guilty of the sin of despair or is admitting that the deceased is in hell. Although

27

defended by only a minority, rigorism remains a potent force throughout the period, as the persistent polemics against it prove. And for the student of poetry rigorism has a particular importance because one of the major poets of Renaissance England, Ben Jonson, writes his funeral poems in accordance with its strictures, as we shall see in chapter 6.

The position of the earliest fathers to concern themselves with mourning is actually harsher than Stoic *apatheia* because it is not an ideal of conduct for the wise man, but a standard which everyone must observe in order to avoid sin.[1] Tertullian, Cyprian, and the authors of the *Epistula ad Turasium presbyterum* and the pseudo-Augustinian *Sermones de consolatione mortuorum* base their position on 1 Thessalonians 4.13–14, which they take as a prohibition of all mourning as evidence of the sin of despair, not just a prohibition of immoderate mourning:

But I would not have you to be ignorant, brethren, concerning them which are asleep, that ye sorrow not, even as the others which have no hope. For if we believe that Jesus died and rose again, even so them also which sleep in Jesus will God bring with him. (KJV)[2]

This important point of doctrine comes down to the interpretation of a conjunction: καθώς in the Greek New Testament, 'sicut' in the Vulgate, 'even as' in the English of the Geneva, Bishops' and King James versions, 'as' in Tyndale's and Coverdale's, and 'as also' in the Rheims. The first interpreters take the 'even as' clause to mean 'not to be sad, which is what the others do who have no hope'. From Ambrose's *De excessu fratris sui Satyri* on, and especially after Augustine's *Sermones* 172 and 173, most interpreters take it to mean 'not to be sad in the manner of the others who have no hope'. Is this a prohibition of all sadness or of a certain mode of sadness? The conjunctions point towards the second interpretation but do not, especially 'sicut', rule out the first.

The patristic period witnesses a steady development from rigorism to moderation, although justification of mourning does not necessarily ease the feelings of the bereaved. Permission to mourn, especially in Augustine, is permission to worry about the bounds of moderate mourning. In sixteenth- and seventeenth-century England rigorism and rigoristic moderation yield to increasingly more tolerant conceptions of moderation. Anxiety about mourning, however, never disappears, as it does in the work of some seventeenth-century poets, and the theologians do not go as far as some poets in their defenses of the humanity of mourning.

Rigorism in England is at its height during the reign of Edward VI. This is also the period during which Calvin publishes his commentary on Thessalonians, which, without naming any names, indicates rigoristic opposition more explicitly than usual.[3] In 1551, a few months before the deaths of the Brandons, Matthew Parker, the future Archbishop of Canterbury, delivered in Cambridge an important funeral sermon for Martin Bucer. Wilson surely heard this sermon (he contributes to the Cambridge collection of funeral poems which mentions it),[4] and his leanings towards rigorism (he cites Paul as prohibiting all grief) may owe something to the distinctions Parker makes. Parker's sermon combines a fiercely logical rigorism with concession to the weakness of human nature. Although Parker ends by justifying a certain kind of grief, the sermon leaves a strong impression of severity.

Parker's sermon strongly recalls Erasmus' letter to Suketus. Like Erasmus, Parker insists that Christians should surpass the self-restraint of pagan philosophers, who had not faith in the resurrection to support them. And like Erasmus, Parker insists that the Christian should rejoice in the good which has befallen Bucer, unless he would reveal his envy of Bucer's felicity. But Parker surpasses Erasmus in his rigoristic exegesis of scripture and asserts that the Bible prohibits mourning:

Moreouer, it agreeth not with the rules of faith, for a christian man to bewayle the dead. For, who can deny that to be against faith, which is flatly forbidden by the scriptures? And how can that be sayed to agree with the rule of fayth, whiche the scriptures most euidentlye prooue to be done by those that haue no hope?[5]

Parker does not rely solely on Paul to the Thessalonians; he argues forcibly that Ecclesiasticus 22.11 does not countenance mourning:

Make small weeping for the dead (sayth the wise man) for he is at rest. If a man do but lightly and superficially consider the words of this scripture, and do not diligently search the bottome and ground of the true meaning and sence thereof, he may (perhaps) thinke that it is thereby permitted yea and after a sort commaunded and enioyned to a man to mourne and bewaile the dead, so that he do it moderatly. (sigs. A4ᵛ–5ʳ)

Parker contends that we must weigh the reason offered by the wise man: then we shall see that we should rejoice. The wise man considers our frailty only because he has no hope of obtaining what he would prefer. If we followed the rule of faith we would rejoice, 'altogether renouncing such womannish wayling, and childish infirmitie' (sigs. A5ᵛ–6ʳ). Parker sums up the first half of his sermon as follows.

Therefore I saye, when wee haue respect and consideration of the party that is dead and departed, it is both vnseemely and wicked to vse any howling or blubbering for him, vnlesse we desire to be accounted creatures endued rather with beastly nature then furnished with the vse of reason: to be deemed Heathen people rather then true christians: enuious caitiues then wel meaning friends: void of hope and faith, not vnderstanding our happy estate, and persons doutful and vncertain of their saluation, rather then constant beleeuers vndoubtedly embracing and crediting the infallible worde of God, therby as by a rule directing all and euery our actions, thoughts and affections, and valiantly subduing and entirely triumphing ouer our imbecillity and weaknes. (sig. A7ʳ)

Until this point, despite an opening assurance that he is going to justify grief for Bucer, Parker has done nothing but equate grief with impiety and unmanliness. Another passage from Ecclesiasticus (38.16) gives Parker the opportunity to make the distinction which is the central thesis of his sermon, since it is impossible that the wise man is contradicting himself.

To make him therefore to agree with himselfe, this must needes bee his meaning: that, as in respect of the party deceased, it is not lawfull to weepe and lament, for that, he enioyeth blisse, and is at rest: so, on the other side, namely in respecte of our selues, that are bereft the company, sight and comfort of his vertuous maners, godly life and excellent learning, we haue most iust and vrgent cause not onely to lament and bee sorie, but euen for a long space to continue the same our griefe and moane, as hauing receiued some great losse and hinderance vnrecouerable. (sig. A8ʳ)

This shift provides ample opportunity to praise Bucer, especially his learning and virtue, but does not lead to any sympathy with the plight of the bereaved. The contrary is the case. The second half of the sermon becomes a fine example of an emotional split characteristic of mourning. The dead is idealized, and the living are blamed for the death. Parker, like Wilson in his letter to the Duchess of Suffolk, harps on the guilt of the survivors. We do have just cause to mourn: Bucer's death is a sign of God's wrath, and we must confess our wicked and detestable lives, repent, beg pardon, and amend them. The allowance of grief for ourselves quickly becomes grief for the wickedness which caused Bucer's death. Mourning is allowed, but it is mourning for sin, not for the dead. Bereavement is a form of punishment.

The most rigorous prohibition of mourning, worthy of Cyprian himself, the main authority behind it, appears in one of the most popular religious tracts of the sixteenth and early seventeenth centuries, Thomas Becon's *The Sicke mannes Salue*. Becon probably composed the book before 1553; after 1560, the year in which it appeared in his *Worckes*, it went through nineteen separate editions, the last in 1632.[6] It was well enough known to be mentioned twice in Jonson's plays, once in the same breath with another immensely popular religious work, Foxe's *Book of Martyrs*.

The Sicke mannes Salue, like the pseudo-Platonic *Axiochus*, is a dialogue that stages the conversion of a dying man from despair at death to resolution to confront it. Epaphroditus is suddenly taken ill and becomes impatient. A group of friends overwhelms him with biblical citations and standard topoi of consolation and succeeds in restoring his faith. Then someone asks how much money he wishes to leave for mourning gowns, and Epaphroditus takes the opportunity to show how well he has learned his lesson. He asks who is to be mourned, is told himself, and replies.

Why for me? Because good things haue chaunced vnto me? Because I haue passed ouer the daungerous sea, and am come vnto the heauen of quietnes? Or because I am deliuered from all euill and set in a blessed and ioyefull state? I thincke that at the burialles of the faithfull, there shuld rather be ioy and gladnes, then mourning and sadnes, rather pleasant songes of thankes geuing: then lamentable and dolefull diriges. Let the infideles mourne for their dead: the Christians ought to reioyse, whan anye of the faithfull be called from this vale of misery vnto the glorious kingdom of God. (fol. 237ᵛ)

Philemon responds with approval, citing Paul, and Theophilus quotes long passages from Cyprian's *De mortalitate* and sums up categorically, 'they whych dye in the lord: are in a blessed state, and therfore not to be mourned nor lamented' (fol. 238ᵛ).

A verse of Paul's letter to the Romans (12.15) is usually cited as a biblical justification of mourning.[7] Becon, however, uses it to show the folly of mourning.

In dede it is a point of fondnesse to mourn for them that ar in ioy, and to be sory for them that are mery. The Apostle saith: Reioyse with them that reioyse, and mourn wyth them that mourn. Seing that the faythful, which are deliuered out of thys world, are in ioy: it is more semely that we should ioy in god wyth them, than mourn and be sory for them, as though they were in worse case now, then they wer afore. Let the heathen mourn whych haue no hope. (fol. 238ᵛ)

The section on mourning concludes with approval of the Trausoi, a Thracian tribe proverbial for weeping at birth and rejoicing at death.[8]

Another Edwardian theologian connected with the Duchess of Suffolk avoids the rigorism of Parker and Becon. In his fifth sermon in Lincolnshire in 1553 Hugh Latimer takes the revival of Jairus' daughter as an occasion to argue for moderation.

Nowe he sayeth to the people, *Quid ploratis*, what wepe ye? You muste vnderstand that our sauiour condemneth not all manner of weepyng, but onelye that whych is without hope: of whyche Saynct Paule speaketh: *tanquam qui spem non habent*, as they that haue no hope: but charitably wepyng is alowed yea commaunded, for S. Paule saieth, *Flete cum flentibus*, weepe with them that wepe, be sorowfull with them that be sorowfull: yet do it measurably as it becommeth christians. In the time of popery, before the gospel came amongest vs, we went to buriales, with wepyng and wailing, as thoughe there wer no god: but sence the gospell came vnto vs, I haue heard saye that in some places they go with the corses girnyng and fleeryng, as though they went to a bearebaiting: which thing is naughte, for lyke as to muche weeping is naught, so to be ἄστοργος without affection is naught to: we shold kepe a meure [sic: for 'mean' or perhaps 'measure'] in al things.[9]

Despite their polemical exaggeration Latimer's examples of lack of moderation are revealing; as far as one can judge, his conception of moderation does not allow much expression of sorrow. Immoderate mourning consists in weeping and wailing at funerals; *apatheia*, grinning and coarse laughing. The mean between these extremes would appear to be a somber composure, a sad self-control. Latimer is more concerned with outward appearances as signs of feelings than with the feelings themselves. He concentrates on behavior at funerals, not the emotional life during a bereavement, and when he goes on to speak against women remarrying too soon after their husbands' deaths, his reason is that such a remarriage is a token of imperfect love. Latimer is interested in regulating conduct, not soothing the bereaved, but he does at least pay lip service to the feelings, something which Becon and Parker refuse to do.

Latimer's attack on *astorgia* is a typical bit of moderate polemic. Moderates find it easier to scoff at stony Stoicism and to require moderate grief than to discuss the emotions of bereavement. This is the case with Calvin and many later justifiers of mourning. Otto Werdmüller, in a treatise on death translated by Miles Coverdale and first published in English around 1555, adopts this strategy in his argument that it is natural to mourn.

Such heauinesse, pitie and compassion doeth God alowe. For he hath not created vs to bee stoanes and blockes, but hath geuen vs fiue senses, and made vs an heart of fleash, that we might haue feelyng, and loue our freendes, beyng sory whan they suffer trouble and die: Yea God hateth vnfrendly and vnmercyfull people: and whose heartes are not moued, whan theyr frendes are vexed or taken away from them.[10]

Werdmüller's defense begins sympathetically, but ends threateningly. His third book is devoted to consolation, but his sympathy is limited to the beginning of the first of twelve chapters, and even here what he emphasizes is God's hatred of absence of grief. This sympathy is really just the equivalent of exordial condolence in the letter of consolation, and in fact the third book shares the bullying tone of Erasmus' *Declamatio de morte*, which is the unacknowledged source for most of it. Werdmüller heaps scorn upon the unmanliness and impiety of immoderate mourning.

In the controversy over the *Admonition to Parliament* moderation of mourning is one of the few things that Thomas Cartwright and John Whitgift agree upon, although Cartwright would like to prohibit mourning gowns as inciters to immoderate grief, while Whitgift argues that there is a lawful use, as well as an abuse, of the attire. Cartwright objects that wearing the gowns is often hypocritical and corresponds to no internal sadness. From this observation one might imagine some sympathy for sadness, but this turns out to be far from the case.

And considering that where there is sorowe in deed for the dead, there it is verie hard for a man to kepe a measure that he do not lament to much: We ought not to vse these meannes whereby we might be further prouoked to sorowe, and so go a greate way beyonde the measure, which the Apostle apointeth in mourning. (p. 161)

Cartwright's notion of moderation is thus severe. His anxiety that even as small an encouragement to grief as the gowns might lead to breakdown is not shared by Whitgift, who contents himself with the retort, 'But there is no suche immoderate mourning for the dead in these days, the contrary rather appeareth' (p. 732). A generation later, in 1597, Richard Hooker, still defending the Church of England against Cartwright, makes the argument seem ridiculous. It is fitting, Hooker says, to show the signs of grief even if there is no internal correspondence of feeling, 'especiallie sith it doth not come oftentimes to passe that men are faine to haue theire mourning gownes puld of their backes for feare of killing them selues with sorrow that way nourished'.[11] Despite the polemical intent, it is fair to say that Whitgift, and especially Hooker, do not fear the excesses of mourning as much as Cartwright and have a more lenient view of moderation.

In a commentary published posthumously in 1583, John Jewel also warns against the inhumanity of not mourning, but has a much keener sense of the pain which bereavement inflicts.

He doth not forbidde natural affection. Our parentes, and our children are deare vnto vs. They are our fleshe and bloude, and the chiefe and principall partes of our bodie. Anye part of our bodie can not be cut off, but wee shall feele it. The father if he feele not the deathe of his sonne: or, the sonne if he feele not the death of his Father, and haue not a deepe feeling of it, he is vnnatural.[12]

He proceeds to command moderation by depicting pagan sorrow for the dead in equally vivid terms.

We are not therfore forbidden to mourne ouer the dead: but to mourne in such sorte as the heathen did, we are forbidden. They, as they did neither beleeue in God, nor in Christe, so had they no hope of the life to come. When a Father sawe his sonne dead he thought he hadde bene dead for euer. Hee became heauie, chaunged his garmente, delighted in no companie, forsooke his meate, famished himselfe, rent his bodie, cursed his fortune, cried out of his gods.... Thus they fel into dispayre, and spake blasphemies. (p. 161)

Jewel's picture of pagan immoderation suggests that he allows for more sorrow and expression of sorrow than Latimer. Weeping and wailing at the funeral are not immoderate, but rather despair and blasphemy. Presumably it is this result which makes pagan sorrow damnable and not the stages which lead up to it, although the inclusion of some of the commonest occurrences in bereavement – depression, inability to enjoy company, loss of appetite – point to an anxiety that giving way to any grief may lead to emotional collapse. Jewel's conception of moderation is an advance on that of his predecessors, but not a great one. Nevertheless, he does not follow Ecclesiasticus 38.17 in restricting mourning to one or two days 'or seven days at the most', as do James Pilkington and Robert Southwell.[13]

In his lectures on Thessalonians, posthumously published in

1606, Robert Rollock gives sorrow its due more than any of his predecessors.

I meane not, brethren, that, that knowledge that workes hope, and that hope that workes joy, will take away from a man altogether all displeasure, all heauinesse, all mourning in the departure of our friendes, and them we loue well. No, it will not, nor should not doe that. There is no grace of God in Iesus, that puts out any naturall affection: none will take away either naturall joy, or displeasure: no, faith and hope will not doe it, but it makes naturall affection sanctified, and puts it in order.

Rollock does not bully his audience by asserting that it is unnatural not to grieve for dead friends. He describes the course of feeling instead of prescribing it. He goes on to make the working of knowledge, hope, and faith natural processes just like sorrow. His rhetoric inspires confidence that sorrow will be overcome instead of threatening that unrepressed sorrow testifies to impiety. His continuation, however, turns towards the old monitory style.

Beware of your mourning, and looke that it be neuer altogether without some joy. Sobst thou? sighst thou vnspeakablie? Looke, that thy sighs be mingled with joy vnspeakable. Will ye haue my counsell? Let neuer joy be the alone, but let euer joy be tempered with sorrow: Haue not sorrow the alone, but let it euer be mingled with some joy.[14]

But even in this passage Rollock does not attack sorrow; he is trying to temper, not obliterate it. 'Will ye haue my counsell?' softens the tone. Rollock is not ordering a mixture of sorrow and joy under threat of punishment, but giving his personal opinion.

In 1619 William Sclater inveighs against the Stoics in familiar fashion and goes to greater lengths than Rollock to justify the 'affections'.

Grace destroyes not Nature but rectifieth it; it doth not abolish Reason, but rectifie it; depriues not of Sense, but teacheth right vse of Senses; proportionally kills not Affections, but only orders them. And *the mortifying of affections* pressed in Scripture, must so be vnderstood, that the Carnalitie of them only is strucken at, not the Affections themselues.... God himselfe hath imprinted such Affections in mans Nature with his owne finger; and they blame Gods workmanship, that condemne them. (pp. 316–17)

Sclater is in an uncomfortable position, however, because he insists on moderation of affections as much as anyone and realizes the difficulties, the temptations of moderation, more than most.

Affections are violent, especially hauing shew of lawfulnesse to set them forward. More frequent are the slips of Saints, in things for their matter lawfull, then in those that are simply vnlawfull. Conscience, euen of good men, sets it selfe loose, hauing plea of lawfulnesse for the action. Herein, Affection growes no lesse then tumultuous, being able to warrant it selfe by instinct of Nature, practice of Christ and his Saints. (p. 320)

Sclater's sympathy for the affections coexists with anxiety that they may overwhelm; he comes close to striking at the affections themselves, not just their carnality. Sclater reveals more clearly than anyone the difficulty of making grief a matter of judgment – where does moderation stop and immoderate grief begin? He does not exploit this boundary to incite fear of excess, like Gervase Babington and Augustine, but it obviously worries him and will probably worry the conscientious reader.

Zacharie Boyd's *The Last Battell of the Soule in Death* (1629) stages a conversation like Becon's among a dying man, his pastor, friends, and family. The conversation would surely kill the hardiest, as it runs for some 1200 pages, and this is easily the most tedious *ars moriendi*. It is also good evidence for a shift towards a more sympathetic attitude towards mourning and thus radically different from Becon. Boyd dedicates his second volume to Elizabeth, Queen of Bohemia, King Charles' sister, who has just lost her first son, Frederick, by drowning. Before offering consolation Boyd advises, 'Yee may MADAME disburden your selfe alittle by powring out your Heart before the Lord in these or such sighes and groanes' (II *5^r). Then follow nine pages of 'The Queenes Lamentation for the death of her Son', which most of Boyd's predecessors would have considered a shameful display of immoderate grief. Boyd, despite his attempt to write in the style of the Old Testament, does not do a bad job representing the desolation which a bereaved mother might feel; the passage could stand comparison with the innumerable hyperbolic expressions of grief in the funeral elegies of the period.

Mine eyes doe faile with teares; my bowels are troubled, my Liuer is powred vpon the earth: I was at ease, but hee hath broken me asunder: Hee hath also taken mee by the necke and shaken mee to pieces, and set mee vp for his marke: His Archers compasse mee round about: Hee cleaueth my reines asunder, and doeth not spare: Hee powreth out my gall vpon the ground: Hee breaketh mee with breach vpon breach. (II *7^v)

Boyd seems to regard this cry of persecution at the hand of God as a preparation for consolation, a valuable part of the process of mourning. In the letter of consolation which follows the lamentation Boyd makes it clear that he does not approve of immoderate mourning and gives no indication that the lamentation has passed the bounds.

Once Boyd has talked his dying Christian into the grave he writes 'A comfortable Speach for the Widow of the defunct'. The justification of mourning is particularly forceful and avoids burdening the widow with the duty not to be unnatural.

I confesse that yee cannot but mourne, beeing depriued of such a pleasure the *fairest jewell* of all your worldlie joy, the staffe of your estate on whom your greatest comforts did depend: what wonder? for many dayes haue ye bene together, so that it is not possible were ye neuer so sanctified, but your heart must be deeplie wounded: Why not? Gods will was neuer against anie moderate mourning for the dead: Grace maketh not men and women *Stoicks and stockes* that cannot bee moued for any thing: Nay, God permits vs to mourne but not to *carke & care* as those *which haue none hope*, who tugging out their haire and downe their cheekes powr[ing] out their roaringes as waters, beeing swallowed vp of discouragement, hauing *none hope* in their griefe, they fome out myre and dirt. (p. 1225)[15]

Boyd focuses on the bond between husband and wife and the pain which its rupture causes. When he mentions immoderation, he goes beyond Sclater, his apparent source for this passage, in his depiction of violent, self-abusing grief. Boyd reiterates the legitimacy of mourning a couple of pages later. Grace will compose violent passions, 'But it neuer dissalloweth *a tempered Turtle crouding* for the absence of our dearest comforts: Such teares the Lord will put vp in his Bottels' (p. 1228).

An *ars moriendi* from 1629, the merchant James Cole's *Of Death a True Description*, is the most compelling instance of compassionate moderation, worlds apart from Edwardian rigorism. Cole's pamphlet is similar in structure to Werdmüller's in that both discuss preparation for death in their first two books and reserve consolation for the third. Werdmüller, as we have seen, begins with our duty to mourn, but quickly proceeds to condemn immoderate mourning for most of his third book. Cole begins in the same way and even cites a number of the Biblical precedents one finds in Werdmüller, but goes on to cite *exempla* of much longer periods of mourning than any which we have seen: the 30 days of lamentation for Moses, the 40 days for the embalming of Jacob, and the 70 days which the Egyptians mourned him. Sclater also refers to the mourning of Jacob and the Egyptians for Joseph, but draws a distinction, '*Aegyptians mourne for IACOB seuentie dayes; Ioseph,* his naturall sonne, onely *seuen dayes*: Not that hee was lesse kind, but more Christian-like prudent' (p. 319). Cole makes no distinction, but remarks approvingly.

And very fitly doth a man take the time of certaine dayes, to ease his heart of the burthen of griefe, it surchargeth it by lamenting and weeping. For this disease hauing so passed the worst, is then the easier to be cured. The sorrowfull finding himselfe wearied out, giues way the more willingly to comfort. Which indeed ought not in due time be neglected, but willingly accepted. For, though the first griefe be not condemnable, yet is the continuance thereof hurtfull. (pp. 166–67)

This is astute psychology; Cole sees mourning as a process that must run its course and realizes that periodic pangs of grief are a necessary and helpful part of the process. At the end of the passage it looks as if Cole is going to revert to the familiar condemnation of immoderate grief, but in fact he does not. For one thing, a period of 70 days – and Cole is not talking about a period of preparation for burial, as his periodic pangs of grief show – would be considered immoderate by many of his predecessors. It is more important, however, that Cole does not say that the continuance of grief is condemnable; he focuses on the suffering of the bereaved: the continuance is harmful. Many earlier authors would have ended the sentence with 'thereof'.

The matter-of-fact way in which Cole greets the passing away of grief with time is particularly interesting, since the standard consolatory topos from Cicero through Erasmus and beyond holds that, while all grief will perish with time, it is shameful not to do for oneself what time will eventually do. Even Boyd, so moderate in most things, uses this topos at the close of his comfortable speech to the widow, 'Nowe that which *Time* can doe to a *Pagane,* let Grace doe it to a Christian' (p. 1237). Once again, Cole is content to let grief take its own course.

Most of Cole's third book is devoted to internal remedies for sorrow which are standard consolatory fare. What is striking, however, is that Cole's compassion for his 'occasions' of bereavement is constantly getting the better of him and blunting the force of his reasoning. He sympathizes with the bereaved husband because marriage is a consecrated delight, but since even a fond mother lets her daughter go off to a foreign land to make an advantageous marriage, the husband should be glad his wife has gone to the eternal Bridegroom. At once Cole qualifies this by saying that it may seem hard to the husband, who should console himself with the thought that he is stronger to bear bereavement than his wife, since he has pastimes out of the house. The plight of the widow stirs Cole's compassion more than the husband's, especially when she and her children are left in want by her husband's death: 'This indeede is a bitter sorrow, and therefore God himselfe seemes to haue compassion on her, who commends her diuers times vnto vs in his word' (p. 185).

I do not wish to suggest that Cole licenses any and all grief; he does insist upon moderation and warns against immoderation. But even while insisting, he recalls the hardships of bereavement: 'Yet ere we leaue, wee would entreat euery one in generall, that (though it seeme harsh vnto them, to be without the louely fellowship of their friends) they would willingly submit themselues to Gods will and ordinance' (p. 190). Here the parenthesis softens the blow; at the very end it is the 'or' clauses, 'Or if we cannot haile our senses out of the graue' (p. 195); 'Or if we cannot wholy keepe our selues from sorrowing' (p. 196). Sympathy and understanding for bereavement displace rigor, and moderation is humane.[16]

Except in Jonson's funeral poetry one does not find total rigorism after Becon. Since, however, many of the supporters of moderation equate it with very brief and restrained periods or insist on the dangers of exceeding the bounds more than on the legitimacy of mourning, a *de facto* rigorism is more common in the sixteenth century than might be supposed. Nevertheless, just as condolence assumes greater importance in precepts for letters of consolation, the right to mourn gradually tempers the severity of moderation and rigorism. Sclater's defense of the affections in general and of sorrow in particular is contemporary with the new interest in condolence, as is Cole's strong sympathy for bereavement. The evidence of both the letter-writing formularies and the theological tracts thus shows that a more tolerant attitude towards grief is emerging at the beginning of the seventeenth century. And the funeral poetry of the period, as we will see shortly, provides even more striking evidence for the new attitude.

Chapter 3

PRAISE AND MOURNING

Funeral elegies represent various aspects of the process of mourning.[1] Obvious as this declaration may seem, it is not generally accepted. Most scholars agree that the major purpose of Renaissance elegy, both in theory and in practice, is to praise the deceased, and that lament and consolation, the other components of elegy, are of secondary importance and often no more than indirect forms of praise. There are two reasons why this view prevails. First, most elegies praise the deceased, and many are little more than excuses for encomium. Second, both classical and Renaissance writers classify funeral orations and elegies as branches of epideictic rhetoric, the traditional functions of which are praise and blame. In this chapter I shall argue that classification of elegy as epideictic does not imply that praise is its primary function and that it is more comprehensive to conceive of elegy as a representation of the process of mourning.

Since O. B. Hardison, Jr., is the most influential interpreter of elegy as the poetry of praise, I shall begin by citing his argument for this position.

The fact that the funeral elegy was always considered an epideictic type has already been mentioned. This resolves the problem by making it clear that praise is the essential element of the form. If consolation were the most important element, funeral elegy would be deliberative rather than epideictic, since *consolatio* was generally classified in the former category. On the other hand, if the poem were primarily a lament with the object of offering either the poet or his audience emotional catharsis, the positive elements of the poem would become subordinate to the negative ones. Threnody can be considered epideictic – a complaint or *vituperatio* against the order of things – but whether considered rhetorically or psychologically, it has no place for the elaborate praise of the *demonstratio*, the philosophical reasoning of the consolation, or the positive and hortatory ending. Naturally, the balance between praise, lament, and consolation varies with individual elegies, but in the majority, the first is dominant and the latter two subordinate.[2]

Hardison oversimplifies. Elegies are too varied to be confined to

40

one pattern; there is no 'essential element'. The combination of praise, lament, and consolation indicates a mixed genre incorporating aspects of epideictic and deliberative rhetoric rather than a type of epideictic. Hardison is more single-minded about the predominance of praise than was Menander the rhetor, the more influential (thanks to Scaliger) of the two rhetoricians who discussed in detail the types of epideictic. The other important rhetorician, the author of the *Ars rhetorica* attributed in the Renaissance to Dionysius of Halicarnassus, insures the predominance of praise by banishing lament from the funeral oration. The major difference between the two (a difference which Hardison, p. 113, ignores) occurs over the status of lament; they do not agree upon a primary purpose for the funeral oration.

After distinguishing between public orations for those who died in battle and speeches at private funerals, pseudo-Dionysius defines the essence of a funeral oration as praise of the dead. Both types of speech have three main parts, although the second is not as important on private occasions: praise of the deceased, exhortation of the living to imitate his virtues, and consolation of the surviving relatives. The author warns the orator not to mix lament and consolation.

It is necessary to understand the method of consolation, for we must not mourn or bewail the dead, since we would not console the survivors, but rather increase their grief. And this will not appear to be praise of the dead, but a lament as if they have suffered something very dreadful.[3]

Far from being an indirect form of praise, lament is incompatible with it. Lament undermines the primary purpose of the funeral oration and contradicts the numerous consolatory efforts to prove that death is good. Pseudo-Dionysius' concern to preserve praise as the primary purpose of the funeral oration leads him to eliminate one of the commonest elements of elegy. He does not draw an inevitable conclusion about lament that writers bent on praise of the deceased would have to honor. Instead, he presents an alternative within the rhetorical tradition to Wilson's observation, 'The loue of all men towardes hym, and the lamentyng generally for his lacke, helpe well moste highly to set furthe his honour' (p. 29)[4] The rhetoricians are by no means unanimous on the subordination of lament to praise or on the status of lament in funeral orations and elegies.

Pseudo-Dionysius describes only one type of funeral oration;

Menander distinguishes three, and praise is not the primary purpose of any of them. In one of them, monody, lament dominates, and praise is a means to lament.

What then is the purpose of monody? To lament and bewail. If the deceased was not a relative, one should only lament him by mixing praises with the laments and continually emphasizing the lament so that the praise is not independent but a pretext for lament.[5]

Menander is trying to make the speaker's lament convincing by providing a reason why he should be so sad. With a relative, Menander implies, praise is not necessary because the speaker does not have to justify his loss.

Nor does Menander see any contradiction between lament and praise in the other two types of funeral oration. Although he does not reduce praise to a pretext for lament, he does insist that the speaker use the topoi of praise to intensify grief: 'Let praises be the material for your laments' (p. 174). In addition, Menander considers lament as a preparation for, rather than counterproductive of, consolation. The first bit of advice he gives the consoler is to magnify the loss and increase grief. Menander does not even worry about the transition from the introductory section of lament to the consolation proper. He is much more concerned about the appropriateness of the speech to its circumstances than about the dominance of praise over lament, consolation, and exhortation. This sense of decorum dictates only one situation in which the *epitaphios* should be pure encomium – when the death is so far in the past that it is unreasonable to assume continuance of grief (pp. 172–74).

Renaissance authors of poetics implicitly side with Menander and counsel the combination of lament with praise and consolation. Julius Caesar Scaliger, the most influential of them, states that an elegy for a person who has died recently should consist of five parts: praise, demonstration of loss, lament, consolation, and exhortation. (An anniversary elegy has no lament because no one grieves for a person dead a year or more; Menander is the unacknowledged source of this distinction as of much else in the chapter on funeral poetry.) Hardison tries to use Scaliger to show that lament is subordinate to praise.

The elegy begins with personal praise, and the lament is a logical consequence – hence dependent on it: 'Since such a noble pledge of glory has been lost, there is nothing else to do but mourn.' Without the praise, the lament would be unmotivated, and conversely, the more hyperbolic the praise, the more intense the mourning. (p. 115)

A closer look at Scaliger reveals that lament depends upon the demonstration of loss, not praise.

Iactura demonstratur suaui primùm, mox incitatiore narratione. in qua immoratio & amplificatio auget amissae rei desiderium. à qua parte statim luctus. Illa enim propter hoc: vt nos in Epicedio regio,
> Quid mihi mentis erit, tam desolata videnti
> Regna tuo lacrymosa obitu: felicia quondam
> Auspicijs seruata tuis, & reddita nobis.
Amisso nánque tam gloriae claro pignore, nihil aliudquàm lugendum.[6]

Loss is demonstrated at first with a gentle, then with a more excited narration, in which lingering over the subject and amplification increase the desire for what has been lost. From which part lament immediately follows. For the demonstration of loss is there to prepare for the lament, as in our 'Royal Elegy': 'What will come to mind when I see the kingdom so desolate and tearful at your death: the happy kingdom formerly preserved and restored to us by your leadership.' For when such a bright pledge of glory has been lost, nothing remains but to mourn.

Scaliger makes lament a consequence of loss, not a form of praise. In some cases, as in the example from his own poem, the demonstration of loss and resultant lament may involve praise of the deceased, but this is a side-effect. Scaliger certainly does not make it the primary purpose of lament.

These rhetoricians show that classification of elegy as an epideictic form does not make praise its essential element. To say that elegy represents various aspects of the process of mourning is not to assert that lament is its essential element, nor that most authors of elegy have experienced personal bereavement at the deaths of their subjects, which is far from true.

The habit of elegy pervades Renaissance culture. Schoolboys compose epitaphs as practice for their Latin.[7] The early seventeenth century in particular is full of collections of elegies on public personages, and these poems are often their authors' only appearance in print. The impulse to compose an elegy seems at times to have been a reflex of learning of a death. One consoler concludes a letter, 'If I can compose any verses that can fit my fancy, I will powre out also my shallow brooke in this great Ocean, whither all the ruines of earthly Paradise runne with strife to pay tribute.'[8] Many elegies are written to gratify a patron or to secure patronage. For his elegy to Sidney, George Whetstone wrote a dedicatory letter to Sidney's uncle, Ambrose,

Earl of Warwick; Whetstone comes close to demanding that he be paid for his work.

> Right Honorable, albeit that sundry of the (manifold) louers, of your most worthy Nephewe, of deare memorie, Sir Phillip Sidney Knight, haue alreadie witnessed, their true affections, in publishing of passionate Poems, Epitaphs, and Commemorations of his neuerdying vertues: yet I hope, my later writing shall finde intertaynment of your Lordship, & fauour amongst those, that truely loued him.[9]

In the early seventeenth century invectives against mercenary grief become very common. W. Towers, a contributor to the 1638 volume on Viscount Bayning, opens his poem with special vividness.

> Hence from This Tomb, you that have only chose
> To Mourn for Ribbands, & the sadder Cloths,
> That Buy your Grief from th' Shop, & desperat lye
> For a new Cloak till the next Lord shall Dye;
> You that shed only wine, and think when all
> The Banquet's past, there's no more Funerall:
> You that sell Teares, and only Weepe for Gaine,
> I dare not say you Mourn, but fill the Traine.[10]

Artificial or insincere grief also comes under attack in the early part of the seventeenth century, as we shall see in the next chapter. In addition, authors often know their subjects slightly or just by reputation (the most notorious example must be Donne and Elizabeth Drury) and not infrequently get simple biographical facts wrong.[11] For all these reasons, the searcher after sincere expression of loss or even informed praise will be disappointed again and again.

The majority of elegists may not be grieving themselves, but they identify with the bereaved, either consciously or unconsciously. Sometimes the identification is a therapeutic strategy. George Puttenham is the only author who is explicit about this, although a related point – that stifled grief is harmful – is a poetic commonplace.[12]

> Lamenting is altogether contrary to reioising, euery man saith so, and yet is it a peece of ioy to be able to lament with ease, and freely to poure forth a mans inward sorrowes and the greefs wherewith his minde is surcharged. This was a very necessary deuise of the Poet and a fine, besides his poetrie to play also the Phisitian, and not onely by applying a medicine to the ordinary sicknes of mankind, but by making the very greef it selfe (in part) cure of the disease.[13]

Puttenham blurs the distinction between therapy for the self and for others; he never explains how the poet's lament will ease the reader's sorrow. His poet consciously acts like a bereaved person in order to play the physician to others, but unconsciously physics his own sorrows, past or to come. Like the consoler, he is proving his own self-control, his own mastery of potentially disturbing emotions. A little farther on, Puttenham explains how grief can cure itself; the poet substitutes a brief and controlled period of mourning for a long and unpredictable one.

Therefore of death and burials, of th'aduersities by warres, and of true loue lost or ill bestowed, are th'onely sorrowes that the noble Poets sought by their arte to remoue or appease, not with any medicament of a contrary temper, as the *Galenistes* vse to cure [contraria contrarijs] but as the *Paracelsians*, who cure [similia similibus] making one dolour to expell another, and in this case, one short sorrowing the remedie of a long and grieuous sorrow. (p. 48; Puttenham's brackets)

Lament is thus an attempt to master grief rather than surrender to it. Sorrow is imagined as an alien object which can be dislodged from the body. Lament, Puttenham hopes, will get rid of it once and for all.

Even when elegy does not enact an abbreviated process of mourning by progressing from praise and lament to consolation and recovery, the recurring features of elegy are psychologically coherent expressions of different parts of the process of mourning. No one will dispute that lament is an expression of mourning, and it is not difficult to see how consolation and exhortation fit into the process, as they can be part of the struggle to accept and recover from loss or anticipatory attempts, upon the part of the consoler, to defend against grief, but how praise of the deceased is part of the process of mourning is not obvious.

What a reader of elegy quickly notices is not merely praise of the deceased, but its exaggeration. The subjects are presented, in Lewalski's phrase, as 'ideal types rather than as peccable individuals' (p. 38). The monotony with which the dead are praised to the skies – 'de mortuis nil nisi bonum' – suggests a psychosocial compulsion rather than unamimous agreement on hyperbolic praise as a spur to virtuous emulation, the traditional defense of flattery. The dead are not merely praised; they are idealized.

Idealization of the dead occurs frequently in bereavement. As Parkes comments in connection with his survey of London widows, 'Memories of the negative aspects of the dead are easily lost and idealization is carried out by most people and encouraged by society' (p. 70). Idealization is a defense against the feelings of ambivalence which accompany most relationships, and it is very difficult to recognize ambivalence, much less to tolerate it. Idealization is an attempt to neutralize the hostility or resentment towards the deceased that has accumulated over time and that is provoked by the death itself: anger at abandonment or at the pain of mourning. Idealization serves to ease feelings of guilt or responsibility for the death, to lull to rest fantasies that hostile thoughts can harm or kill. Idealization solaces the bereaved by proving the purity of their feelings towards the deceased and propitiates the dead to ward off retaliation.

Lament and consolation complement idealization. Exaggerated lament insists on the prostration of the bereaved, and the general thrust of consolation, its emphasis on the miseries of this life, debases the value of existence. Lament and consolation are thus forms of self-abasement and the opposite of idealization of the other. In many poems – for example, Surrey's 'Wyat resteth here' and Spenser's *Dapnaida* – the deceased and bereaved form a contrasting pair: the deceased is a saint, the bereaved a sinner. Probably the most extravagant example of the splitting of ambivalence occurs in Donne's *Anniversaries*, where Elizabeth Drury is portrayed as the pattern of perfection and the world is hyperbolically vilified.

By exaggerating positive feelings towards the deceased, idealization defends against negative ones, but when the latter are strong, they make themselves felt in some indirect way. *Dapnaida* is an extreme instance of extravagant idealization and not-so-hidden anger at the idealized person. Anger at the deceased for abandoning the bereaved occasionally results in reproach, for example, in one of Lodovick Bryskett's elegies on Sidney or in Cowley's elegy on Hervey.[14]

A major reason for conceiving of elegy as part of the process of mourning rather than the poetry of praise is that on this view of the matter anger and domineering consolatory tones are easier to understand. If lament were primarily an indirect form of praise, it would be difficult to understand why the bereaved should be severely urged to lay aside grief or even chided for it. Aside from disguised anger at the idealized dead and consolatory anger at the bereaved for abandoning rational self-sufficiency, one finds a third kind of displaced anger: anger towards others as a diversion from painful feelings of loss. Even when 'manly' action is not taking the place of sorrow for the dead, it is striking how much more easily some authors, Surrey and Herbert for example, express anger than sorrow.[15]

Expressions of sorrow in Renaissance elegy tend to be either hyperbolic – as exaggerated as most of the praise – or else only implicit: the poet, like Scaliger in the lines quoted above, hints at, rather than openly expresses his grief. Both modes honor cultural strictures against mourning. That implied grief does so is obvious. Hyperbolic grief (the desolation of all nature in pastoral elegy, for example) satisfies two contradictory desires: to express overwhelming sadness and to deny its existence. Grief is expressed, but is also distanced, sometimes projected onto inanimate objects. The grief is less disturbing because so patently fictional. Since poet and reader do not have to take it seriously, they have no need to worry about its being excessive.

At the end of the first chapter, I argue that the angry tone of consolation is part of the consoler's own defense against grief. In order to clarify some of the other assertions in the preceding paragraphs I shall examine Nicholas Grimald's 'A funerall song, vpon the deceas of Annes his moother'.[16] The poem idealizes the dead mother and yet is angry with her; it is filled with implied grief and and at the same time expresses anger with others as a diversion from the pain of mourning.

Grimald begins very defensively.

> Yea, and a good cause why thus should I playn.
> For what is hee, can quietly sustayn
> So great a grief, with mouth as styll, as stone?
> My loue, my lyfe, of ioye my ieewell is gone.
> This harty zeale if any wight disprooue,
> As womans work, whom feeble minde doth mooue:
> Hee neither knowes the mighty natures laws,
> Nor touching elders deeds hath seen old saws.

Grimald is more concerned about the appropriateness of his feelings than with pouring forth his sorrow. He is at pains to justify himself, both to defend his grief and to avoid a charge of insensibility. He is afraid of excess in opposite directions; he does not want to appear unmanly or a Stoic stock or stone, to others or to himself. He goes to greater lengths to defend his right to lament than his actual lamentation requires. Even though he refers to the poem as 'waylful verse, and doolfull song' and asks indignantly, 'And should not I expresse my inward wo, / When you, most louyng dam, so soon hence go?', in point of fact he does not wail at all. The closest he comes is the fourth line above, his only direct expression of loss or sorrow in the entire poem. Throughout the poem he avoids his sorrow instead of expressing it. In the lines just quoted Grimald quickly turns from his loss to an aggressive, intellectual argument; he chides the potential chider. This shift gives him occasion to digress for eighteen lines on respect bestowed on mothers and nurses. It would be a mistake to regard this parade of learning solely as a humanist showing off: the digression permits an intellectual escape from emotion and an opportunity to act vigorously rather than suffer.

The digression also offers a clue to one of the reasons why Grimald cannot confront the feelings roused by his mother's death: four of his eight examples show a marked ambivalence towards mothers or mother figures (nurses) and thereby suggest ambivalence towards his own. Judging from the way in which Grimald leads up to them, one expects examples of valiant sons who intensely mourned their mothers' deaths. This is true of only one, Sertorius, and Grimald does not mention his grief, but merely says, 'Into Hesperian land Sertorius fled, / Of parent aye cheef care had in his hed'.[17] Instead, in three of the four examples of deference or dutiful behavior towards mothers (and to the father in one case) the deference proves fatal to the sons. Coriolanus' yielding to his mother's plea that he spare Rome leads to his death. He foresees this in Plutarch: 'Oh mother, what have you done to me? And holding her hard by the right hande, oh mother, said he, you have wonne a happy victorie for your countrie, but mortall and unhappy for your sonne: for I see my self vanquished by you alone.'[18] The 'Sicil brethren' are Amphinomus and Anapias; they died in saving their parents from an eruption of Mount Etna. Grimald's reference to Cleobis and Biton suggests bondage to their mother, 'No more of Tyndars ymps hath Sparta spoke, / Than Arge of charged necks with parents yoke'. In this story the sons drag their mother in a chariot 45 furlongs to the temple of Hera, who grants their mother's prayer to reward them with the greatest good which can befall a mortal. It turns out to be death.[19]

After deference to mothers come four cases of honor for nurses. These do not show how dangerous mothers can be to their children, and but one of them recalls a scandal while supposedly praising: 'Acca, in dubble sense Lupa ycleaped, / To

Romane Calendars a feast hath heaped'. Acca nursed Romulus and Remus after the she-wolf and was thought to be a prostitute ('lupa' can mean both).[20] These examples present a very different picture of mothers and mother figures from Grimald's idealized mother, totally devoted to her son.

In his efforts to justify his grief Grimald uses the prescribed topoi of praise in an unusual and revealing way. The two time-honored patterns for praise are the stages of life and the virtues.[21] Wilson's presentation, which acknowledges its dependence on Quintilian (3.7), is typical of the first pattern. Wilson recommends dividing an encomium into things before, during, and after a person's lifetime. Before the life one should consider the realm, shire, town, parents, and ancestors; during the life, the birth and infancy, childhood, 'stripelyng age, or spryng tide', man's estate, old age, and time of death; after the life, the tomb, coat of arms, and funeral honors (pp. 25–27).

What distinguishes Grimald's use of this structure is that he describes his mother's actions, which are often regarded as the most essential part of encomium,[22] in terms of the stages of his own life. He does not mention her ancestry, place of origin, or parents. His description of his mother's life is completely centered on himself; he writes only about what she has done for him. She carried him in her womb, gave birth to him, nursed him, directed him to the Muses, paid for his lessons out of her spinning, and made clothes for him while he was at Cambridge and Oxford. Some rhetoricians recommend the inclusion of any signs, prophecies, or prodigies that occurred at the subject's birth.[23] Grimald modifies this topos to insist that he is his mother's favorite.

> You mee embraced, in bosom soft you mee
> Cherished, as I your onely chylde had bee.
> Of yssue fayr with noombers were you blest:
> Yet I, the bestbeloued of all the rest.
> Good luck, certayn forereadyng moothers haue,
> And you of mee a speciall iudgement gaue.

Given the ambivalence towards mothers in the examples and the frustration at abandonment which follows this passage, Grimald's claim to be her favorite sounds very suspicious and suggests a feeling of deprivation. Grimald is protesting too much, just as he is exaggerating the grief which he is expressing. He does not act like a favored child secure in the possession of his

mother's affection. He only presents himself as a passive recip-
ient of all this maternal care; he does not express gratitude or
sorrow. He acts as if he expects to receive his due and feels that
he is owed more.

At the news of her sickness Grimald describes the open grief
of her neighbors, her kinswomen, her 'charge, the maydens', and
her daughters, and the hidden grief of his father. Of his own feelings he says nothing. As with the earlier stages of life, the death
scene is also centered on the favorite child, even though he was
not present.

> You, not forgetting yet a moother's mood,
> When at the dore dartthirling death there stood,
> Did saye: Adeew, dear spouse, my race is roon:
> Wher so he bee, I haue left you a soon,
> And Nicolas you naamed, and naamed agayn:
> With other speech, aspiring heauenly raign.

Everything in the poem so far suggests that Grimald wants to
view his mother as his personal caretaker, that he looks to her
for continuous emotional and material support. He clings to a
belief in a special intimacy with her. He takes her death as desertion of him (and his sisters), and for one moment his anger at
losing his source of support gently surfaces as a reproach.

> Ah, could you thus, deare mother, leaue vs all?
> Now, should you liue: that yet, before your fall,
> My songs you might haue soong, haue heard my voyce,
> And in commodities of your own reioyce.
> My sisters yet vnwedded who shall guide?
> With whose good lessons shall they bee applyed?

This is the poem's first 'us', and Grimald's shift to the plural at
this point shows once again how he shies away from his own
emotional response. When he approaches his sense that he has
been abandoned, he diffuses his loss by sharing it with his sisters,
who have had no place in the poem except as second bests in his
mother's affections. He continues to deflect attention from himself with another 'us': 'Haue, mother, monumentes of our sore
smart'. The monuments turn out to be this poem. He is now the
poet expressing the family's loss, not just that of a bereaved
child. He is paying his debt to his mother with interest; she may
have given him life, but he is immortalizing her name. At the
end of the poem he bids farewell until the last judgment. The
grief which he was at such great pains to justify has vanished
without explanation.

Despite certain infelicities of style, in particular awkward inversions, this is a moving poem, not because of the sorrow which it expresses but because of Grimald's inability to express it directly. It is a case of emotional blockage instead of conscious reserve because Grimald believes that he is overindulging his grief. He is so anxious about what it is appropriate to feel and about what his conduct should be that he cannot come to terms with what he actually does feel. Nevertheless, through his confusion there emerges resentment at care to which he felt that he was entitled and never received and anger at his abandonment by this idealized, all-giving mother.

Chapter 4

THE SHIFT FROM ANXIOUS ELEGY

Grimald is not the only sixteenth-century poet who is more concerned with what he is supposed to feel than with what he is
actually feeling. His anxieties about the legitimacy of grief are
characteristic of elegy throughout the greater part of the century.
Setting aside elegies which are primarily panegyric or which
indulge in hyperbolic grief, one finds much more defensiveness
about mourning than actual expression of sorrow. Anxiety about
violating the various cultural norms is often the dominant feeling in the poem. None of the sixteenth-century poets, consolers,
or theologians can express grief as simply and unself-consciously
as Henry King does in 'An Exequy', the moving poem on the
death of his wife in 1624.

> Accept, thou Shrine of my dead Saint!
> Instead of Dirges this Complaint;
> And, for sweet flowres to crowne thy Hearse,
> Receive a strew of weeping verse
> From thy griev'd Friend; whome Thou might'st see
> Quite melted into Teares for Thee.[1]

King is not inhibited about his grief and does not exaggerate it;
nor does his poem show a trace of anxiety about moderation or
the legitimacy of mourning. He celebrates a private funeral rite
and focuses on his memories of his wife and his sense of loss.
He does not take refuge in hyperbolic grief, nor does he merely
hint at the great depths of his sorrow by means of an inexpressi-
bility topos. He expresses his loss and affection directly, without
struggling to overcome them. This directness and lack of anxiety
about the irrationality, weakness, impiety, and effeminacy of
grief make King seem worlds apart from Grimald. This chapter
will briefly sketch the course between them. The elegy of the
period, like the letter-writing formularies and the theological
tracts, shows the emergence of a more sympathetic, less anxious
attitude towards mourning.

One finds elegies throughout the sixteenth century, but published collections of elegy, so familiar because 'Lycidas' appeared in one, are a surprisingly late phenonemon and arise in the Cambridge of Cheke, Wilson, and Haddon, the Cambridge so lovingly memorialized in Ascham's *Scholemaster*. In fact, printed elegy of any form is not very common before late in the century. Before 1551 I find only four prints, all of single poems: *The Epitaffe of the most noble and valyaunt Iasper late duke of Beddeforde* (1496), Surrey's and Leland's poems on the death of Wyatt (1542), and *A lamentation of the death of Henry the eyght* (1546?). Between 1551, the year of the first two collections (on Bucer and the Brandons), and 1587, the year which saw three for Sidney, I am able to find only one other, in late 1583 or early 1584 for Sir William Butts. The collections on Sidney's death may have helped to set the fashion, but it is not until the seventeenth century that they are truly common. Oxford University and its colleges were responsible for more volumes than any individual or other institution, and it is instructive to note that whereas only four of their volumes appeared between 1587 and 1603, seventeen were published between 1603 and 1638. The greatest outpouring of elegy occurred after the death of Prince Henry late in 1612. The collective production of elegy thus increases markedly during the period in which attitudes towards mourning are becoming more sympathetic, although the sheer fact of more elegy, however interesting in itself, is not nearly as important as the change in the mood and tone of elegy.[2]

The two earliest collections of elegy, those of 1551, were organized by proponents of the new learning at Cambridge and are closely related in theme, form, and tone. (In fact, the poems by the subjects of the second volume, Henry and Charles Brandon, occupy the place of honor in the first.) Both collections are preoccupied with the theological repercussions of mourning and writing elegy; poem after poem defends or rebukes grief or qualifies its own tentative expression of grief. None of the poems is totally rigoristic, but many, especially in the volume for Bucer, follow Matthew Parker's severe restriction of grief to the loss the living have suffered and to their sins. Since the two volumes are so similar and many of the contributors to the Cambridge section of elegies for the Brandons also wrote on Bucer, I will restrict my examples to the earlier volume.[3]

Parker's sermon for Bucer, as we saw in chapter 2, insists on the impiety of mourning the dead in the Lord, but allows mourning for the loss of the survivors. This legitimate mourning, however, is then focused on the sins of the living, which were responsible for the death of Bucer. Parker is relentlessly logical in this distinction, and the energy with which he condemns mourning for the dead is much more striking than his justification of mourning for loss. With Parker's words ringing in their ears (the prefatory letters refer to his sermon), it is hardly a surprise that defensiveness about mourning and about the publication of the collection is an important issue. The apparent editor, Nicholas Carr, takes great pains in his letter to Sir John Cheke to justify the mourning for Bucer:

...et causas intexam, cur necesse fuit in tali nos moerore esse. Que cum omnia audieris, nec me ut spero reprehendas, qui luctum nostrum mandarim literis: & omnes nos quod ita luxerimus, pio amicorum officio perfunctos iudicabis. (sig. c1^{rv})[4]

...and I shall weave in the reasons why it was necessary for us to be in such sorrow. When you have heard them all, you will not, I hope, blame me for committing our grief to print and will judge that all of us who have grieved in this way have performed the pious duty of friends.

Many of the poets share this defensiveness, and a number of them make sure that no one can accuse them of mourning the dead.

Mors grauis est nobis orbatis lumine tanto:
  Non grauis est tibi, quae vita beata tibi est. (Sir John Cheke, sig. i2^v)
Death is oppressive to us deprived of such a light, but not to you, for whom it is the blessed life.

      Quod occidit, non angimur,
      Sed nostra quod Respublica
      Suo carebit lumine
      Quo clara fulsit vndique. (Christopher Carleil, sig. i4^v)
We are not distressed that he died, but that our republic will lack his light, by which it shone bright everywhere.

Nostram deploro sortem, sed gratulor illi
  Nunc patriam quod habet, qui prius exul erat. (John Herd, sig. m3^v)
I lament our lot, but rejoice with him because he, formerly an exile, now has his fatherland.

Although all of these authors express some grief, they are careful to qualify and justify it. Others are more severe; they devote their poems to setting forth reasons not to grieve and rail against grief. John Frerus, in a Greek poem, asks, 'Why, stranger, do you weep the death of such a man?' (sig. k2^v), proceeds to standard consolatory topoi, and concludes with the ominous implication that anyone who weeps for Bucer does not believe in the resurrection. William Thalesius orders England to abandon weeping.

> Quid fles Bucerum gens Anglica funere raptum?
>   Num lachrymis illum posse redire putes?
> Frontem porge tuam, miseras depone querelas,
>   Viuit, non moritur uir pietatis amans. (sig. m2^r)

Why do you weep Bucer snatched away by death, people of England? You don't think your tears will enable him to return? Relax your brow, put aside your wretched complaints; the lover of piety does not die: he lives.

Francis Newton begins the same way as Thalesius.

> Pone graues fletus, mentem nec confice luctu:
>   Mors etenim secum gaudia magna tulit. (sig. m^r)

Put away your heavy weeping and do not consume your mind with grief, for death brings great joys.

Both poets then move on to familiar reasons not to grieve.

The only anonymous poem is the best example of the tone and themes of the collection. I quote it in full.

> Anglia quid luges Bucerum morte peremptum?
>   Cum Christo superos possidet ille polos.
> Carmine lugubri tua dicas turpia facta,
>   Bucerum nobis haec rapuere mala.
> Flagitijs motus, mortalibus arma mouere
>   Vult Deus, & poena nos grauiore premet.
> Inditium est irae Bucerus morte peremptus:
>   Noluit hunc Dominus tanta uidere mala.
> Anglia te defle, luge tua facta nefanda,
>   Bucerum magnum quae rapuere tibi.
> Buceriçue memor, docuit quae dogmata constans
>   Persequere, & colito cum pietate fidem.
> Hic honor est illi summus: sic ira recedet
>   Magna, Dei vanas reddet & ipse minas. (sig. l2^{rv})

England, why do you mourn Bucer destroyed by death? He possesses the heavens above with Christ. You should tell in mournful song your shameful deeds; our wickedness has snatched Bucer from us. Moved by our crimes, God wishes to wage war with mortals, and he will afflict us with a heavier punishment. Bucer destroyed by death is a sign of wrath; God did not wish him to see such wickedness. England, weep for yourself; mourn your evil deeds which have snatched the great Bucer from you. Mindful of Bucer, follow the teachings which he steadfastly taught, and practice faith with piety. This will be his greatest honor; in this way the great wrath will depart, and God himself will make his threats vain.

55

The poet redirects grief from Bucer to the wicked deeds of the living which have caused Bucer's death. The assertion that Bucer is in heaven suffices to silence grief, and most of the poem concerns the survivors, not the deceased. Bucer is idealized as the just man who is taken away so he will not have to see evil, while the survivors are guilty wretches threatened with further punishment. The only justifiable mourning is for sin, since the poet follows Parker's emphasis on sinfulness instead of his explicit permission of mourning for loss.[5]

The volume on Sir William Butts edited by Robert Dallington around the end of 1583 is not as severe on grief as the ones on Bucer and the Brandons, but the difference is not great. Butts, knighted for his service at the battle of Musselburgh in 1547, died at age 72, and it was a commonplace that grief for the death of the elderly would be much less than for the young – which makes the restraint in the Brandon collection all the more remarkable. The balance of grief and rejoicing rather than the suppression of grief by rejoicing is a keynote of the Butts collection.

> Lament and mourne, that BVTS is gone, you godly that remaine,
> But BVTS is gone from earth to heauen, therefore reioice againe.[6]

Mourning is given its due, however briefly, just as in a poem by Henry Gosnolde: 'Then mourne his want, but laugh because he wants no good, / Lament our losse, triumph his gain, that growes where vertue stood' (sig. D1ᵛ). Gosnolde, like the earlier poets, is careful to state that what is to be lamented is the loss of Butts, not Butts himself, but the lines lack the anxiety about mourning characteristic of the earlier collections.

The Butts volume, however, contains a number of poems which check the expression of sorrow. Anthony Cade begins with a series of angry questions about the power of death and fate over men; the questions justify mournful verse, and Cade has Apollo, Athena, and the Dryads, Fauns, Nymphs, and Muses weep for Butts. Cade even goes so far as to assert that his only pleasure is in weeping ('sola est mihi flere voluptas'), but this goes too far and leads to the poem's reversal.

> Sed quid ago demens, quid luctibus aethera pulso?
> Num lachrymasse iuuat? num gemuisse iuuat? (sig. C4ʳ)

But what am I – a madman – doing? Why do I beat the skies with my laments? Weeping is of no use, is it? Or groaning?

Cade retracts the complaints which begin his poem. His grief is blocked after a brief indulgence.

The tragic death of Sir Philip Sidney at age 32 in November 1586 elicited an unprecedented amount of elegy – and of elegy which reveals a much more tolerant attitude towards mourning – but it would be a mistake to regard the outpouring solely as genuine grief for Sidney. Cambridge scored a great coup by bringing out a volume the day of Sidney's burial, 16 February 1587; the volume is headed by an English sonnet by James VI with five Latin translations (one by the king himself), several poems in Greek, and even one poem in Hebrew. (This does set a fashion; it becomes *de rigueur* in the later university collections to have at least one poem in Hebrew.) Alexander Nevill, the editor, dedicated the volume to Sidney's uncle, the Earl of Leicester, the chancellor of Oxford. This volume was a considerable embarrassment to that university, which responded with two of its own (one from New College, one from the university as a whole) and numerous excuses.

William Gager's dedication to Leicester of *Exequiae Illustrissimi Equitis, D. Philippi Sidnaei*, a few days over a year after Sidney's death, explains the delayed appearance of the collection as due to the immensity of grief at Oxford. The Trojan women wailed for Hector, Gager argues, but how does that compare with Hecuba's silence? Oxford men were too shocked to write, and those who did wrote for themselves, not for display – an obvious hit at Cambridge. The *Exequiae*, following upon New College's *Peplus*, takes the last place in the procession of mourning collections, 'qui est inter lugentes & honorificus, & luctuosus maximè' ('which is the most honorific and mournful among the mourners'). Gager allows that his major difficulty as editor was to avoid being overwhelmed by the multitudinous crowd of elegies, for which reason he had to exclude 'the Hebrew, Greek, French, Italian and even not a few of the Latin' poems. Several poems in the collection, not to mention one in *Peplus*, take up Gager's theme that great grief is silent, while superficial grief finds easy expression.[7] The most genuine emotion in much of the *Exequiae* is irritation at Cambridge.

Nevertheless, several poems in the Sidney collections reveal a different attitude towards mourning. Expressions of grief – many hyperbolic and none particularly convincing – abound to an unprecedented degree, and it is especially significant that they are rarely blocked and rarely lead to self-rebuking reversals. A few of the poems even set themselves up for a reversal and then studiously avoid it.

Roger Morrell begins a poem with what looks like a common-place about the futility of grief: if only tears could bring back the dead. One expects him to conclude: then weeping would be commendable, but since tears are useless, stop them. But Morrell takes another direction. If tears could bring back Sidney, all nature would melt into tears, and, in fact, nature did mourn at the moment of his death. Morrell proceeds to praise Sidney for his service to Mars and the Muses, perhaps the commonest theme in the collections, and to declare their grief, as well as Parma's (the enemy's) and Queen Elizabeth's. His conclusion asks for a continuation, not a diminution, of grief.

> Cumque satis nullus decoret tua funera fletus,
> (Nec nimis esse potest quod satis esse nequit)
> Plangamus palmas, lachrimarum flumina manent,
> Sitque tuae mortis tristis & atra dies.[8]

Since no weeping can sufficiently honor your death (and what cannot be sufficient cannot be excessive), let us beat our hands, let rivers of tears flow, and let the day of your death be sad and black.

The poem does not completely escape from anxiety about mourning, as the defensive parenthesis indicates.

A poem apparently by William Gager attacks the efficacy of two standard consolatory topoi. The poet asks for consolation but

> Non vel quale solet legi libellis
> Audiriue Scholis, vetus leuamen:
> Nempe pro patria occidit Philippus,
> Omnibúsque semel mori statutum est;
> Sunt haec nota satis, nimisque trita,
> Vincuntúrque meo statim dolore. (*Exequiae*, sig. C3ʳ)

not the kind which is usually read in books or heard in the schools, the old comfort – that yes, to be sure, Philip died for his fatherland, and it is ordained that we all die sometime. These are well enough known and too trite and are immediately defeated by my sorrow.

The ending of the poem implies that no consolation will be able to still the poet's grief; there is no hint of anxiety about lack of moderation.

Another poem, an anonymous one, tries to stir up grief which is passing away.

Quis desiderio sit pudor, aut modus
Tam chari capitis? lugubris Anglia,
Exhausta quamuis sit dolore,
Denuò iam renouat dolorem. (*Exequiae*, sig. F4ʳ)

What restraint or measure can there be for the loss of so dear a person?
Let mournful England, though exhausted by sorrow, renew its sorrow
again.

By borrowing the first couple of lines of Horace's *Odes* 1.24, this
poet comes very close to a defense of immoderate grief. Contrary
to Gager's preface, this poem was apparently written long after
Sidney's death, and yet it wishes to renew grief, not suppress it.
One final example actually does vilify anyone who would impose
any bounds to grief.

Audio nescio quos nostris finemqué modumqué
Iudicio lacrymis imposuisse suo.
Cedite vecordes, ignari cedite rerum,
Saepe solet medicam vincere morbus opem. (*Peplus*, p. 12)

I hear that I know not whom has imposed a limit and measure of their
judgment on our tears. Go away, madmen, ignoramuses: the disease
often defeats medical aid.

The lines are another example of the way in which anger at others can take the place of direct expression of sorrow, but it is still
significant and unprecedented to defend immoderate mourning.[9]

Two poems from Thomas Campion's *Poemata* of 1595 show a
further relaxation of the restraints on grief and also a reversal of
previously rigoristic topoi. Shortly before the publication of the
volume, Francis Manby died at sea.[10] Campion opens his elegy
by asking Phoebus why, since the grief-stricken prefer darkness,
he brings daylight. This leads the poet to imagine himself as
another Orpheus following his friend to the underworld.

Heu heu sequar quocunque me rapiet dolor,
Et te per atra Ditis inferni loca
Manbaee lachrymis ora suffusus petam
Flectamque manes planctus & immites deas,
Liminaque dira molliam, ac vsque horridas
Acherontis vndas, cuncta nam pietas potest,
Quâ quâ redibis moeror inueniet viam.[11]

Alas, I shall follow wherever sorrow takes me and seek you, Manby, my
face drenched with tears, through the black regions of infernal Hades. I
shall make the dead and the harsh goddesses relent and soften the hard
threshold and even Acheron's rough waves with my lamentation, for
dutiful affection can do anything. Grief will find whatever way will
allow you to return.

Campion is diverting his sorrow with the fantasy that grief felt deeply enough will restore his friend to life. For a moment he is able to master his suffering and envisions a revivified world, in which the hateful light complained of in the first line will turn kindly again.

> Tùm rursùs alma luce candebit polus,
> Vltroque flores terra purpureos dabit,
> Omnia virebunt, sentiet mundus suum
> Decus reuerti, sentiet tremulum mare,
> Suumque flebit ipse Neptunus nephas. (sigs. F5^{rv})

Then again the sky will glow with kindly light, and the earth will spontaneously put forth purple flowers. Everything will bloom. The world will feel its ornament return; the quivering sea will feel it, and Neptune himself will weep for his crime.

Death intrudes into the vision even amidst the flowers, for purple flowers are traditionally offerings to the dead,[12] and the reality of death finally dispels the fantasy.

> Ah siste vanos impetus demens furor,
> Sperare nostrûm nemini tantum licet,
> Fac ergo quiuis iure quod miser potest,
> Luge, supersit hic tibi semper labor. (sig. F5^{v})

Oh, check your futile impulses – a mad frenzy; none of us is allowed to hope for so much. Do, then, what any wretch justly can: mourn; let this wearying toil always be present to you.

Campion does reverse himself; he renounces his impossible fantasy of restoration and even calls it insanity. One might expect that the poet would conclude with some stiff consolatory precept about the futility of grief, thus rejecting all the sorrow and affection embodied in the fantasy. Instead, Campion tells himself to mourn. 'Labor' – emphatically placed as the last word in the poem and carrying all its Virgilian connotations of long-suffering, persistent toil – is the future to which Campion pledges himself, not resigns himself (as 'supererit' would have suggested). The poem ends by embracing grief instead of rejecting it – embracing a simple grief stripped of self-important fantasies and freed from the easy excesses of hyperbole.[13]

A consolation for the poet Edward Mychelburne on the death of his sister takes a surprising turn away from consolation.[14] The poem begins severely enough.

> Ergòne perpetuos dabit vmbra sororia fletus?
> Inque fugam molles ossea forma deas?
> Sic Edouarde situ ferali horrenda Thaleia

60

> Antiquosque sales, delitiasque abiget?
> Carmina nequaquam tangunt funebria manes.
> Impetrabilior saxa ad acuta canas.
> Parce piam temerare animam, si cara sorori
> Extinctae superest, nè sit iniqua tibi. (sig. D3ᵛ)

So then, the shade of your sister will cause perpetual weeping? The bony form will put the soft goddesses to flight? So, Edward, fearful Thalia will lead the old wit and delights away from the deadly site? Funeral poems by no means touch the dead. You would more easily get your desire by singing to the sharp rocks. Stop profaning the pious soul, if it remains dear to your dead sister, lest it be harsh to you.

Campion complains that Mychelburne is allowing morbid feelings to divert him to futile funeral elegies when he should be writing witty epigrams and love elegies. The first line implies that the grief has lasted long enough; it is time to return to lighter poetry before he alienates both his Muse and his dead sister. 'Ossea forma' ('bony form') is a shock tactic and hardly sympathetic. After the indirections of the first four lines Campion asserts sarcastically and forcefully that grief is a waste of time: Mychelburne might as well sing to the rocks, symbols of inhumanity since the *Iliad*.

The next section of the poem describes the exhaustion of 'Elegeia' from grief and leads to an exhortation to put mourning aside and return to former poetic pursuits. Campion urges Mychelburne to banish his sister's image from his mind and forget her last words, since oblivion cures grief. So far the poem has been nothing but hard-nosed consolation, but the conclusion, totally unprepared for, changes all that.

> Verba dolorem acuunt, soluunt obliuia curas,
> Immemores animos cura dolorque fugit.
> Sed tua si pietas monitis parere recusat,
> Aegraque mens constans in feritate sua est,
> Nulla sit in terris regio, non ora, nec aetas
> Inscia moeroris, moestitiaeque tuae.
> Non Hyades tantum celebrent fulgentia coelo
> Sydera fraternus quas reparauit amor:
> Quantùm fama tuas lachrimas, obitusque sororis,
> O benè defleto funere digna soror!
> Et tibi si placet hoc indulge Edouarde dolori,
> Singultuque grauem pectore pasce animum.
> Tristitiam leuat ipsa dies, gaudebit & vltro
> Ascitis tandem mens vegetare iocis. (sig. D4ʳᵛ)

Words sharpen sorrow, forgetting dissolves cares, and care and sorrow flee the forgetful mind. But if your dutiful affection refuses to obey this

61

advice, and your sick mind is constant in its wildness, let there be no region, shore, or age on earth that does not know about your grief and sadness. Don't let the Hyades, whom love for their brother revived, make their constellation shining in the sky as famous as your tears and the death of your sister, O sister worthy to be well wept for in death. And, if it pleases you, Edward, indulge your sorrow and nourish your heavy mind with deep sobs. Time itself will relieve your sadness, and your mind will at last of itself take pleasure in quickening to its habitual sports.

As in the poem on Manby, Campion uses *pietas* to describe respectful devotion to the memory of the dead; he avoids the rigoristic paradox of 'impia pietas', which will be discussed in the section on Jonson. At the end of this poem *pietas* silences the earlier arguments against grief, especially any lurking implication of its impiety. Campion encourages Mychelburne to give himself wholly over to his sorrow and to funeral poetry, thereby making himself a more famous monument to grief than the Hyades, whose weeping for the death of their brother led to their stellification ('reparauit' is odd). In Erasmus and elsewhere we have seen the consolatory argument that grief consumes health and destroys the body; here Campion urges his friend to nourish ('pasce') himself on his sorrow. And the final couplet ignores another rigoristic commonplace. For Campion, as for Cole 30 years later, there is nothing shameful about waiting for time to cure grief. In fact, Campion's lines are truly consoling; they inspire the confidence that grief will run its course and allow Mychelburne to resume his former poetry. He is urged to indulge his sorrow, freed now from the worry that indulgence in sorrow will lead to uncontrollable, interminable excess.[15]

Another indication of the change in attitude towards mourning is the development, long before Johnson's famous strictures on 'Lycidas', of criticism of artificial grief in elegy. This criticism is implicit in the Oxonians' rationalizations of the tardy appearance of their verses on Sidney (great grief cannot speak) but now becomes more pointed, as in Towers' previously quoted attack on mercenary grief. The criticisms of artificial grief protest too much to secure their apparent rhetorical purpose – to persuade the reader of the sincerity of the poet's grief – but for that very reason testify to an emerging ideal of sincere expression of heartfelt sorrow rather than to the former ideal of somber self-restraint. The opening of Davenant's 'Elegy on the Duke of Buckingham's Death', probably of 1628, is a good example.

> No Poetts triviall rage, that must aspire
> And heighten all his hymnes by inforced fire,
> Shall his loud dirges mix with my sad Quire.
> Such sell their teares, like Inke, for sordid hire.[16]

Clement Paman deplores with unusual force the hypocritically lachrymose practice of contemporary elegy in a poem concerning the collection for Ben Jonson, who is praised for his 'wise greife'.

> Now we but kick the urne & blow about
> Those ashes into sport wch sorrow ought
> Preserue in balme, not Pickle. For though y^{ere}
> May be a touch of salt in euery teare
> Yett sure there is more churlishnes in them
> W^{ch} are wrung out & forc't then those wch streame
> From full & easy chanells, T'one's art
> Foames from the teeth, t'others melt from the hart.[17]

Since the famous collection on Edward King contains three modifications of this theme, a brief consideration of that collection and two others also published in 1638 will conclude this chapter.[18]

Jonsonus Virbius is striking for its single-minded devotion to praise and contains few expressions of sorrow. Only the first poem, Lord Falkland's pastoral elegy, goes to any lengths to grieve and seems to be a case in which grief is intended as an indirect form of praise. Robert Meade explicitly equates moaning with praising (p. 471). There is no defensiveness about mourning, but there is considerable defensiveness about Jonson and his achievement and the authors' own poetic talent.[19] In particular a number of elegists attempt to clear Jonson of charges of malicious satire and ill temper and to explain away his setbacks on the stage as due to envious ignorance.

Only one poem in the collection appears to brood over mourning. Dudly Diggs begins.

> I Dare not, learned *Shade*, bedew thy Hearse
> With *teares*, unlesse that *impudence* in Verse
> Would cease to be a *sinne*; and what were *crime*
> In *Prose*, would be no *injurie* in *Rime*.
> My *thoughts* are so *below*, I feare to act
> A sinne, like their black *envie*, who detract. (p. 444).

The first four lines might suggest pure rigorism; weeping for the dead is a crime or reveals a suspicion that the dead is in hell. The next couplet, however, shows what Diggs really means. He

63

is declaring his own inadequacy for the task of praising Jonson and fears that his bungling will do more harm than good. The sin that bothers him is defamation, not grief. This becomes more apparent in the lines which follow and spell out the poet's 'weaknesse'. Diggs is using weeping as a shorthand for praising:

> O could we *weepe* like *Thee*! we might convay
> New *breath*, and raise *men* from their *Beds* of Clay
> Unto a *life* of *fame*.

That an elegy on the one consistently rigoristic poet reveals no understanding of its subject's attitude towards mourning is evidence of the demise of rigorism.

From *Jonsonus Virbius* one might conclude that anxiety about mourning was a thing of the past, but the other collections from 1638 tell a different story. Later in the year Christ Church College honored the untimely death of a great benefactor, Paul, Viscount Bayning. Several of the poets – Jasper Mayne, William Cartwright, Robert Meade, and Richard West, among others – had written for Jonson because that collection had been edited by Brian Duppa, the current Dean of Christ Church. West's elegy for Bayning is particularly severe, although his poem on Jonson gives no hint of a corresponding severity.

> Forbeare yee whining Wits to rayle at Fate
> In viler termes then Scolds at *Billings-gate*:
> Nor brand poore Death with baser Epithites
> Then *Textor* has when of the Divell he writes:
> All such ill-sounding Dirges yee can have
> Are but as Mandrakes planted on his grave.
> Your teares are now ridiculous; were I
> A Poet, I would write Deaths Elogie. (p. 9)

West resorts to the bullying rhetoric of *consolatio* and its reasons not to grieve, including the accusation that mourning is envy of the dead's felicity. Meade (p. 12) and Thomas Isham (p. 16) ask pardon for their tears. Nevertheless, these three authors are exceptions. None of the others worries about grieving, and some even want to heighten their grief. H. Benet writes: 'Pardon my grief, that dares assume that Dresse, / For scatter'd in wild Fancies 'twould seem lesse' (p. 41). F. Palmer apologizes if the college's grief seems less now than when Bayning went on his travels (p. 26). And I. Fell, although careful to indicate that he disapproves of immoderation, says that it is a sorrow not to have sorrowed enough.

Non tamen hoc credam, iuvat usque favere dolori,
   Sed nequeo, hoc dolor est, non doluisse satis. (p. 30)

Now I don't believe that it is good to indulge sorrow constantly, but I can't help it: not to have sorrowed enough – this is sorrow.

The *Justa Edovardo King* contains the widest range of attitudes towards mourning of the three collections of 1638. Some poets maintain an anxious self-restraint, some disapprove of artificial grief, two defend immoderate mourning, and a number curse the sea and express sorrow with no care for strictures against mourning. 'Lycidas', as we shall see in the last chapter, serenely rises above any anxiety about mourning.

One poem is even a full-blown attack on grief. It is by Thomas Farnaby, the famous schoolmaster, who is apparently the oldest contributor to the collection. The poem reads as if it belongs to the generation before Farnaby – with one difference which indicates the change in times. Here are the opening lines.

Stultus trecentas ingerit plagas freto,
Et nectit arctas compedes maris Deo,
Impius in Austros arma Psyllorum movet,
Quicunque summi Numinis legi obstrepit.
Gestare silices Stoici cordis tamen
Arguerer, & adamanta duri pectoris,
Me nisi moveret cladis acceptae dolor:
Qui fraena justus poscit immitti sibi;
Si non abominarer Austros, & fretum,
Scopulos, ratem, improbúmque rectorem ratis,
Cujus scelere juvenis spei ingentis meus
Periit alumnus morte acerba, ingloria. (p. 25)[20]

Whoever clamors against the law of the highest godhead foolishly heaps three hundred blows on the deep and binds the sea-god with tight shackles or impiously takes up the arms of the Psylli against the south winds. Nevertheless, I should be accused of bearing the Stoic's flinty heart and hard, adamantine breast if sorrow for the disaster I've heard about didn't move me – sorrow which rightly demands restraints – and if I didn't detest the south winds and the deep, the rocks, the ship and its wicked helmsman, by whose crime a youth of great hope, my pupil, perished immaturely and ingloriously.

Farnaby stigmatizes the folly and impiety of grieving with two allusions to Herodotus. After his bridge over the Hellespont was destroyed by a storm, Xerxes ordered that the sea receive three hundred lashes and that a pair of fetters be thrown into it for defying him, its master. This dreadful instance of *hubris* is a sure indication of Xerxes' downfall.[21] The Psylli perished to a man for waging war with the south wind after it dried up their water (Herodotus 4.173 and Gellius 16.11). Farnaby is suggesting that murmuring against God's decrees is not only impious and foolish: it is fatal. It would thus seem obvious that one should avoid grief. What distinguishes Farnaby from the rigorists of earlier days is his defensiveness about his rigorism. Realizing that his severity will appear outmoded, he tries to blunt censure by anticipating it. Despite the impious folly of murmuring against God's will, he will be called a Stoic stock and stone if he does not grieve. It used to be that those poets who wished to mourn justified themselves; now it is the rigorist who feels he must do so. This attempt to silence criticism is the closest Farnaby comes to a concession to grief. He proceeds to prove that King is not without glory because his fame remains and he escaped to heaven from the prison of the body.

> Lessus inanes mittite ergò & naenias:
> Virtute cassos impii & stulti fleant;
> Lugere felices nefas est & furor.

So stop your empty laments and dirges. Let the impious and foolish weep for those lacking in virtue. It is sacrilege and madness to mourn for the blessed.

There is no expression of sympathy for grief; no allowance is made for the loss of the survivors. This is one poem Becon would have approved of.[22]

He would not have approved of some of the others, especially two which argue that it is reasonable to mourn immoderately, not just within bounds. These authors go to the opposite extreme from Farnaby. They are defensive about grief, but differ from the earlier justifiers who make their justifications more acceptable by granting that immoderate mourning is prohibited. Thomas Norton concludes his poem without even a nod to moderation.

> I'th' Irish sea, there set our Sun;
> And since he's set, the day's undone.
> Perpetuall night, sad, black, and grim,
> Puts on her mourning-weeds for him.
> What man hath sense, or dare avouch
> H' ath reason, and yet hath no touch?
> Reason not limits them that weep,
> But bids them lanch into the deep;
> Tells us they not exceed, that drain
> In tears the mighty Ocean;

Nor all that in these tears are found
As in a generall deluge drown'd. (pp. 19–20)

Norton is not simply asserting that natural affections are wounded at the death of a dear friend. Like Falkland in *Jonsonus Virbius* (p. 431), Norton is asserting that this grief is reasonable. Someone who did not mourn for King would not merely be a Stoic stock, but irrational. One of the commonest consolatory weapons against grief, its irrationality, is thus stood on its head.[23]

This brief survey of elegy from 1551 to 1638 shows a decided reduction of anxiety about mourning, but not the disappearance of anxiety. The late sixteenth- and early seventeenth-century elegist is much less likely to worry about justifying his laments. Chiding retractions of grieving verses become uncommon, and swerves away from consolatory severity take their place beside more serene progressions from grief to comforting resolution. Defenses of mourning continue, but some defenders dispense with the earlier adherence to moderation and argue that no bounds should be set to mourning. Some poets begin to attack artificial displays of grief, thereby revealing an ideal of sincere sorrow rather than silent self-restraint. Simple expressions of sorrow, instead of hyperbolical escapism, are still infrequent, although a poem like Campion's on the death of Manby shows a poet wrestling with unexaggerated sorrow. There are some triumphs over inhibitions to grieve; we shall see them when we come to King and Milton.

Chapter 5

SURREY AND SPENSER

Surrey

Surrey writes with greater ease when he is restraining or hinting at his grief or attacking the enemies of the deceased. Some of his efforts to lament are peculiarly awkward, and his most moving elegy is a poem which disguises the fact that it is an elegy. Suppressed grief is the dominant note instead of anxious reflection on the legitimacy of mourning, even though one of the elegies is a justification of grief for Wyatt.

Some time before 8 August 1537, in the grounds of Windsor, Surrey struck Edward Seymour, presumably for spreading the rumor that Surrey and his father, the Duke of Norfolk, were in sympathy with the Pilgrimage of Grace.[1] Violence within the court was considered a personal threat to the king, and an offender ran the risk of losing his right hand, his goods, his lands, and of imprisonment at the king's pleasure. Norfolk was worried that his son would lose his hand, but Surrey was only confined to the grounds of Windsor. 'So crewell prison' is a product of that confinement, perhaps a protest against it. One of Surrey's motives for writing the poem may have been to call attention to his special friendship with his brother-in-law, Henry VIII's illegitimate son, Henry Fitzroy, Duke of Richmond, in an effort to persuade the king to release him from Windsor. In any event, beneath the poem's surface lies indignation, which Surrey prudently does not declare openly, at his imprisonment. This indignation makes it easier for Surrey to recall his intimacy with Richmond and to express grief at his death. Richmond had died a year before, 22 July 1536, and his death was a heavy blow to Surrey, according to Norfolk's letter to Cromwell, 12 July 1537. Norfolk was requesting permission for Surrey to join him at York because he had just had word that Surrey was 'very weak, his nature running from him abundantly'. Norfolk comments, 'He was in that case a great part of the last year, and as he

68

showed me came to him for thought of my lord of Richmond, and now I think is come again by some other thought.'[2]

'So crewell prison' is often called an elegy, for example by W. J. Courthope in his fine tribute, 'I know of few verses in the whole range of human poetry in which the voice of nature utters the accents of grief with more simplicity and truth; it seems to me to be the most pathetic *personal* elegy in English poetry.'[3] Tottel, however, publishes it with the title 'Prisoned in windsor, he recounteth his pleasure passed there', which is an accurate description of most of the poem and allows the reader to be surprised by line 46, the turn towards lament for Richmond. For Surrey leads even the reader who immediately recognizes the 'kinges soon' (Fitzroy) of line 3 as Surrey's recently dead friend to expect not an elegy but a contrast between past pleasure at Windsor and his current imprisonment. For most of the poem the reader assumes that 'eche swete place retournes a tast full sowre' because Surrey has lost his freedom, not because of associations with Richmond. Thus Surrey's grief, when it does emerge, is seen to be a noble lament for a lost friend rather than irritation at imprisonment; the potentially hostile reader for whom the poem seems to have been written, perhaps Henry VIII himself, is thus forced into admiration for the poet. This, at any rate, seems to be the poem's rhetorical strategy.

Nevertheless, the poem is an elegy. Surrey reviews the sites of his various activities with his friend, as if mental revisitation might bring him back to life. When his meditation brings him indoors to 'The voyd walles eke, that harbourde us eche night', his solitary situation within those walls reveals the frustration of the search and leads to an emotional outburst.

> And with this thought the blood forsakes my face,
> The teares berayne my chekes of dedlye hewe;
> The which, as sone as sobbing sighes, alas,
> Upsupped have, thus I my playnt renewe:
>
> O place of blys, renewer of my woos,
> Geve me accompt wher is my noble fere,
> Whome in thy walles thow didest eche night enclose,
> To other lief, but unto me most dere.
>
> Each wall, alas, that dothe my sorowe rewe,
> Retournes therto a hollowe sound of playnt.
> Thus I, alone, where all my fredome grew,
> In pryson pyne with bondage and restraynt,

> And with remembraunce of the greater greif,
> To bannishe the lesse, I fynde my chief releif.

Two things are striking about this expression of grief. First, as scholars have noticed, the diction is that of love-lament and has parallels in Surrey's own love poetry.[4] Surrey is himself aware of this; he points to the connection by calling his lament 'my playnt' only a few lines after writing 'Of pleasaunt playnt and of our ladyes prayes'. Later in the century Puttenham links laments for death, war, and disappointments in love, and modern psychologists agree in regarding mourning as a reaction to loss in general, not just loss through death. The language of love-lament to express sorrow for Richmond's death is thus wholly appropriate, since Surrey's grief stems from the rupture of a loving relationship. And this language hardly intrudes into the poem; most of the earlier stanzas recall various moments of the friends' amorous service of their ladies and use the standard diction of love poetry. In fact, the major bond between the two is companionship in love; Surrey and Richmond sound like models for Musidorus and Pyrocles in Sidney's *Arcadia*.

> The statelye sales, the Ladyes bright of hewe,
> The daunces short, long tales of great delight,
> With wordes and lookes that Tygers could but rewe,
> Where eche of us did plead the others right.

These tigers are the counterparts of 'Each wall, alas, that dothe my sorowe rewe', for tigers and stones are conventional types of unpitying heartlessness.[5] The hyperbole of love poetry proves to be no exaggeration of Surrey's grief; the stony walls are sympathetic, but their hollow reverberation only underscores his isolation. The continuity of diction between the recollection of the past and the lament emphasizes the affection for Richmond which is declared with such restraint.

Even more striking than the language of love poetry is the control of grief. Surrey presents himself as directing the emotional cycle of the poem. He is following the Paracelsian method of expelling one sorrow with another, 'And with remembraunce of the greater greif, / To bannishe the lesse, I fynde my chief releif'. He is calling to mind his friendship and inducing his tears, sobs, and plaint; he is not overwhelmed by them. The poem does not describe something that happened to the poet unexpectedly, as does 'When Windesor walles sustain'd my wearied arme'. In that poem, probably not from the period of

70

Surrey's imprisonment at Windsor because of the references to spring, the scene before the poet triggers a memory – 'Than did to mynd resort' – and makes him sad, even to the point of considering suicide. We are to imagine one chance occurrence, but 'So crewell prison' asks us to imagine the poet reproducing his mental search through Windsor and the sorrow which it releases. The grief is tamed; it comes when Surrey calls it, not of its own accord. The poem allows Surrey to remain faithful to his society's ideal of self-control and to express sorrow at the same time.

Surrey shares this ideal and is uncomfortable and awkward when he tries to express grief. In 'So crewell prison' his mastery of the situation allows him to mourn more naturally than in his other elegies. He is most at ease with understatement; he hints at his grief more effectively than he can declare it. In the sonnet on Thomas Clere, 'Norfolk sprang thee, Lambeth holds thee dead', which was inscribed on a tablet in the Howards' chapel at Lambeth, Surrey effaces himself from his public commemoration. The poem addresses Clere in the second person and gives no indication that its author is Surrey, to whom it refers by name or calls 'Thine Earle'. The closest the poet comes to lament is one exclamation, 'Shelton for love, Surrey for Lord thou chase: / Aye me! while life did last that league was tender'. The other exclamation points to depths of affection, and by implication, of grief: 'Ah Clere, if love had booted, care, or cost, / Heaven had not wonn, nor earth so timely lost'. Although an isolated reading of this sonnet might find 'less the restraint of inhibition than the orderliness of contemplation',[6] setting it within the context of Surrey's other elegies and the repressive attitudes towards grief in the first part of the sixteenth century suggests that the orderliness of contemplation is a defense and an inhibition.

The public epitaph 'Wyat resteth here, that quicke coulde never rest' is even more restrained and impersonal than the sonnet for Clere.[7] The first 36 lines praise Wyatt's virtues in anatomical order, and the last two lines blame 'us' for his death: 'Thus, for our gylt, this jewell have we lost; / The earth his bones, the heavens possesse his goost'. Wyatt personifies all the virtues; poet and reader are sinners. The praise expiates society's offenses against Wyatt, and the poem enacts the split of ambivalence into an idealized dead person and vilified survivors.

Surrey conforms to the ideal of self-restraint for which he

praises Wyatt: 'In neyther fortune lyfte, nor so represt, / To swell
in welth, nor yelde unto mischaunce'. This ideal is often held up
to the bereaved, as when Servius Sulpicius Rufus tells Cicero
that everyone has seen how well he has borne good fortune and
now is his opportunity to show how well he can bear ill fortune
(*Epistulae ad familiares* 4.5.6). Surrey does not miss his chance
to avoid yielding to misfortune. The only emotion is expressed
at the recollection of Wyatt's enemies.

> A valiaunt Corps, where force and beautye met,
> Happy, alas, to happy but for foos,
> Lyved, and ran the race that nature set;
> Of manhodes shape, where she the mold did loos.

This emotion is not even Surrey's own; it is borrowed from one
of Dido's last speeches in the *Aeneid*.

> I lived and ranne the course fortune did graunt,
> And under earth my great gost now shall wende.
> A goodly town I built, and saw my walles,
> Happy, alas to happy, if these costes
> The Troyan shippes had never touched aye.[8]

The inappropriateness of this imitation reveals the difficulty
which confronts Surrey when he tries to interject a note of sorrow; he is too constrained to express his own feelings and has
recourse to a Virgilian tag.

A similar inappropriateness occurs in 'Dyvers thy death doo
dyverslye bemone' just at the moment that Surrey is trying to
express his intense grief for Wyatt. The sonnet is the most
explicit treatment of the theme that Wyatt was greatly envied, a
point insisted upon by each of the elegies. Surrey contrasts the
feigned and envious tears of Wyatt's enemies – some shed hypocritical tears as Caesar did for Pompey's death in Wyatt's translation of Petrarch, and some shed envious tears because of Wyatt's
fame after death – with his own sincere grief.

> But I that knewe what harbourd in that hedd,
> What vertues rare were tempred in that brest,
> Honour the place that such a jewell bredd,
> And kysse the ground where as thy coorse doth rest
> With vaporde eyes; from whence such streames avayle
> As Pyramus did on Thisbes brest bewayle.

Pyramus sheds tears for Thisbe because he misinterprets her
bloody veil as a sign that a wild beast has killed her; his tears are
the prelude to his suicide (Ovid, *Metamorphoses* 4.105–21). His

tears and death are thus based on an illusion. Surrey's couplet also suggests an odd pun, inappropriate to the occasion. Pyramus sheds his tears over Thisbe's veil; Surrey's tears 'avayle'. It is difficult to understand why Surrey would want to associate his grief for Wyatt with this macabre story, and the couplet has been condemned since Nott.[9] Is Surrey implying that he is so upset by Wyatt's death that he is contemplating suicide?[10] Such hyperbole seems too implausible. Discomfort with the expression of grief prevents Surrey from thinking through the implications of his comparison and of the language he uses to make it.

The third poem on Wyatt's death reads like a defense of the tears shed in the other sonnet. It is addressed to one of Wyatt's enemies, who finds fault with grief at his death. The syntax is tortuous and has given trouble; the poem has yet to receive an accurate paraphrase.[11]

> In the rude age when scyence was not so rife,
> If Jove in Crete and other where they taught
> Artes to reverte to profyte of our lyfe,
> Wan after death to have their temples sought;
> If vertue yet in no unthankfull tyme,
> Fayled of some to blast her endles fame
> (A goodlie meane bothe to deter from cryme
> And to her steppes our sequell to enflame);
> In dayes of treuthe, if Wyattes frendes then waile
> (The onlye debte that ded of quycke may clayme)
> That rare wit spent, employde to our avayle,
> Where Christ is tought deserve they monnis blame?
> His livelie face thy brest how did it freate,
> Whose Cynders yet with envye doo the eate.

The general sense of the first twelve lines is: if benefactors of humanity and the virtuous have been praised even in barbarous, ungrateful times, should Wyatt's friends be blamed for mourning his death? The lines thus praise Wyatt for his virtuous life and his intellectual service to mankind, probably his translation of the penitential psalms, to which Surrey refers at the end of the 'Epitaffe' and which he praises in 'The greate Macedon that out of Persy chased'. The couplet then turns against Wyatt's enemy who presumes to blame such mourning, and suggests that only envy could prompt his censure. It is much easier for Surrey to attack this enemy than to express sorrow; the couplet has a directness and pungency lacking in Surrey's attempts to mourn.

The first quatrain has caused the greatest difficulty. Tottel changes 'where they' to 'were that'. Nott and Rollins take 'wan' to be the past tense of 'ween'. Jones sees a reference to the uncertainty of Jove's birthplace. 'Wan', however, is the past of 'win' in the sense of 'succeed in doing, manage to' (OED 13). 'Other' is the plural form of the pronoun (OED 6b), and 'other where' does not mean 'elsewhere', as it often does in the sixteenth century. The first quatrain presupposes an euhemeristic interpretation of ancient deities: Jove and other human benefactors of mankind were worshipped as gods after their deaths.[12] Jove was worshipped in Crete; the others, where they taught. 'In Crete' and 'where they taught / Artes to reverte to profyte of our lyfe' are thus parallel, although the clause also provides the reason why the others were worshipped.

'Blast' has proved the stumbling block in the second quatrain. It can mean 'blight' or 'bring discredit upon', but these meanings do not suit the two lines which follow because discrediting virtue is hardly the way to make it attractive and to deter people from vice. 'Blast' here means 'proclaim' (OED 16): not even in times noted for ingratitude has virtue lacked someone to praise her. 'Sequell' is a bit of a puzzle. The meaning required is something like Sylvester's 'to inflame us so that we might follow her (Virtue's) footsteps', but the word is not attested in a sense equivalent to 'following'. OED, in fact, gives this line as one of its examples for the meaning 'posterity'. This, however, is unlikely. In all of the other citations the sense is clear from the context, and it is hard to understand why Surrey would wish to restrict the effect of praising virtue to posterity and not extend it to the present generation.

The third quatrain is the easiest of the three to understand, even though Nott, perhaps Surrey's best commentator, wished to emend 'if' to 'let'. Surrey reasons *a fortiori* in a way that recalls Erasmus' introduction of Christianity in the *Declamatio de morte*: if pagans worshipped virtue, shouldn't Christians? Mourning is here conceived as a tribute to the dead, an indirect form of praise. Surrey, like the elegists for Bucer and the Brandons, is careful to specify the kind of grief he is defending: not grief for Wyatt as if he had suffered something dreadful, but grief for the loss of Wyatt's genius, which had been so beneficial. ('Spent' probably means 'consumed, extinguished' rather than just being a synonym for 'employde'.) 'Where Christ is tought' is parallel to 'where they taught' and goes better with the words that follow than those that precede: do Wyatt's friends deserve blame *among Christians?* In other words, someone who does condemn this grief – the person whom the poem addresses – is not a Christian.

Spenser

Anger at Wyatt's enemies is the emotional response to his death which Surrey can express most forcefully. Surrey laments with greatest success when he makes grief his own action rather than something which takes possession of him and which he must suffer passively. Spenser, on the other hand, is a master of lament. His poetry contains wild, uncontrolled displays of grief, and he is more sympathetic even towards excess, provided that it is temporary. Surrey is at pains to justify mourning for Wyatt, but his justification is part of an attack on the dead poet's enemies. Spenser is more concerned about the moral problem of grief; his elegies explore the boundaries between moderation and excess.

Daphnaida, written in 1590 after the death of Douglas Howard, the eighteen-year-old wife of Spenser's friend Arthur Gorges, presents a picture of excessive mourning as a counterexample to moderation.[13] An instructive parallel comes from Seneca's *Consolatio ad Marciam* (2–3), which contrasts the reactions of Augustus' sister and wife to the deaths of their sons. Octavia never stops mourning Marcellus' death; she becomes a monument to her own grief and an enemy to his memory. She rejects all attempts at consolation and refuses to have a picture of her son, to hear his name mentioned, or to receive any poems commemorating him. She hates all other mothers, especially her sister-in-law Livia, despises the good fortune of her brother, and irritates the rest of her family, who resent her perpetual bereavement, as if they mean nothing to her. She leads a wretched life in darkness and solitude. Livia, on the other hand, puts aside her grief for Drusus after his burial and never ceases to celebrate his memory.

Although Seneca spells out the consequences of following Octavia's example, Spenser allows the reader to draw his own conclusions from Alcyon's grief. In fact, Spenser never passes judgment on Alcyon, feels the greatest sympathy for his loss, and offers all the consolation and aid in his power. Spenser describes himself as heavily grieving, and Alcyon represents his darker side, a self-torturing penchant for despair. Spenser is meditating on 'this worlds vainnesse and lifes wretchednesse', and Alcyon appears, almost a fantasy in the flesh.

> So as I muzed on the miserie,
> In which men liue, and I of many most,
> Most miserable man; I did espie
> Where towards me a sory wight did cost,
> Clad all in black, that mourning did bewray. (36–40)

The example of stubborn, self-centered, destructive grief stands as a warning to Spenser as well as to his bereaved friend, Arthur Gorges. Spenser does not recoil with horror from Alcyon because he realizes the temptation to yield to despair himself.[14]

What is so disturbing, so pathological, both for Spenser and for the modern psychologist, about Alcyon's grief is not so much its violence as its obsessiveness: the fixation of chronic mourning. Alcyon's determination to become a monument to grief like Octavia is the surest indication that something is wrong, for Spenser is relatively tolerant of outbursts of sorrow provided that they subside. In comparison with Surrey or, better yet, Jonson, Spenser's tolerance of mourning is very high indeed.

Two episodes in *The Faerie Queene* reveal this tolerance and show what is wrong with Alcyon. When Una spies the dwarf with Red Cross's armor, shield, and spear, she faints, and after the dwarf revives her she breaks into a two-stanza lament, a miniature of Alcyon's. She wishes for death and orders the sun to hide its beams. This is, however, her immediate reaction; she recovers enough to ask for the story of Red Cross's misfortunes.

> She heard with patience all vnto the end,
> And stroue to maister sorrowfull assay,
> Which greater grew, the more she did contend,
> And almost rent her tender hart in tway. (1.7.27)

Spenser does not underestimate the difficult struggle to recover from bereavement. Una's struggle with grief is by no means over; Arthur has a difficult time persuading her even to tell him why she is so sad. Unlike Alcyon, however, Una at least makes an effort to control herself.

Una's despairing lament is not belittled as womanish, and Spenser does not imply that it would be inappropriate for a man. At the news of Pastorella's (supposed) death Calidore is much wilder.

When *Calidore* these ruefull newes had raught,
  His hart quite deaded was with anguish great,
  And all his wits with doole were nigh distraught,
  That he his face, his head, his brest did beat,
  And death it selfe vnto himselfe did threat;
  Oft cursing th'heauens, that so cruell were
  To her, whose name he often did repeat;
  And wishing oft, that he were present there,
When she was slaine, or had bene to her succour nere.

But after griefe awhile had had his course,
  And spent it selfe in mourning, he at last
  Began to mitigate his swelling sourse,
  And in his mind with better reason cast,
  How he might saue her life, if life did last. (6.11.33–34)

Calidore's initial reaction is more self-destructive than Una's or Alcyon's, for he beats himself, behavior which Spenser usually reserves for women.[15] The difference between Calidore and Alcyon is obvious: an overwhelming, immediate outburst which lasts a short while versus an attempt to perpetuate grief. Spenser allows for the power of grief, but also recognizes that it is a process that should run its course.

When Spenser encounters Alcyon on the gloomy autumn afternoon, Daphne's death has already occurred. Alcyon's mourning is not a first reaction, but the result of a resolution, 'So will I wilfully increase my paine' (378). Alcyon wills his grief, but (unlike Surrey in 'So crewell prison') not to show his mastery over it. Alcyon's motivation is quite different. He asserts he is doing penance to Daphne and is hastening his reunion with her by hastening his death, but his penance is actually disguised aggression, an effort to strike back at Daphne, the white lion whom he captured and tamed, for daring to leave him. Anger at this desertion is determining the course of his grief.

Anger, in fact, is the most noticeable aspect of Alcyon's behavior. When Spenser first addresses him, 'He lookt a side as in disdainefull wise' (59), and when Spenser makes a final attempt to comfort him, he casts 'vp a sdeinfull eie at me' (549). Alcyon is angry at heaven for taking Daphne (197–203), curses all of nature (322–42), wishes the wolves will devour his flock (344–50), and hates everything and everyone in the world (393–434). This destructive rage is completely self-centered. Alcyon does not care for anyone or anything – not even, presumably, his daughter Ambrosia, whom Daphne entrusts to him on her deathbed and whom he never refers to again.[16] He does not care for Daphne's own well-being and thus would be stigmatized by Spenser's contemporaries, saturated as they were in the literature of consolation, as a lover of himself rather than of the deceased.[17]

While she was alive, Alcyon cared for Daphne as a possession, a tame animal which enhanced his stature among his fellow shepherds; he did not love her as a person with an independent existence. Alcyon turns his courtship into lion-taming. He saw 'a faire young Lionesse' (107) and

> gan to cast, how I her compasse might,
> And bring to hand, that yet had neuer beene:
> So well I wrought with mildnes and with paine,
> That I her caught disporting on the grene,
> And brought away fast bound with siluer chaine. (115–19)

No wonder Daphne is glad to be 'freed from wretched long imprisonment' (273).

Alcyon thinks he has made Daphne his own creature and is frustrated and angry to discover that she does not belong to him. In his eyes her death is an act of defiance, and he cares no more for her welfare after death than during her life. Spenser insists upon this self-absorption. Alcyon reports the consoling speech which Daphne delivers from her deathbed, but does not even understand it, much less take comfort from it. Spenser uses part of the poem's complex numerological structure to emphasize this point.[18] There are two midpoints, the center of the poem and the center of Alcyon's lament, and they offer radically different interpretations of Daphne's death. At the center of the poem Daphne describes the peace of heaven to which death is leading her; at the center of the lament Alcyon declares that the purpose of Daphne's death is to torture him. The center of the poem offers a vision of Christian community in the afterlife; Alcyon's center is his private hell, his inability to see anything from another's point of view or to escape for a moment from his sole self. By placing Daphne's vision at the very center of the poem Spenser is affirming its superiority.

> I goe, and long desired haue to goe,
> I goe with gladnesse to my wished rest,
> Whereas no worlds sad care, nor wasting woe
> May come their happie quiet to molest,
> But Saints and Angels in celestiall thrones

> Eternally him praise, that hath them blest;
> There shall I be amongst those blessed ones. (281–87)

Daphne assumes that Alcyon is grieving for her, not for himself. She is attempting to comfort him with her faith that she has suffered nothing evil and is going to heaven.

> Or why should he that loues me, sorie bee
> For my deliuerance, or at all complaine
> My good to heare, and toward ioyes to see? (278–80)

For Alcyon, however, her consolation is nothing but 'those piercing words', 'those last deadly accents, which like swords / Did wound my heart and rend my bleeding chest' (295, 297–98). She is tormenting, not comforting him.

Alcyon's self-absorption leads him to a view of Daphne's death which contradicts her own. For her, death is deliverance from wretchedness; for him, punishment of himself, as the central stanza of his lament makes clear.[19]

> Therefore my *Daphne* they haue tane away;
> For worthie of a better place was she:
> But me vnworthie willed here to stay,
> That with her lacke I might tormented be.
> Sith then they so haue ordred, I will pay
> Penance to her according their decree,
> And to her ghost doo seruice day by day. (365–71)

Alcyon feels that Daphne dies to spite him, as the shift in this stanza reveals. Why should Alcyon do penance to Daphne rather than the gods unless he feels that she is the one who is tormenting him? His penance is an effort to torment her in turn because, by her own account, she is now enjoying the 'happie quiet' of heaven and is insensible to human woes.

> And she my loue that was, my Saint that is,
> When she beholds from her celestiall throne,
> (In which shee ioyeth in eternall blis)
> My bitter penance, will my case bemone,
> And pitie me that liuing thus doo die:
> For heauenly spirits haue compassion
> On mortall men, and rue their miserie.
>
> So when I haue with sorowe satisfide
> Th'importune fates, which vengeance on me seeke,
> And th'heauens with long languor pacifide,
> She for pure pitie of my sufferance meeke,
> Will send for me; for which I daylie long,
> And will till then my painfull penance eeke.

Alcyon cannot recognize his anger at Daphne. His ambivalent

feelings towards her are split: she is idealized and invested with all of the beneficent aspects of God, while heaven or the fates are blamed for persecuting him. His suffering is his way of seeking vengeance on her; he is trying to reassert his control over her, to make her suffer for his suffering. Martha Wolfenstein sounds as if she is describing Alcyon rather than a bereaved child.

A rankling sense of having suffered an injustice may develop, with a vindictive need to prove how mistreated the child is. He may feel impelled to turn himself into a living and dying reproach. At the same time he may cherish the fantasy that his demonstration of suffering must eventually force the lost parent to return and care for him.[20]

Alcyon is turning himself into a living and dying reproach to Daphne's cruel desertion. This explains his ancient mariner compulsion to traverse the globe bearing witness to his grief. Even though he protests that he cannot talk about his woes and does not care what people think about him, he requires little persuading to tell his fable of the lion and then bursts into his long lament. He concludes with a series of six apostrophes, in which he insists upon his 'vndeserued paines' (522), his 'vndeseru'd distresse' (531). In order to preserve his sense of injury Alcyon rejects Spenser's proffered assistance of shelter for the night and proceeds on his self-tormenting way. Spenser's final comment is, 'But what of him became I cannot weene', but the poem compels one to the conclusion that unless Alcyon can come to terms with his rage at Daphne's death, he will become another Octavia, a monument to grief.

Spenser does not intrude into *Daphnaida* to judge Alcyon's grief; he lets the excess speak for itself. He does not close off the possibility that Alcyon will overcome his sorrow and is thus tactfully allowing Gorges the opportunity to learn from Alcyon's excess. A year later, in *Colin Clouts Come Home Againe*, Spenser portrays Alcyon as still grieving and gently urges him to leave his plaints for songs of mirth; one senses that Alcyon's grief is no longer excessive, but the passage is too short and vague to be sure (384–91).[21] Whether or not Gorges took the warning against stubborn, self-absorbed grief is impossible to say, but his imitation of Alcyon's lament some twenty years later in his memorial to Prince Henry, *The Olympian Catastrophe*, shows that he follows traditional notions about moderation of mourning. Unlike Alcyon, who has been mourning so long that Spenser can hardly recognize him, Princess Elizabeth wails out

her lament 'when she heard the newes' (p. 176).[22] Gorges frames
the lament, which follows brief indications of the grief of other
members of the royal family, by underscoring its futility.

> And thus she playnd (but death hath eares of stone
> Else would have pitied this sweete virgins moane)....
>
> But plaintes and teares no whit at all avayl'd...
> And these laments theire want of him exprest,
> That findes no want of them wheare he doth rest. (p. 178)

Gorges strips Alcyon's lament of its anti-social excesses, not to
mention its excessive length (26 lines as opposed to 343). Elizabeth is self-abusing, but does not strike out angrily at the rest of
the world, and does not angrily challenge the gods. Her lament
progresses from self-abuse to concern for Henry. Most important, the reader knows that this lament is the result of the
overwhelming news of her brother's death and that the passionate outburst is just temporary, for the dedicatory sonnet to
Elizabeth praises her victory over grief, her maintenance of 'Reasons Empery'. Gorges' imitation of *Daphnaida* strongly suggests
that he recognizes the excesses of Alcyon's grief.

Spenser also recognizes the excesses. His other elegies, despite
their sympathy for bereavement and for human vulnerability,
wrestle with the moral problem of grief. He tries to redirect grief
from the deceased, who has finally escaped the miseries of this
world for the bliss of heaven, to the sorrowing condition of the
survivors without implying that they are selfish lovers of themselves like Alcyon. Erasmus, we recall, has Suketus' son reject
this excuse with a chilling rebuke.

But ye say, that you on your part wepe and make lamentation. For soth
therin ye do nat like louers: but like vnto them that haue a respecte to
them selfewarde, and that wyll (to others discommoditie) se to their
own busines. (sig. C3ʳ)

Spenser turns the topos into a lament for the miseries of human
existence; he mourns 'our' condition, not just an individual's, as
in the conclusion of the 'dolefull lay' of Clorinda.[23]

> But liue thou there still happie, happie spirit,
> And giue vs leaue thee here thus to lament:
> Not thee that doest thy heauens ioy inherit,
> But our owne selues that here in dole are drent.
> Thus do we weep and waile, and wear our eies,
> Mourning in others, our owne miseries. (91–96)[24]

These lines suggest the tension between grief and the comfort of heaven which is a central aspect of Spenser's first and finest funeral elegy, 'November'. An ambivalent attitude towards grief, a need to explain and justify it, directs Spenser's imitation of his model, Clément Marot's 'Eglogue sur le Trespas de ma Dame Loyse de Savoye'. After departing from Marot in his consolation, Spenser concludes the poem by returning to him.

> O franc Pasteur, combien tes Vers sont pleins
> De grand doulceur & de grand amertume!
> Le chant me plaist, & mon cueur tu contraincts
> A se douloir plus qu'il n'a de coustume.[25]

> Ay francke shepheard, how bene thy verses meint
> With doolfull pleasaunce, so as I ne wotte
> Whether reioyce or weepe for great constrainte? (203–5)

Spenser sharpens the lines into a paradox. Marot's Thenot links sweetness and bitterness, but then proceeds, in the lines which follow this passage, to emphasize the sadness of Colin's song. Spenser's Thenot mingles sorrow and pleasure into one phrase and focuses on the Christian dilemma: shall he 'reioyce or weepe'? 'Doolfull pleasaunce' is Spenser's version of this dilemma, and Colin's song for Dido has just dramatized it.

Although Spenser omits a number of passages which Marot takes from Theocritus' *Idyll* 1, he closely follows Marot in the first part of the song, the stanzas of mourning. The openings are nearly identical.

> Tu me requiers de ce dont j'ay envie. (p. 325)

> *Thenot* to that I choose, thou doest me tempt. (49)

Spenser adds a modesty topos of three lines, and the song proper begins with Marot's 'Sus donc': 'Up then'. The second stanza takes over the 'Plorons' anaphora, but significantly omits the excuse for weeping: 'Plorons, Bergers, Nature nous dispense!' (p. 326).

This justification of tears does not satisfy Spenser, but Marot gives only one other indication that grief poses a problem. Louise is in the Elysian fields, 'Et nous ça bas, pleins d'humaines raisons, / Sommes marriz (ce semble) de son aise' (p. 334). Marot is implying that grief under such circumstances reveals envy of the dead.[26] The 'humaines raisons' suggest a failure to see Louise's death from her vantage point in heaven. They hint at a conflict between human grief and divine consolation, but are hardly preoccupied with the impiety of mourning. 'Ce

semble' undercuts the force of the accusation, and in any event
Marot only touches on the problem; the lines introduce a
description of Louise's joys in heaven.

Spenser is preoccupied with the legitimacy of mourning the
dead. Besides adding to Marot's slight reservations two stanzas
that reflect on the grief of the first part of the poem, he redirects
the grief from Dido, the dead individual, towards the condition
of the world. Marot uses a topos of pastoral elegy first found in
'Moschus', and Spenser imitates him.

> D'où vient cela qu'on veoit l'herbe sechante
> Retourner vive alors que l'Esté vient?
> Et la personne au Tombeau trebuchante,
> Tant grande soit, jamais plus ne revient? (p. 333)

> Whence is it, that the flouret of the field doth fade,
> And lyeth buryed long in Winters bale:
> Yet soone as spring his mantle doth displaye,
> It floureth fresh, as it should neuer fayle?
> But thing on earth that is of most availe,
> As vertues braunch and beauties budde,
> Reliuen not for any good. (83–89)

Spenser shifts the emphasis from the death of a person to the
disappearance of beauty and virtue from the world. Dido's death
is an emblem of earthly transience; this is what Spenser is
lamenting, not Dido the individual. This movement towards
lament for the world reaches its climax immediately before the
consolatory reversal, in a stanza that has no parallel in Marot,
but which expresses Spenser's major obsession, for he is always
relearning Petrarch's lesson 'Che quanto piace al mondo è breve
sogno'.

> O trustlesse state of earthly things, and slipper hope
> Of mortal men, that swincke and sweate for nought,
> And shooting wide, doe misse the marked scope:
> Now haue I learnd (a lesson derely bought)
> That nys on earth assurance to be sought:
> For what might be in earthlie mould,
> That did her buried body hould,
> O heauie herse,
> Yet saw I on the beare when it was brought
> O carefull verse. (153–62)

Dido slips into the background, and the earth, which appears
three times, moves to center stage. Her death represents the
world's fragility, a justifiable target for grief.

This stanza provides a smoother transition to Dido's

apotheosis than Marot's abrupt reversal. Marot does not worry at all about proceeding from lament to consolation; he just decides he has wailed enough.

> Chantez, mes vers, fresche douleur conceue.
> Non, taisez vous, c'est assez deploré;
> Elle est aux champs Elisiens receue,
> Hors des travaulx de ce Monde esploré. (p. 334)

There is something charmingly defiant in this neglect of transition, but the two parts of the poem are hardly unified. Marot's poem is the only one I know in which the joys of heaven are felt so intensely that sorrow drops away and seems superfluous, a form to be gone through before jubilation can begin. Spenser cannot approach such joy, but he does unify his poem. 'That nys on earth assurance to be sought' implies that it must be sought in heaven.

The reassurance of the afterlife, however, makes mourning for Dido problematic.

> Why then weepes Lobbin so without remorse?...
> Why wayle we then? why weary we the Gods with playnts,
> As if some euill were to her betight? (167, 173–74)

As in the conclusion of *Astrophel*, Spenser resorts to human imperfection to account for grief.

> Vnwise and wretched men to weete whats good or ill,
> We deeme of Death as doome of ill desert:
> But knewe we fooles, what it vs brings vntil,
> Dye would we dayly, once it to expert. (183–86)

These lines are considerably harsher than anything in Marot's poem, *Astrophel*, or *Daphnaida*. What should bring joy emphasizes stupidity, failure, and woe. Disgust at misery displaces sympathy for it, and Spenser comes his closest to the rigoristic tradition of condemning grief.

Chapter 6

JONSON AND KING

Jonson

Spenser may approach rigorism; Jonson subscribes to it. Even if we did not have Selden's assurance that Jonson was well read in the Church fathers and possessed many of their works, Jonson's references to *The Sicke mannes Salue* indicate an acquaintance with this important source of Renaissance rigorism.[1] His epigram 'Of Death' implies its major position: 'He that feares death, or mournes it, in the iust, / Shewes of the resurrection little trust' (VIII 37). Most significantly, over a period of 30 years Jonson wrote about twenty funeral poems which contain very little mourning. The poems that do mourn exhibit great restraint, never exceed the feeling of loss allowed by such strict fathers as Tertullian and Cyprian, and struggle to overcome even this. The restraint is not merely a matter of genre, for it characterizes all the poems, the two long elegies and the ode on Cary and Morison as well as the epigrams. In fact the elegies, to which Puttenham assigned lamentation, are more severe than some of the epigrams. In addition to avoiding or tempering expressions of grief Jonson exhorts himself and others not to mourn and chides those who do; his poetry continues the tradition of angry consolation which was examined in chapter 1.

In order to understand the appeal of rigorism for Jonson one should remember how much he prided himself on his manly accomplishments, in particular the single combat in the Netherlands in which he killed his man and took 'opima spolia' and the duel in which he killed Gabriel Spencer. He boasted of both feats twenty years after their occurrence. Jonson's concern with manhood goes hand in hand with a fear of the emotions, especially with those which weaken self-control. Jonson, who shares Wilson's obsession with the rule of reason, exalts 'reason, our affections' king', as he calls it in 'Epode', but has nothing but suspicion for the 'passions'.

Two passages from *Sejanus* capture Jonson's suspicions and ideals. Silius attributes the fall of the Roman republic and subsequent political decay to the usurpation of the affections.

> We, that (within these fourescore yeeres) were borne
> Free, equall lords of the triumphed world,
> And knew no masters, but affections,
> To which betraying first our liberties,
> We since became the slaues to one mans lusts;
> And now to many. (IV 357)

A strong commitment to the ideal of rational self-sufficiency makes it very difficult to acknowledge or accept feelings of loss. Arruntius' description of Germanicus' funeral sketches Jonson's ideal of mastering grief.

> What his funeralls lack'd
> In images, and pompe, they had supply'd
> With honourable sorrows, souldiers sadnesse,
> A kind of silent mourning, such, as men
> (Who know no teares, but from their captiues) vse
> To shew in so great losses. (IV 359)

As his marginal note indicates, Jonson is reworking Tacitus, *Annales* 2.72–73. The 'souldiers sadnesse' and 'silent mourning' are Jonson's additions, and one recalls Jonson's own military career and his admiration for soldiers ('To True Souldiers'). The response which Jonson desires in the face of loss is an increase in gravity, reason's tribute to death.

Only twice in his elegies does Jonson ask the reader to weep for the dead. 'An Epitaph, on Henry L. La-ware' requests the bare minimum of grief, one tear: 'If, Passenger, thou canst but reade: / Stay, drop a teare for him that's dead' (VIII 233). The most unrestrained appeal for sympathy occurs in the poem with the lightest tone, the 'Epitaph on S. P.'

> Weepe with me all you that read
> This little storie:
> And know, for whom a teare you shed,
> *Death's* selfe is sorry. (VIII 77)

The witty conceit that the young actor impersonated old men so well that death mistook him for one hardly stirs up sorrow. The epitaph 'On Margaret Ratcliffe' does not ask the reader for a tear, but it does begin: 'Marble, weepe, for thou dost couer...' (VIII 39). No other mourning for Margaret occurs.

This last epitaph illustrates Jonson's one concession to mourning, which, although not strictly consistent with rigorism, is traditional. From Archilochus' admonition to Pericles, 'Endure and cast aside womanish grief', a consolatory commonplace condemns grief as effeminate, weak, and unworthy of a man, or deems it more fitting in a woman.[2] In accordance with this sexual stereotype Jonson makes Margaret's grief at her brother's death one of her praiseworthy accomplishments and, in a passage that barely disguises its misogyny, praises grief for a husband, even though it brings on the wife's death, in 'To yᵉ memorye of that most honoured Ladie *Jane*'.

> But, I would have, thee, to know something new,
> Not usuall in a *Lady*; and yet true:
> At least so *great* a *Lady*. She was *wife*
> But of one *Husband*; and since he left life,
> But *Sorrow*, she desir'd no other *ffriend*. (VIII 394)[3]

The distinction between masculine and feminine grief enters one of the few poems in which Jonson expresses any personal loss, 'On My First Daughter'.

> Here lyes to each her parents ruth,
> MARY, the daughter of their youth:
> Yet, all heauens gifts, being heauens due,
> It makes the father, lesse, to rue.
> At sixe moneths end, shee parted hence
> With safetie of her innocence;
> Whose soule heauens Queene, (whose name shee beares)
> In comfort of her mothers teares,
> Hath plac'd amongst her virgin-traine:
> Where, while that seuer'd doth remaine,
> This graue partakes the fleshly birth.
> Which couer lightly, gentle earth. (VIII 33–34)

A struggle between reason and emotion takes place in the first four lines. Jonson admits his sorrow, but quickly asserts that recognizing life is a loan – his favorite consolatory commonplace – diminishes it.[4] His phrasing is ambiguous, however, and reveals his uneasiness with mourning, his fear that it might deplete him. 'It makes the father, lesse, to rue' suggests that mourning will make him less of the person he should be. Jonson makes himself more reasonable than his wife, since both mourn but only he is consoled. He swerves away from his own emotional response, since it might diminish him; he mentions his wife's tears, not his own. She requires more comforting, special intervention from the Virgin Mary in fact. He is completely resigned to his daughter's death by the end of the poem. His faith in her resurrection is unassailable, and he modifies a traditional close to epitaphs – may the earth cover you lightly – by calling the earth 'gentle'.[5] The epithet turns the earth into a trusted protector, a temporary guardian of his daughter's body, and reveals Jonson's confidence that his request will be fulfilled. Grief has been contained, reason has won the struggle, and the strictures of rigorism have not been violated.

Feelings of loss are much stronger in 'On My First Sonne', and no quiet resolution is achieved.

> Farewell, thou child of my right hand, and ioy;
>> My sinne was too much hope of thee, lou'd boy,
> Seuen yeeres tho'wert lent to me, and I thee pay,
>> Exacted by thy fate, on the iust day.
> O, could I loose all father, now. For why
>> Will man lament the state he should enuie?
> To haue so soone scap'd worlds, and fleshes rage,
>> And, if no other miserie, yet age?
> Rest in soft peace, and, ask'd, say here doth lye
>> BEN. JONSON his best piece of *poetrie*.
> For whose sake, hence-forth, all his vowes be such,
>> As what he loues may neuer like too much. (VIII 41)

This is a poem of leave-taking; Jonson is trying his hardest to say goodbye to his son and to lay his feelings of loss to rest, to exorcise them. The poem is much more personal than the one on his daughter, which immediately adopts the public stance of epitaph ('Here lyes') and speaks of the parents' loss. One does not realize that 'On My First Sonne' is an epitaph until line 9, and Jonson's relation with his son excludes his wife. We know that Jonson was not with his family when his son died in 1603, although not enough evidence exists to say whether or not he was estranged from his wife at the time.[6] In any event what is striking is not so much that Jonson does not mention the mother as that he refers to his son as if he alone were responsible for his birth: 'thou child of my right hand'. The phrase, as has been pointed out so often, translates the Hebrew 'Benjamin'; it also suggests the child is the product of Jonson's pen and thus anticipates 'his best piece of *poetrie*'. In either case Jonson's attachment is fiercely possessive: the child is his creation.

The entire poem is centered on Jonson; the son has no existence independent of his father. One can guess his name only from 'thou child of my right hand', and that name is the father's. His age is mentioned in terms of how long the father had him. Jonson takes the responsibility for his son's death by implying that it is a punishment for his own sin. For a moment the son seems to be addressed for himself, but in the next is told to speak of his father. Although Jonson addresses his son, the poem is really an internal dialogue; the questions are ones he is arguing with himself. Jonson cannot separate himself from his son even though he fears that his attachment and expectations were excessive and even fatal. His son is very much a part of himself, a part about which he could feel proud and hopeful.

The last two lines of the poem show that Jonson is no longer willing to pay the price for this attachment, heartfelt though it has been. 'For whose sake' does not mean that Jonson is making his vow for his son's advantage, but rather that Jonson is making the vow for his own sake 'on account of' what has happened to his son. Jonson is attempting to cut off the possibility of another painful loss by sacrificing in advance the type of attachment which he felt for his son. He shares some of the superstitious sense of nemesis that animates his model, Martial.

> Inmodicis brevis est aetas et rara senectus.
> quidquid amas, cupias non placuissse nimis. (6.29)

The life span of extraordinary things is short; rarely do they reach old age. You should desire that whatever you love does not please too much.

Jonson does not want to provoke the jealousy of the gods by too much contentment, for they might kill the object of his affection. In other words he is afraid of having strong feelings of attachment because they leave him vulnerable to loss.

The conflict between reason and emotion is most powerful in the center of the poem. Rigorism tells Jonson he should rejoice in his son's death, but phrasing the consolatory commonplaces as questions rather than statements and desiring to annihilate all fatherly feelings testify to the failure of reason. Jonson is fighting his feelings as much as he can; he does not express his loss personally, but takes refuge in abstractions: 'O, could I loose all father, now. For why / Will man lament the state he should enuie?' In order to satisfy rigorism, which is warding off a confrontation with the pain of loss, Jonson longs for insensibility. He is willing to sacrifice all feelings if he can avoid being overwhelmed by this pain. Yet at the same time something within him longs to give way to his feelings, to pour out his sorrow. Part of Jonson wants to lose his paternal feelings, but

another part wants to 'loose' them, to free them from restraint
(OED 1–2). The conflict between these opposed desires is too
painful, and Jonson tries to suppress it by committing himself to
a future of expendable attachments.

'An Epitaph on Master Vincent Corbet' reveals a similar,
though not as intense, conflict between familial feeling and restraint.

> I Have my Pietie too, which could
> It vent it selfe, but as it would,
>   Would say as much, as both have done
>   Before me here, the Friend and Sonne;
> For I both lost a friend and Father,
> Of him whose bones this Grave doth gather. (VIII 151)

These lines refer to the elegy which Richard Corbet wrote for his
father and perhaps to a lost poem by an unidentified friend.
Corbet by no means indulges in extravagant grief, but does insist
on his own bereavement and does ask the reader's tears for his
father.

> Besides his fame, his goods, his life,
> He left a greiv'd Sonne, and a wife.
> Straunge Sorrow, not to be beleiv'd,
> When the Sonne and Heire is greiv'd.
> *Reade* then, and *mourne*, whate're thou art
> That doost hope to have a part
> In honest Epitaphs; least, being dead,
> Thy life bee *written*, and not *read*.[7]

Corbet has no difficulty expressing his grief; if anything 'Straunge
Sorrow ...' suggests that he may feel a bit defensive about not
meeting an emergent ideal of sincerely felt sorrow (his father
died in 1619). Unlike Jonson he is under no constraint not to
grieve.

The reference to 'Pietie' helps to explain Jonson's restraint; he
is alluding to a paradox that had some currency among the
Church fathers. The paradox turns on the double meaning of
pietas: dutiful respect towards one's family, especially parents or
children, and reverence for God. In English the second meaning
has displaced the first, which was still common in Jonson's day,
but in classical Latin they were often not separated, or if they
were, the first predominated as in Cicero's definition of different
types of justice, 'eaque erga deos religio, erga parentes pietas'
(*Partitiones oratoriae* 78: 'the one towards the gods is religion,
towards parents and ancestors, piety'). With Christian Latin

pietas comes more and more to refer to God, and the paradox of 'impia pietas' becomes possible.

Paulinus of Nola can thus present the Christian reaction to death as a struggle between piety and faith. Near the beginning of *Carmen* 31 he does not know whether to grieve or rejoice.

> heu! quid agam? dubia pendens pietate laboro,
> gratuler an doleam? dignus utroque puer:
> cuius amor lacrimas et amor mihi gaudia suadet,
> sed gaudere fides, flere iubet pietas.[8]

Alas, what shall I do? I am afflicted and waver with uncertain piety: should I rejoice or grieve? The boy deserves both, love for whom urges me to tears and to joy. But faith bids me rejoice, piety to weep.

'Uncertain piety' produces emotional civil war until Paulinus resolves the struggle by condemning piety.

> inpia nam pietas animam lugere beatam,
> gaudentemque deo flere nocens amor est.
> nonne patet quantum tali pietate trahatur
> peccatum? arguimur fraude tenere fidem
> aut reprobare dei leges errore rebelli,
> ni placeat nobis quod placuit domino. (ll. 45–50)

For it is impious piety to mourn a blessed soul, and harmful love to weep for one who is rejoicing in God. Is it not plain how great a sin comes from such piety? We accuse ourselves of holding our faith by fraud or of finding fault from rebellious error with God's laws unless what the lord has decreed pleases us.

Paulinus appears to resolve his dilemma in favor of joy, and he does relegate mourning to the faithless later in the poem (385–92), but towards the end one sees that the tension is not resolved: 'Celse, dolor patribus, gloria, Celse, patrum / Celse, amor et desiderium' (592–93: 'Celsus, a grief to your parents, Celsus, the glory of your parents, Celsus, love and longing'). Weeping and rejoicing prove inseparable.[9]

Like Paulinus and Spenser, Jonson does not know whether to rejoice or weep. He hints at a depth of emotion, a struggle against the knowledge that it is sinful to mourn the dead. Consequently he focuses on Corbet's virtuous life and his own deprivation and suffering, as he did not learn as much as he could have from his dead 'father'. When Jonson requests tears at the poem's close, they are for himself, not Corbet. The lines, gently and quietly, correct the tears at the close of Richard Corbet's elegy by directing them away from the dead.

> Now I conceive him by my want,
> And pray who shall my sorrowes read,

> That they for me their teares will shed;
>> For truly, since he left to be,
>> I feele, I'm rather dead then he! (VIII 152)

In these poems Jonson appears to be trying to suppress all grief, but he may simply be trying to moderate it. Other poems are more severe. Consider the first lines of the consolatory epigram to King Charles and Queen Mary on the death of their infant son.

> Who dares denie, that all first-fruits are due
>> To God, denies the God-head to be true:
> Who doubts, those fruits God can with gaine restore,
>> Doth by his doubt, distrust his promise more. (VIII 235)

Jonson expresses no sympathy, allows no mourning, and proceeds to order the king and queen not to complain. The tone – that of an angry consoler – is remarkably harsh for an address to royalty. No doubt Jonson was pleased with this tone, as ten years earlier he boasted to Drummond that he wished he could deliver one sermon to the king, 'for he would not flatter though he saw Death' (I 141). In the epigram Jonson adopts the persona of the religious teacher who makes no concessions to human frailty, even though he ends with an assurance that God will grant the royal couple a large posterity for their patience.

The death of the Marchioness of Winchester inspired elegies by Jonson and John Eliot, among others. Jonson's is by far the most severe, although Eliot's makes confused use of rigoristic topoi. Eliot awkwardly combines them with assertions that future generations will mourn the marchioness and that he himself is so overcome that he can hardly write for his tears.

> Shall I rub natures sores, and once again,
> From tender parents eyes press drops of rain;
> That were a Crime that would beget a storie,
> To mourn for her they know is crown'd with glory,
> But they religious are, and will repent
> The sighs, and groans, and teares already spent;
> For being married thus before they die,
> To Ioyes long liv'd, as is eternitie,
> Part of her hapiness they shall destroy
> That weep for her, unless they weep for Ioye.[10]

Should her husband weep for her?

> That were a Crueltie her gentle soul
> Would sharply in his sleep and dreams controule,
> For if the Saints our actions doe discover,
> To weep for her would show he did not love her.

So far Eliot appears as rigoristic as Jonson ever does; any grief is criminal unless for the damned. After some bizarre conceits on the marchioness' dead infant as a diamond, Eliot reverses himself. Will no one weep? Future generations will; they will go on pilgrimage to the grave of mother and babe. The poet, so overcome that he cannot write for the tears falling on his paper, concludes: 'Rest then in peace, the world to dust shall turne / When tears are wanting to keep moyst thy urne' (p. 39). Rather than begin with feigned condolence and proceed to arguments to suppress grief, Eliot inverts the traditional pattern of consolation: his condemnation of grief seems feigned, a preparation for eternal sorrow. As in Diggs' elegy for Jonson, topoi of rigorism are used in so confused a manner that rigorism must be an unfamiliar position. Diggs and Eliot unwittingly attest to the disappearance of rigorism and the shift in attitude towards mourning.

Jonson ignores the marchioness' untimely death and does not mention her pregnancy. He deliberately avoids stirring the reader's compassion. Instead he sketches a death scene of such resolution and fortitude that she converts her family's tears and fears into joys. Her fervor for death receives its reward in heaven, at which point Jonson turns to her parents.

> Goe now, her happy Parents, and be sad,
>   If you not understand, what Child you had.
> If you dare grudge at Heaven, and repent
>   T'have paid againe a blessing was but lent,
> And trusted so, as it deposited lay
>   At pleasure, to be call'd for, every day!
> If you can envie your owne Daughters blisse,
>   And wish her state lesse happie then it is! (VIII 271)

The strong irony of *concessio* condemns and forbids grief by equating it with impiety, impatience, and envy.

Jonson can be just as severe on himself. The last of the three epigrams on Sir John Roe, printed immediately before 'Of Death', rebukes the tears shed in the first.

> Ile not offend thee with a vaine teare more,
>   Glad-mention'd ROE: thou art but gone before,
> Whither the world must follow. And I, now,
>   Breathe to expect my when, and make my how.
> Which if most gracious heauen grant like thine,
>   Who wets my graue, can be no friend of mine. (VIII 37)

The poem depends on the rigoristic position that one should mourn only the deaths of those whose souls are going to hell, as, for example, in Jerome's formulation, 'lugeatur mortuus, sed ille quem gehenna suscipit, quem tartarus deuorat, in cuius poenam aeternus ignis exaestuat' ('Let the dead be mourned, but the one whom hell receives, whom Tartarus devours, for whose punishment the eternal fire burns').[11] This explains why the tears are offensive to Roe and why a weeper over Jonson cannot be his friend; the tears imply that they are in hell. Besides being offensive, Jonson's tears are vain. Not only are they useless – they cannot bring the dead back to life – they are self-indulgent and reveal more self-love than affection for the dead.

The opening of 'Elegie on my Muse' indulges Jonson's 'wounded mind' and leads to an imprecation on nature. But Jonson quickly stops himself.

> My Passion
> Whoorles me about, and to blaspheme in fashion!
> I murmure against *God*, for having ta'en
> Her blessed Soule, hence, forth this valley vane
> Of teares, and dungeon of calamitie!
> I envie it the Angels amitie!
> The joy of Saints! the *Crowne* for which it lives,
> The glorie, and gaine of rest, which the place gives!
> Dare I prophane, so irreligious bee
> To 'greet, or grieve her soft Euthanasee? (VIII 283)

These lines ignore any human aspect of grief and take it as blasphemy. Grief affronts God's ordering of the world. Jonson uses self-rebuke to check Sir Kenelm Digby's grief for his wife; he is offering himself as an example of the victory of faith over the emotions.[12]

This poem shows how unswervingly Jonson holds to rigorism. He is writing 30 years after the death of his first son, almost 30 years since the death of Roe. If anything, he is more severe than he was earlier in his life because here, and in the almost contemporary 'Elegie on the Lady Jane Pawlet', he dwells on the offense to God. His confidence that reasoned reflection on the sin of grief can curb the emotions is at its height. His portrayal of the resurrection is more elaborate than anywhere else in his funeral poetry. After this description, he pauses to ask a question similar to one in 'On My First Sonne'.

> This being thus: why should my tongue, or pen
> Presume to interpell that fulnesse, when
> Nothing can more adorne it, then the seat
> That she is in, or, make it more compleat?

> Better be dumb, then superstitious!
>   Who violates the God-head, is most vitious
>   Against the Nature he would worship.

The differences between the passages are striking. In the earlier
poem grief is inevitable though mysterious; man 'will' lament the
state he should envy. Here grief is under control. The 'should'
implies options, and 'presume' hints at self-indulgent rebellion.
The pause ends with a generalizing condemnation; the questions
are answered, not left as mysteries as in the poem on his son.
Jonson's struggle with grief is over.

King

Because of his adherence to rigorism, Jonson does not lament
the subjects of his elegies with a clear conscience. Either he feels
that he should overcome his grief while he is expressing it or he
criticizes himself after its expression. Unlike Spenser, Jonson
does not excuse grief by appealing to human weakness; he is too
committed to the ideal of rational self-sufficiency. The tenacity
with which Jonson adheres to rigorism makes him an anachron-
ism, since despite isolated examples like Farnaby's poem for
Edward King one has to return to Edwardian England to find
comparable severity. Indeed, there is evidence that his contemporaries did not understand Jonson's funeral poems because they
did not understand rigorism. We have already seen the
contradictory use of rigoristic commonplaces in Diggs and Eliot.
This is how Lord Falkland describes the effect of Jonson's elegy.

> Whil'st Johnson forceth with his Elegie
> Teares from a griefe-unknowing Scythians eye,
> (Like Moses at whose stroke the waters gusht
> From forth the Rock, and like a Torrent rusht.)
>   (Donne, *Epithalamions*, p. 91)

Jonson tries to force his readers to suppress their tears, and his
attitude towards mourning is closer to that of the Trausoi than
Falkland realizes. Nevertheless, Jonson has more in common
with Surrey and Spenser than his rigorism might suggest. What
distinguishes the three of them from poets of a later generation is
the anxious conviction that grief requires a defense. Jonson takes
the further step that grief is indefensible, while the others cannot
rid themselves of that suspicion or fear that they may be over-
stepping the bounds of defensible grief.

Henry King, on the other hand, does not share these anxieties, even though one of the elegies by this 'poet of the funereal'[13] insists that grief does not reveal envy of the dead. King's finest poetry expresses grief in an unprecedentedly direct way, and he is most moving on the occasions which seem to have caused the greatest personal loss.

King writes funeral poetry over a period of 45 years and does not always express grief simply and movingly. Some of his earliest elegies, especially the one from the Oxford collection on Queen Anne, are full of conventional hyperbole, but even the hyperbole occasionally indicates a more relaxed attitude towards mourning. In this respect King's Latin elegy on Prince Henry is more interesting than his more hyperbolical English elegy, which asserts that the dissolution of the earth will be less grievous than Henry's death. For the Latin elegy is another example of a poem that looks as if it is going to criticize the grief it has been expressing. After asserting that no greater calamity could have befallen England, and praising Henry's precocious virtue and wisdom, King stops short with a question.

> Sed luctuoso quid iuuat questu malum
> Grauare nostrum?[14]

But what good is it to aggravate our woe with a mournful plaint?

Where one expects the customary chestnuts about the futility of grief and an exhortation to give it over, King proceeds to describe *English* grief and to insist that the whole world, from pole to pole, partake of the mourning for Henry. It turns out that King is emphasizing 'nostrum', since this 'Herculean sorrow' must not be confined to England. The occasion for a severe reversal is introduced only to be ignored.

King's poem on Sir Thomas Bodley not only avoids a severe reversal, but argues that it is criminal to impose any limitation on mourning.

> Sed nostras, celebris BODLEIE querelas
> Extendisse juvat. Non hora, diesvè, nec aetas,
> Non chelys Odrysij vatis pulsata loquaces
> Mulcebit gemitus. Scelus est imponere legem
> His curis, vllumvè modum censere dolendi.[15]

But it is good, famous Bodley, to have extended our laments. Not an hour, day, or age, not the lyre struck by the Thracian bard will soothe our clamorous groans. It is criminal to impose a law on these cares or to decree any limit to grieving.

96

This passage goes beyond its Horatian and Statian models and is as strong an assertion of a right to boundless mourning as any we have seen. In a much later elegy for Lady Anne Rich, who died 24 August 1638, King again uses the futility-of-grief topos without reversing himself and in fact concludes, 'So with full Eyes wee close thy Vault. Content / (With what Thy Losse bequeaths us) to Lament' (p. 95). 'Content' conveys the acceptance of grief which is a striking characteristic of King's elegies.

Acceptance of grief is most pronounced in 'An Exequy', the only Renaissance elegy which rivals 'Lycidas'. The poem has been deservedly admired for its metaphysical conceits,[16] but one of its triumphs is the coexistence of direct expression of affection and sorrow with elaborate metaphors. The imagery is systematic and complex, yet the emotions are very simply expressed.

The poem creates the impression of overhearing a conversation with a dead spouse – or, rather, a conversation with a dead friend, for it is not until the poem is exactly half over that one knows that the friend is a woman, and not until it is two-thirds over that one knows that the friend is King's wife. The full title, 'An Exequy To his Matchlesse never to be forgotten Freind', and King's early reference to himself as 'thy griev'd Friend' (line 5) do not reveal whether the poem is addressed to a man or a woman or what type of relationship existed between poet and friend, since besides its modern meaning 'friend' could mean 'lover'. (King uses 'friend' in the titles of his elegies on Donne and Jonson.) Although 'friend', especially in the plural, could mean 'relation', it rarely refers to a wife. 'Friend' stresses the mutual affection between King and his wife and helps to create the illusion of overhearing a conversation. He is addressing his wife so intimately that he ignores outsiders; unlike most elegists and unlike his own practice in other poems, in 'An Exequy' King never uses a generalizing 'we'. The reader witnesses a private funeral ceremony – apparently also the point of the distinction between 'Dirges' and 'Complaint' in the first two lines – not a public commemoration. The reader witnesses the process of mourning, not a funereal display as in King's elegies for Prince Henry.

The first part of the poem focuses on the commonest sign of grief, tears: the 'strew of weeping verse', the 'griev'd Friend' 'Quite melted into Teares'. In the second stanza King develops these images from the first.

> Deare Losse! since thy untimely fate
> My task hath beene to meditate
> On Thee, on Thee: Thou art the Book,
> The Library whereon I look
> Though almost blind. For Thee (Lov'd Clay!)
> I Languish out, not Live the Day,
> Using no other Exercise
> But what I practise with mine Eyes.
> By which wett glasses I find out
> How lazily Time creepes about
> To one that mournes: This, only This
> My Exercise and bus'ness is:
> So I compute the weary howres
> With Sighes dissolved into Showres. (pp. 68–69)

The images describe the mental searching characteristic of the second stage of mourning. King's daily exercise is to pore over his memories of his wife even though he is almost blind from tears. This concentration on the day-to-day occupations of bereavement and the simple observation that time passes more slowly are unusual. King dwells on the quiet, lonely aspects of a period of mourning and on the daily struggle with memories and pangs of grief, not on the grand public gestures of sorrow.

One image of the poem leads to another just as the search to recover the dead follows trains of memories and associations. The slowing of time requires an explanation, and King employs the common image – we will see several examples in connection with 'Lycidas' – of death as sunset.

> Nor wonder if my time goe thus
> Backward and most praeposterous;
> Thou hast Benighted mee. Thy Sett
> This Eve of blacknes did begett,
> Who wast my Day, (though overcast
> Before thou hadst thy Noon-tide past)
> And I remember must in teares,
> Thou scarce hadst seene so many Yeeres
> As Day tells Howres. (p. 69)

Time is moving so slowly that it seems to be moving backward, which is true in that King is living in the past with his memories of his wife. King personalizes the sunset topos. His recollection of his wife's premature death produces another pang of grief, as every image leads back to her: the sun's meridian and the hours of the day recall her age at death.

The searching, which depends upon the unconscious premise

that it is possible to recover the dead, continues with solar images, culminating in the eclipse of the grave, but sunset and eclipse hold out the hope of a return of light, a fantasy of reunion.

> I could allow Thee for a time
> To darken mee and my sad Clime,
> Were it a Month, a Yeere, or Ten,
> I would thy Exile live till then;
> And all that space my mirth adjourne,
> So Thou wouldst promise to returne,
> And putting off thy ashy Shrowd
> At length disperse this Sorrowe's Cloud. (p. 69)

King tries to master his grief by a bargain: he will agree to suffer if the suffering will bring back his wife. Once he becomes conscious of the unconscious desire behind his imagery, he realizes that his desire to regain his wife will be frustrated, and he bursts into grief.

> But woe is mee! the longest date
> Too narrowe is to calculate
> These empty hopes. Never shall I
> Be so much blest, as to descry
> A glympse of Thee, till that Day come
> Which shall the Earth to cinders doome,
> And a fierce Feaver must calcine
> The Body of this World, like Thine,
> (My Little World!) That fitt of Fire
> Once off, our Bodyes shall aspire
> To our Soules' blisse: Then wee shall rise,
> And view our selves with cleerer eyes
> In that calme Region, where no Night
> Can hide us from each other's sight. (p. 70)

Exposing the emptiness of the hopes leads to no self-condemnation; King does not rebuke himself for his folly, but proceeds to substantial hopes. He does not deny the existence of his longings, but transfers them to religion. The last judgment and resurrection enter the poem as a natural elaboration of the solar and temporal imagery rather than dogmatic intrusions to silence the passions. The conflagration which will end time is presented from the private point of view of King and his wife, merely the 'fitt of Fire' which separates them from one another. The resurrection of the body and heaven do not promise the beatific vision or any of the traditional joys of union with God, but the desired resolution of the search of mourning, personal reunion with the assurance of no subsequent separation.

The last line of the passage I have just quoted is at the poem's center, and the faith in restored sight of the beloved is extended by a train of images in the second half of the poem. This faith does not cancel grief, even though the tears which dominated the first half of the poem do not reappear.

> Meane time, thou hast Hir Earth: Much good
> May my harme doe thee. Since it stood
> With Heaven's will I might not call
> Hir longer Mine; I give thee all
> My short liv'd right and Interest
> In Hir, whome living I lov'd best:
> With a most free and bounteous grief,
> I give thee what I could not keep.
> Be kind to Hir: and prethee look
> Thou write into thy Doomsday book
> Each parcell of this Rarity,
> Which in thy Caskett shrin'd doth ly:
> See that thou make thy reck'ning streight,
> And yeeld Hir back againe by weight;
> For thou must Auditt on thy trust
> Each grane and Atome of this Dust:
> As thou wilt answere Him, that leant,
> Not gave thee, my deare Monument. (p. 70)

Life as loan is a common consolatory topos; it is Jonson's favorite. Recalling the topos reduces his grief in 'On My First Daughter'. The version in 'On My First Sonne' suggests a punishment or the type of loan Shylock might make: 'Seuen yeeres tho'wert lent to me, and I thee pay, / Exacted by thy fate, on the iust day'. In 'An Elegie On the Lady Jane Pawlet' the topos appears in the ironic permission that the parents may grieve, and refusal to submit to its force is castigated as complaining against God. Jonson is worried about paying back something that is due and fears the charge of ingratitude. Jonson pays back; King gives. And by giving up his 'short liv'd right and Interest', King does not give up his grief. He retains his grief and entrusts his wife to the earth, which receives her as a loan. This final transformation turns a topos which at best urges resignation into evidence of King's mastery of his grief and his faith in reunion with his wife. He now feels confident enough to complete his private funeral ceremony and, before returning to direct address to his wife, to acknowledge his relation: 'So close the ground, and 'bout hir shade / Black Curtaines draw, My Bride is lay'd'.[17]

King continues to express his affection and sorrow unobtrusively while imaging his daily journey towards death and reunion. The remaining sections conclude with statements of his progress towards reunion or of his assurance of eventual arrival. The end of the poem echoes the end of its first part and restates this faith in reunion as the ground for resuming life, but a life which must continue to acknowledge the presence of grief.

> The thought of this bids mee goe on,
> And wait my dissolution
> With Hope and Comfort. Deare! (forgive
> The Crime) I am content to live
> Divided, with but half a Heart,
> Till wee shall Meet and Never part. (pp. 71–72)

What distinguishes 'An Exequy' from most Renaissance elegy is the extraordinary degree to which King can confront, accept, and express his grief at his wife's death. The poem shows that for him the process of mourning is running its course. He begins in a backward-looking stage of searching and pining, in which he dwells among his memories and experiences pangs of grief. Once he becomes conscious of the futility of his desire to recover his wife in this life, he does not renounce his grief, but shifts the goal of his searching to a future reunion in heaven and sorrowfully resolves to go on.

King never again writes so simple and moving an elegy and later shows some impatience with the process of mourning. Here are the concluding lines of 'On two Children dying of one Disease, and buryed in one Grave'.

> You Pretty Losses, that revive the fate
> Which in your Mother, Death did Antedate,
> O let my high-swol'n Grief distill on You
> The saddest dropps of a Parentall Dew:
> You ask no other Dowre than what my eyes
> Lay out on your untimely Exequyes:
> When once I have discharg'd that mournfull skoare,
> Heav'n hath decreed you ne're shall cost mee more,
> Since you release, and quitt my borrow'd trust,
> By taking this Inheritance of Dust. (p. 72)[18]

This tearful conceit, especially the third and fourth lines, has none of the immediacy of 'An Exequy'. Grief is imagined to be a debt which can be paid and forgotten; a few baroque tears will cancel it. Six years after his wife's death, in 'The Anniverse', King complains that this is not the case.

> How happy were mankind, if Death's strict Lawes
> Consum'd our Lamentations like the Cause!
> Or that our grief, turning to dust, might end
> With the dissolved body of a freind! (pp. 72–73)

In these passages King fights against his earlier acceptance of mourning as a process which must run its course, but he again approaches that acceptance in 'An Elegy Occasioned by the losse of the most incomparable Lady Stanhope, daughter to the Earl of Northumberland' of 1654. In fact, what chiefly distinguishes this poem – besides King's customary ease of tone – from anxious defenses of mourning is a sense of mourning as process. The elegy begins with a contrast between the 'Ceremonious Rites', which are over, and the continuing heartfelt sorrow of the survivors, obsequies 'Which to thy precious memory are due' (p. 132). This section presents sincere inward grief as a duty rather than a natural process, but the affection behind the duty is more apparent than the disgrace of not performing it. King assures Lady Stanhope that this grief is no attempt to disturb her peace or murmur against God; nor is it envy or doubt of her bliss. He explains, 'Know then blest Soul! we for our selves not thee / Seal our woe's dictate by this Elegie' (p. 133). This formulation of the old defense that one is mourning for oneself not for the deceased grants a greater stature to mourning because woe, like reason or conscience, conforms to its own dictates or principles instead of being just a passionate impulse. Nevertheless, it is a defense, and King's difference in attitude does not emerge until the final lines.

> Thus like religious Pilgrims who designe
> A short salute to their beloved Shrine,
> Most sad and humble Votaries we come
> To offer up our sighs upon thy Tomb,
> And wet thy Marble with our dropping eyes
> Which till the spring which feeds their current dries
> Resolve each falling night and rising day
> This mournfull homage at thy Grave to pay. (p. 133)

This conclusion avoids the histrionics of eternal grief. Instead grief is seen to be a process which will flow until it runs its course. The mourners are not trying to control their grief; they let their feelings guide them and thus produce a natural sign of their affection and duty to the dead.[19]

Even though he takes on the role of spokesman for a grieving circle of survivors, King is able to sustain a tone of intimate address to Lady Stanhope. In 'An Elegy Upon my Best Friend L.K.C.' he maintains that tone and achieves as simple an expression of grief as one can find except for 'An Exequy'. Lady Katherine Cholmondeley died 15 June 1657, by which time King had written 24 elegies (counting the six published Latin elegies and a seventh preserved in manuscript). He was thus in a good position to reflect upon mourning verse.

> Should we our Sorrows in this Method range,
> Oft as Misfortune doth their Subjects change,
> And to the sev'rall Losses, which befall,
> Pay diff'rent Rites at ev'ry Funeral;
> Like narrow Springs drain'd by dispersed Streams,
> We must want Tears to wail such various Themes,
> And prove defective in Death's mournfull Laws,
> Not having Words proportion'd to each Cause. (pp. 133–34)

These lines suggest exhaustion. King is afraid he will not be able to discharge the social duty of elegy and implies that grief is overwhelming him. These fears and the generality of the opening make the personal directness of the next lines all the more moving.

> In your Dear loss my much afflicted Sense
> Discerns this Truth by sad experience,
> Who never Look'd my Verses should survive,
> As wet Records, That you are not Alive;
> And less desir'd to make that Promise due,
> Which pass'd from Me in jest, when urg'd by You. (p. 134)

As in 'An Exequy' (line 7), King uses the simplest phrase for his affection and sorrow, 'Dear loss'. The universalizing tone of the moralist or preacher gives way to a private, shared reminiscence. For a moment King seems to be writing only for his dead friend.

103

Chapter 7

MILTON

Direct expression of sorrow distinguishes King's elegy at its finest, for even though he is writing during the period in which attitudes towards mourning are becoming more sympathetic and anxieties about grieving verse are diminishing, hyperbolic display is still the rule. It is much easier to find passages which attack artificial grief than ones which satisfy the ideal the attacks demand. King can meditate on his grief, look squarely at his loss, and describe his feelings without letting notions of what he should be feeling block them and without sacrificing metaphorical and logical complexity. Milton's elegy is not distinguished by direct expression of sorrow, although a passage in 'An Epitaph on the Marchioness of Winchester' and some of 'Lycidas' are as simple and direct as most elegy other than King's. What distinguishes Milton's elegy, especially 'Lycidas' and 'Epitaphium Damonis', is the lack of anxiety with which Milton protests against death and bereavement, the freedom with which he indulges the angry outbursts of grief. For with one early exception the Christian visions of heaven which conclude several of his elegies do not lead to a rejection of the sorrow and angry protest which precede them. A brief examination of the way in which Milton handles these visions in particular, and consolation in general, reveals his customary sympathy for mourning and is a good approach to the vexed question of the unity of 'Lycidas'.

Consolatory Visions

The second half of 1626 was a busy time for Milton the elegist; the Vice-Chancellor and Beadle of Cambridge and the Bishops of Winchester and Ely all died during this period. The elegy for the Vice-Chancellor severely intones the inevitability of death and gently concludes with the prayer that he walk with the blessed in the Elysian Fields. Like the elegy for the Beadle, which concludes by urging the university to mourn, no reversal from sorrow to joy occurs and no consoling vision of heaven appears. In both elegies Milton adopts the voice of a detached observer and makes no attempt to dramatize personal grief.

The elegies for the bishops do dramatize the poet's grief and thus anticipate the personal involvement of the pastoral elegies. The elegy for Launcelot Andrewes, Bishop of Winchester, begins with a simple declaration of sorrow.

> Moestus eram, et tacitus nullo comitante sedebam,
> Haerebantque animo tristia plura meo.[1]

I was mournful and silently sitting without a companion, and many sad things were clinging to my mind.

Recollections of the plague and of the deaths of famous men assault the poet. These sorrowful memories, especially of Andrewes, lead to a complaint against death which questions the order of the universe. Then the poet falls asleep and has a dream vision of heaven and the bishop's reception there. Dawn dispels the dream, and the poet concludes with a wish for more dreams of this kind.

What the poem does not do is more interesting than what it does. The imperfect tenses of the opening couplet set the scene for an event, and the reader familiar with elegy might well expect that this event will be a conversion from sorrow to resignation or joy. But despite the vision of heaven no conversion takes place; Milton does not say what effect the vision has on his grief, only that he weeps at the disturbance of his sleep and wishes for dreams like the one he has just had: 'Flebam turbatos Cephaleiâ pellice somnos, / Talia contingant somnia saepe mihi'. The lines imply that the poet has been comforted by his dream, but not that it has made him wholly give over his grief. Strictly speaking, one cannot even say whether he has understood the Christian significance of the dream. It is important to see that the complaint against death goes unrebuked, even though the vision suggests that human death leads to a better life. Grief and the questioning of death's place in the universe are allowed to remain even after a vision of heaven.

This is not the case in the elegy for the Bishop of Ely, Nicholas Felton, which does rebuke rage against death. The structure of the elegy is similar to the one for Andrewes. The poet is still grieving for Andrewes, when news of Felton's death reaches him. This time he is even angrier and curses death instead of just complaining. Then comes the reversal; Felton's spirit chides him from heaven.

> Caecos furores pone, pone vitream
> Bilemque et irritas minas.
> Quid temerè violas non nocenda numina
> Subitoque ad iras percita? (27–30)

Lay aside your blind rage; lay aside your bile and vain threats. Why do you recklessly profane powers which cannot be harmed and are quickly moved to wrath?

The violence of the tone may obscure the fact that Felton is not attacking grief *per se*, but rather the poet's angry threats at death. Nevertheless, the departed spirit is very harsh and recalls the prosopopoeias of the dead sons in Lucian and Erasmus. Felton dispels pagan illusions about death and describes his ascent to heaven; he was happy to leave the prison of the body.[2] As in the elegy for Andrewes, the poet does not consciously bring about the reversal of grief. In neither poem does the poet check his own sorrow or anger. Since the poem ends with Felton's speech, we once again do not learn how the intervention affects the poet's grief, but this time the anger released by death is rebuked.[3]

We have already seen how Jonson suppresses the circumstances of the Marchioness of Winchester's untimely death in childbirth to avoid arousing pity for her, and how he grants bitterly ironic permission to her parents to grieve. In his elegy on the marchioness Milton dwells on the untimeliness and double death of mother and child. He does not call for lamentation or mourn himself, but exploits the pathos of the event before addressing the marchioness.

> Gentle Lady may thy grave
> Peace and quiet ever have;
> After this thy travail sore
> Sweet rest sease thee evermore,
> That to give the world encrease,
> Short'n'd hast thy own lives lease;
> Here besides the sorrowing
> That thy noble House doth bring,
> Here be tears of perfect moan
> Wept for thee in *Helicon*,
> And som Flowers, and som Bays,
> For thy Hears to strew the ways,
> Sent thee from the banks of *Came*,
> Devoted to thy vertuous name;
> Whilst thou bright Saint high sit'st in glory.... (47–61)

These lines are much simpler than the conceits which precede them (and much simpler than anything in Milton's Latin elegies), although they do not match King's 'Exequy' for intimacy of address. The only expression of sorrow in the poem introduces the heavenly vision instead of being criticized or qualified by it. Funeral duties to the earthly remains proceed *while* her spirit is in heaven with Rachel. The marchioness is addressed both in the grave and in heaven, and Milton stresses her place in natural cycles of generation before picturing her as a saint in heaven. Although the marchioness is not genius of her shore, she is still firmly connected to the earth and her family even while her spirit dwells in the other world.[4]

'Epitaphium Damonis' has none of the serenity of the epitaph on the marchioness. It is an angry protest against the loss of a friend, not a lament for him, and hardly even a commemoration despite a few professions to the contrary. Donald C. Dorian rightly emphasizes the 'concentration on the emotional problem of [Milton's] personal bereavement'.[5] Milton himself makes this clear both in the headnote, 'se, suamque solitudinem hoc carmine deplorat' ('he bewails himself and his forlornness in this song'), and in line 7, 'Dum sibi praereptum queritur Damona' ('while he complains that Damon was untimely snatched from him'). It is instructive to glance at the headnote to 'Lycidas': 'the Author bewails a learned Freind'. Milton is unobtrusively situating 'Epitaphium Damonis' in the tradition we have seen in Parker's sermon, the collection for Bucer, Spenser, and elsewhere: he is lamenting his loss, not Diodati.

From the very beginning of the lament Thyrsis knows that Damon is in heaven.

> Ite domum impasti, domino jam non vacat, agni.
> Hei mihi! quae terris, quae dicam numina coelo,
> Postquam te immiti rapuerunt funere, Damon;
> Siccine nos linquis, tua sic sine nomine virtus
> Ibit, et obscuris numero sociabitur umbris?
> At non ille, animas virgâ qui dividit aureâ,
> Ista velit, dignumque tui te ducat in agmen,
> Ignavumque procul pecus arceat omne silentum. (18–25)

Go home unfed, lambs; your master has no time for you now. Ah me, what shall I call gods in earth or heaven, after they have seized you, Damon, with a harsh death? And do you leave us thus, will your virtue go nameless, and will you be merged with the group of unknown shades? But he who divides the spirits with his golden rod would not wish this, would lead you to a host worthy of you, and would keep all the ignoble, silent herd far at a distance.

Thyrsis has no qualms about presenting himself as the bad shepherd; the hungry sheep look up and are not fed (they are fed in the Virgilian models for this refrain, *Eclogue* 7.44, 10.77). He is neglecting the care of his flock, although this care was a reason for his return to England (14–15). After defying the heavenly powers, he persuades himself that Hermes *psychopompos* will escort Damon to heaven, for Milton imagines that Hermes uses his *virga* to divide the good from the bad souls.[6]

Damon's presence among the good souls and enduring fame on earth – fame which Thyrsis will ensure – are not enough to comfort Thyrsis for his loss. In fact they exacerbate it: 'At mihi quid tandem fiet modò?' (37: 'But what about *me*?'). In the sections introduced by this cry, Thyrsis almost rivals Spenser's Alcyon in self-absorption. The repetition of the refrain suggests rejection after rejection of the hungry sheep, and Thyrsis also neglects his agricultural duties. He avoids all consolers and complains about the difficulty of finding a companion and the injustice of having one snatched away. He feels guilty for going to Italy and not being present at Damon's deathbed to remind Damon to think of him in heaven (123: 'nostri memor ibis ad astra'). He recalls his successes in Italy and states his plans for an English epic.

This sketch may exaggerate Thyrsis' self-absorption, for he does imagine Damon as a separate person with a life of his own, but the exaggeration serves a purpose because it emphasizes the freedom with which self-indulgent grief is presented. When the train of associations which begins with absence from the deathbed leads back to the starting point of the lament – Damon in heaven – there is no severe reversal or condemnation of the rather petulant grief.

> Tu quoque in his, nec me fallit spes lubrica, Damon,
> Tu quoque in his certè es, nam quò tua dulcis abiret
> Sanctáque simplicitas, nam quò tua candida virtus?
> Nec te Lethaeo fas quaesivisse sub orco,
> Nec tibi conveniunt lacrymae, nec flebimus ultrà,
> Ite procul lacrymae, purum colit aethera Damon.... (198–203)

You also, Damon, are among these [holy minds and gods] – no unreliable hope is deceiving me – you also are surely among them, for where would your sweet and holy simplicity, your shining virtue go? It is not right to seek you below in Lethaean Orcus, and tears do not suit you, and we will not weep further. Go far away, tears, Damon dwells in the pure ether.

The picture on Manso's cup of Olympus with Amor firing worthy souls with divine love recalls Thyrsis to his first surmise that Damon had been conducted to his reward by Hermes. The transition has been carefully prepared. Thyrsis resumes his musing about where Damon's 'virtus' will go. Damon with the blessed has been in Thyrsis' mind all along and has not dulled the pain of his personal loss or nullified its legitimacy or significance. In these lines, too, Thyrsis does not reject the weeping he has done, which has been for his forlornness, but for the first time considers the relation of his tears to Damon. They are *inappropriate* to Damon, a very mild expression; they are not blasphemous or insulting, for instance. The lament has run its course and served its purpose of relieving Thyrsis' immense sorrow, so he resolves to stop his tears. There is no guarantee that Thyrsis' mourning has come to an end; he might soon say 'what about me' to himself. This poem, unlike 'Lycidas', has no conclusive coda; it ends with the ecstatic vision. The line which introduces the lament declares it is the *beginning* of an effort to disburden sorrow: 'Coepit et immensum sic exonerare dolorem' (17: 'and he began to relieve his immense sorrow as follows'). The lament dramatizes an episode of grief and a variety of angry and sorrowing emotions, not a recovery from the process of mourning.

'Lycidas'

[Milton] is a writer of centos, and yet in originality scarcely inferior to Homer. (William Hazlitt)

This survey of Milton's elegy should make two points which will aid our understanding of 'Lycidas'. First, the visions of heaven which conclude several elegies do not negate the sorrow and anger aroused by death (the elegy for the Bishop of Ely is a partial exception). Feelings of loss are allowed to coexist with confidence that the dead are in heaven, and this is real coexistence, not, as in Spenser, a concession to a sinfully frail human nature which cannot take sufficient comfort from the resurrection. To put it simply, for Milton there is no conflict between mourning and faith; his elegies show almost no struggle to overcome grief. Milton is exceptionally tolerant of angry protests against bereavement, especially in 'Epitaphium Damonis'. Second, Milton is very careful to preserve dramatic unity in the three elegies in which the poet pours forth his own grief. In particular, he ensures that the transition from grief to a vision of heaven does not disrupt the poem by splitting it into grieving and rejoicing parts. Marot's 'Chantez, mes vers, fresche douleur conceue. / Non, taisez vous, c'est assez deploré' is not for Milton. In the elegies for the bishops a dream vision and a voice from heaven bring the consolations of the afterlife; in the 'Epitaphium' Damon is with the blessed before Thyrsis' lament for his own forlornness begins, and the final vision, triggered by a train of memories, elaborates the earlier suggestions.

'Lycidas' is full of angry protests, but not against being left alone by the death of a dear friend.[7] Whereas 'Epitaphium Damonis' only touches on the injustice of untimely death, 'Lycidas' angrily challenges God's ordering of the world and ruthlessly exposes the insufficiency of pagan pastoral to offer adequate consolation for death. Yet despite repeated revisionary, defiant gestures, the poem does not wholly reject pastoral and does not turn against its earlier expressions of sorrow and indignation. The vision of Lycidas in the company of the saints is the gentlest, most sympathetic consolation in Renaissance England. More than any other the vision respects the painful doubts and feelings which it is intended to assuage.

But how does the consolation fit into the poem? This question goes to the heart of the debate over the unity of 'Lycidas', which has been raging since Johnson's famous strictures on the 'irreverent combinations' of 'trifling fictions' and 'the most awful and sacred truths'.[8] Todd in 1801 particularly objects to the mingling of angels wiping the tears from Lycidas' eyes with Lycidas as genius of the shore.[9] Stanley E. Fish in 1981 correctly observes of the 'Weep no more' passage, 'It is at this point that the orthodox reading of the poem, in which "the troubled thought of the elegist" traces out a sequence of "rise, evolution, and resolution", founders.'[10] Merely remarking the poem's 'natural and agreeable wildness and irregularity' (Thyer) does not satisfy the blessed rage for unity of most modern critics, who deny the emergence of a new voice (Alpers), speak of 'an infusion of grace' (Friedman), assign the speech to St. Michael (Madsen), or discover anonymity of voice in the second half of the poem (Fish).[11] Except for Alpers, all these critics sense that a new speaker has been introduced: but is it a regenerated speaker, St. Michael, or an anonymous, choral voice?[12] I agree that there is a new speaker, and I shall argue that it is the spirit of Lycidas himself. In order to make the argument it is necessary to go in some detail into the history of the poem's interpretation, into its relation to its poetic traditions, and even into matters of punctuation.

Madsen's attempt to assign the speech to Michael has met with little acceptance because, as Friedman (p. 33) points out and Fish (p. 2) agrees, he does not explain why Michael is alone introduced 'without comment or identification'.[13] The question at once arises: since Lycidas is not explicitly identified as speaker, how can a reader be expected to realize that Lycidas is in fact speaking? The answer lies in Milton's manipulation of poetic traditions, especially, though not exclusively, the pastoral.[14] Even while defying and criticizing pastoral conventions, Milton depends upon them for the overall shape and significance of his poem. And even though Milton imitates a wide range of pastoral, one model stands out: Virgil's *Eclogue* 10.[15] In fact, Milton maintains an interrupted but running dialogue with this poem, and these tantalizing allusions to Virgil are a major key to the identity of the speaker of the 'Weep no more' passage.

Newton remarked in 1752 that 'Lycidas' 'begins somewhat like Virgil's Gallus' (p. 480). Only somewhat, however. Whereas Virgil sounds weary or reluctant (pastoral song is no longer play but *labor*), Milton sounds indignant at being compelled to write. Lycidas' death is an interruption, an inconvenience which forces him out of his studious retirement. That Milton is imitating Virgil does not become apparent until 'Who would not sing for *Lycidas?*' (10), which almost translates 'neget quis carmina Gallo?' (3), but even at this point the reader still does not know whether the imitation is going to prove structurally significant. The next several lines do not help to answer that question. Although 'Begin then' might recall Virgil's 'incipe', the phrase also recalls the Greek pastoral refrains in ἄρχετε, is hardly distinctive (unlike a later Virgilianism, 'meditate the Muse'), and does not lead into anything akin to *Eclogue* 10. The opening lines set a pattern for the oblique allusiveness that is characteristic of the poem.

In comparison with its predecessors 'Lycidas' takes a long time to look like a pastoral elegy: the singer has trouble beginning his

111

song. 'Begin then' does not begin the promised song for Lycidas; nor does 'Hence with denial vain, and coy excuse' (18), which leads the singer to a fantasy of being elegized at his own death and then to memories of times spent with Lycidas. The memories of pastoral comradeship call forth a poignant outburst of grief.

> But O the heavy change now thou art gone,
> Now thou art gon, and never must return!
> Thee shepherd, thee the woods and desert caves
> With wild Thyme, and the gadding vine o'ergrown,
> And all thir echoes mourn.
> The willows, and the hazel copses green
> Shall now no more be seen,
> Fanning thir joyous leavs to thy soft layes.
> As killing as the canker to the rose,
> Or taint-worm to the weanling herds that graze,
> Or frost to flowrs that thir gay wardrope wear,
> When first the white thorn blows;
> Such, *Lycidas*, thy loss to shepherds ear. (37–49)

When Milton comes to express grief and hence reaches the point at which many earlier elegists take refuge in hyperbole, he expresses sorrow simply and addresses Lycidas for the first time in the poem. The personal relationship is emphasized for a moment, and then it looks as though Milton is going to resort to the most hyperbolic of all evasions of grief, the pathetic fallacy. The inversion of object and subject leads the reader to expect the active lamentation of the 'woods and desert caves'; instead, the next line shifts attention from action to the image of the caves, and 'echoes' raises the possibility that the mourning sounds are human voices – perhaps those of the shepherds mentioned in the last line. ('Shepherds ear' is the first hint that the poet may be representing other shepherds as well as personally grieving.) In any case, Milton is toying with the convention and has outdone Virgil's restraint (trees, streams, and Mount Maenalus wept for Gallus), not to mention the excesses of 'Moschus' and other pastoral elegists. Here are no jackals howling, no trees dropping their fruit. The projection of sympathy onto nature is hinted at by 'no more be seen', and the lines suggest that nature's sympathetic response ends with Lycidas' death. The poet is superior to his tradition by calling attention to the artificiality of its conventions: he is not so naive as not to see through the pathetic fallacy.

The poem now returns to *Eclogue* 10 and its model, Theocritus' *Idyll* 1, with 'Where were ye nymphs' (50). Although it
takes Virgil only six lines to move from 'who would not sing' to
'where were ye nymphs', it takes Milton 40, and as soon as the
address ends, this traditional beginning of pastoral lament almost
causes the poet to give up his poem in despair: 'Ay me, I fondly
dream!' (56). In the passage that follows, the strategy of using
pastoral conventions in order to point up their inadequacy
becomes obvious. The poet may be foolish enough to cry out to
the nymphs, but at least he, unlike Virgil and Theocritus, sees
the futility of the gesture.

It is becoming a commonplace of 'Lycidas' criticism that the
poem questions what Fish calls 'pastoral efficacy' (p. 7), but critics of the poem do not sufficiently realize that this very questioning is a central theme in Virgil and, through Virgil, of the
pastoral tradition in general. This turning against the invocation
of the nymphs finds its parallel in *Eclogue* 10 itself. Gallus is
imagining that hunting will ease his unrequited love for Lycoris;
he spins out a lovely fantasy and then stops himself short with
'tamquam haec sit nostri medicina furoris, / aut deus ille malis
hominum mitescere discat' (60–61: 'as if this could cure my
love-madness or that god [Cupid] could learn to soften at men's
misfortunes'). Gallus' realization that pastoral provides no
remedium amoris colors Virgil's own leave-taking of pastoral,
which, in *Eclogue* 9, has just been disintegrating in the face of
political realities. The questioning of pastoral efficacy in *Eclogue*
10 leads to its abandonment, but in 'Lycidas', which calls into
question the value of all poetry, even all action and ambition,
and reaches a profounder level of despair, the questioning finds
some answers. The answers come from pastoral itself but at the
same time transcend it. For just at the moment at which
Milton's sorrow and indignation are about to force him to give
up 'the homely slighted shepherds trade', he brings his poem
back to the point at which he left *Eclogue* 10. The address to the
nymphs introduces a procession of speakers, although it takes
the reader a while to recover from the shock of what Milton is
doing to this convention.

Phoebus' intervention *is* shocking; it is more than 'a noble
abruptness of transition', as John Scott remarks in 1785.[16] Fish
is quite right to quote Ransom's 'an incredible interpolation' and
'a breach in the logic of composition'. All of a sudden we are not

overhearing a lament in the present, but listening to a report of a speech delivered sometime in an unspecified past. But it is the reader who is overwhelmed, not the poet. The reader is jarred loose from a complacent sense of witnessing someone else's sorrow and doubts and is made to participate in the disturbing, confusing process of mourning. The poet's independence is not at all compromised, as Fish would have it. On the contrary. The poet is defiantly asserting his independence of the pastoral convention he is transforming by introducing the procession of speakers with flagrant, unprecedented disregard for transition. While the reader scrambles for bearings, the poet takes charge of the poem after the starts and hesitations of the opening lines. He introduces and listens to the procession, and from this point the poem sticks rather closely to the form, if not the spirit, of pastoral elegy. Moreover, the startling past tense of 'repli'd' is the first hint that there will be a resolution to the grief and angry questionings we hear before Phoebus' speech and prepares the way for that resolution through a speech by someone other than the poet.

The author, as he calls himself in the headnote to the 1645 edition, the uncouth swain, as he calls himself in the coda, the speaker or persona, as has been fashionable to call him since the New Critics, in other words Milton the poet, is taking charge in another way, revising another convention, with the allusion to the opening of Virgil's *Eclogue* 6. Fish misinterprets this allusion and the passage in Virgil. Although it appears that Apollo is quashing Virgil's presumptuous desire to rise above the pastoral, Virgil is using Apollo to assert his poetic independence. Virgil imitates the programmatic passage at the beginning of Callimachus' *Aetia* in order to refuse, politely but firmly, to write an epic on Varus' military exploits. Callimachus and Virgil, not to mention their many Roman imitators, introduce Apollo to defend their choice of genre, to insist on their integrity as poets, and the name given to these passages – *recusatio* – stresses that integrity.[17] Moreover, in the rest of the poem, if Virgil does not rise above pastoral, at least he extends it with Lucretian cosmology and Alexandrian *epyllia*. Virgil is using Apollo to declare his allegiance to a Callimachean poetics, to make a place for himself rather than be put in one by someone else.

The allusion to Virgil does not voice a desire to rise above pastoral and does not rebuke ambition. Phoebus strengthens a weakening resolve to sing for Lycidas, even though he corrects a misguided notion of fame with some severity (not with as much severity as the Son condemns glory in *Paradise Regained* 3, however). The poet is losing so much confidence in the value of pastoral poetry that he is not far from abandoning his poem out of despair. Far from quashing a desire to rise above pastoral, Phoebus tells the poet to quit worrying about earthly rewards and reputation: it is the business of 'all-judging *Jove*' to mete out true fame, and this implies that merit will receive its due, will not be cut short by death. The rebuke, if such it is, is liberating, and the poet resumes his song in better spirits. In *Eclogue* 6 and the other *recusationes* Apollo warns the poet not to attempt something beyond his powers; Milton's Apollo, for all his brusqueness of tone, comes to encourage. Milton has inverted the tradition he is using, and this is also true of the content of Apollo's speech, 'Fame is no plant that grows on mortal soil' (78). One of the greatest consolations of pastoral elegy is continued fame *on earth*.

> dum iuga montis aper, fluuios dum piscis amabit,
> dumque thymo pascentur apes, dum rore cicadae,
> semper honos nomenque tuum laudesque manebunt.
>
> (Virgil, *Eclogue* 5.76–78)

As long as the boar loves the mountain ridges and the fish the streams, as long as bees feed on thyme and cicadas on dew, honor of you, your name and praises will always remain.[18]

Virgil's 'semper' is linked to nature and does not promise the eternity of fame which Phoebus expounds. The fame which pastoral promises depends on the continuance of natural cycles and the pastoral community itself. Phoebus' speech is 'of a higher mood' because it introduces a conception of fame alien – or rather superior – to pastoral. Once again Milton has criticized the tradition he is using.

The poet is in control of the form of his poem – 'But now my oat proceeds' – but the speakers after Phoebus bring no consolation and cannot explain why Lycidas was doomed to early death. St. Peter's withering denunciation of the Bad Shepherds only increases the sense of a world out of joint, without justice, and once his 'dread voice' has passed, the poet seeks consolation from another pastoral convention, the strewing of flowers over the grave of the dead shepherd. Once again the convention is used to be criticized: 'For so to interpose a little ease, / Let our frail thoughts dally with false surmise' (152–53). Lycidas' body is not lying on a bier, and flowers strewn on the grave are small consolation for death. Nevertheless, this funeral rite does 'interpose a little ease' and soothes some of the pain of bereavement; as Richardson says, this self-deception is 'extremely natural and tender'.[19] The convention is criticized but not rejected, and once again the criticism has a Virgilian precedent: Corydon's realization that Alexis will not care a bit for his garland (*Eclogue* 2.56–57).

It is at this point that the poet makes one last effort to find consolation. He addresses Lycidas.

> Ay me! Whilst thee the shores, and sounding Seas
> Wash far away, where ere thy bones are hurld,
> Whether beyond the stormy *Hebrides*,
> Where thou perhaps under the whelming tide
> Visit'st the bottom of the monstrous world;
> Or whether thou to our moist vows deny'd,
> Sleep'st by the fable of *Bellerus* old,
> Where the great vision of the guarded Mount
> Looks toward *Namancos* and *Bayona's* hold;
> Look homeward Angel now, and melt with ruth.
> And, O ye *Dolphins*, waft the hapless youth. (154–64)[20]

No one has ever denied that the 'thee' addressed in these lines is Lycidas, but since Thomas Warton's edition in 1785 most scholars have assumed that the angel in line 163 is St. Michael.[21] Warton was the first to spot an allusion to St. Michael's Mount; in Newton's edition only a general reference to Cornwall (because of '*Bellerus*') was noted. Here is the heart of Warton's argument that the angel is Michael.

The Great Vision and the Angel are the same thing: and the verb *look* in both the last two verses has the same reference. The poet could not mean to shift the *application* of LOOK, within two lines. Moreover, if in the words *Look homeward angel now* – the address is to Lycidas, a violent, and too sudden, an apostrophe takes place; for in the very next line Lycidas is distantly [for 'distinctly'?] called THE *hapless youth*. To say nothing, that this new *angel* is a *hapless youth*, and to be *wafted by dolphins*. (p. 30)[22]

Warton also observes against Thyer's supposition that the angel is Lycidas, 'But how can this be said to *look homeward*? And why is the shipwrecked person to *melt with ruth*? That meaning is certainly much helped by placing a full point after *surmise*, v. 153.' Warton then points out that the 1638 edition has a semicolon for the period at line 153; he regards this as the correct punctuation, but curiously enough does not print it in his text.[23]

Not everyone agrees that 'the great vision of the guarded Mount' is Michael. No one, to my knowledge, has suggested that a similar phrase, 'the fable of *Bellerus* old', refers to the giant instead of Cornwall. 'Looks toward *Namancos* and *Bayona's* hold' suggests the position of the mountain, not an act of vision, and I take the vision to be the mountain, not the archangel. But this is a minor point. If Milton would not shift the 'application' of 'look' in adjacent lines, would he address one person for nine lines and then suddenly and violently apostrophize someone introduced obliquely even for this poem? The shift of 'thee' is more startling than a shift of subject for 'look'. In addition, the 'now' in 'Look homeward Angel now' is otiose if Michael is the angel, but essential if the angel is Lycidas: Lycidas, once a shepherd, is now an angel.

Warton's more persuasive point is the incongruity of calling Lycidas an 'Angel' in one line, 'the hapless youth' in the next. But he fails to note another incongruity, one which troubles Todd so much: Lycidas is about to join the saints in heaven *and* become 'the Genius of the shoar'. I think these two 'incongruities' are closely related. There are two Lycidases or rather two aspects to the dead Lycidas, the 'hapless youth', whose 'bones' are imagined to be in the sea somewhere between the Hebrides and St. Michael's Mount, and an angelic part, a spirit to which the poet in a moment of mingled hope and desperation appeals. The poet begins to address Lycidas as if his spirit were separate from his corpse: 'Whilst thee ... where ere thy bones are hurld'. In other words, addressing Lycidas allows the possibility that his spirit continues to exist, even while the bones, which are metaphorically endowed with life, 'visit' the northern shores of England or 'sleep' by the southern. The shipwrecked corpse is not asked to melt with ruth. It is the spirit of Lycidas that is asked to look toward the grieving survivors and take pity on them because of their perplexity and sorrow, which have been greatly increased because they have not had even the earthly comfort of burying his bones and paying their last respects. The thought of the body lost at sea, 'the haplesss youth', dispels the temporary hope embodied in the prayer, and the poet appeals to the dolphins to bring the bones to shore. For lines 154–63 are a prayer. The spirit is invoked, and the form of invocation should settle the angel's identity. Milton is using the most prominent feature of the 'cletic hymn', the summoning of a god – or the spirit of a dead person – to come and answer a prayer.

The most prominent feature of the cletic hymn is the specification of the places where the god is likely to be. Part of Scaliger's chapter on hymns 'Euocatorii, siue Inuocatorii' makes this clear.

Euocatorii, siue κλητικοὶ dicuntur à Graecis ii, quibus deos vel inuocamus, vel etiam euocamus. Non quemadmodum prisci Romani cùm eorum oppidorum, vrbiúmue, quae obsideant, numina euocabant. sed quo modo Orpheus in Hippan liberi patris nutricem. vbi non vnius loci facit mentionem:

> Κλῦθι μου εὐχομένου χθονία μῆτερ βασίλεια
> Εἴτε σύγ' ἐν φρυγίῃ κατέχεις ἴδης ὄρος ἁγνόν,
> Εἴ τμῶλος τέρπει σε, καλὸν λυδοῖσι θέασμα
> Ἔρχεο πρὸς τελετάς. (p. 162)[24]

The Greeks call those hymns in which we invoke or summon the gods summoning or cletic hymns. Not summoning in the way that the ancient Romans called the gods out of the towns and cities of people they were besieging, but as in Orpheus' hymn to Hippas, Dionysius' nurse, in which he mentions more than one place: 'Listen to me praying, earth-mother, queen, whether you are dwelling in Phrygia on the holy mountain, Ida, or Tmolos, a beautiful sight to Lydians, is delighting you, come to these rites.'

Milton is fond of this convention and of hymn form in general. A beautiful version appears in the invocation to *Paradise Lost*, which mentions Oreb and Sinai before

> Or if *Sion* Hill
> Delight thee more, and *Siloa's* brook that flow'd
> Fast by the Oracle of God; I thence
> Invoke thy aid to my adventrous Song.... (1.10–13)

Another beautiful example occurs at the end of *Paradise Regained* in the 'Heavenly Anthems' which celebrate the son's victory over temptation.

> True Image of the Father whether thron'd
> In the bosom of bliss, and light of light
> Conceiving, or remote from Heav'n, enshrin'd
> In fleshly Tabernacle, and human form,
> Wandring the Wilderness, whatever place,
> Habit, or state, or motion, still expressing
> The Son of God.... (4.596–602)

A not so beautiful example is more relevant to 'Lycidas'.

> Resolve me then oh Soul most surely blest
> (If so it be that thou these plaints dost hear)
> Tell me bright Spirit where e'er thou hoverest

Whether above that high first-moving Sphear
Or in th'Elisian fields (if such there were).
  Oh say me true if thou wert mortal wight
And why from us so quickly thou didst take thy flight. (36–42)

Milton is addressing the spirit of the fair infant and asking her to
resolve a doubt. The situation is similar in 'Lycidas', but, in
keeping with the perpetual obliqueness of the greater poem, Milton proceeds allusively. It is the very use of the convention
which alerts the reader to Lycidas' apotheosis, and it is not just
the 'whether ... or' itself, but the elaborate, chiastic 'where'
clauses that show we are listening to a prayer.[25] Given this convention from cletic hymn, a shift of addressee to Michael at line
163 is impossible. The spirit of Lycidas is the angel.

And 'Angel' is a very carefully chosen word because it suggests
more than the survival of Lycidas' spirit. 'Angel' suggests that
Lycidas is going to preach, since one of the word's meanings,
thanks in particular to Revelation, the book of the New Testament which is about to play so prominent a role in the consoling
speech, is 'minister'. Here is Milton in *Animadversions Upon the
Remonstrants Defence, against Smectymnuus* of 1641.

'Tis not Ordination nor Jurisdiction that is Angelicall, but the heavenly
message of the Gospell, which is the office of all Ministers alike; in
which sense *John* the *Baptist* is call'd an *Angel*, which in Greeke
signifies a Messenger ... the reason of this borrow'd name is meerely to
signifie the preaching of the Gospell....[26]

Lycidas, by bringing the good news (*evangelium*) of his reception
in heaven, becomes the good minister whose loss was deplored
by St. Peter.

The poet, then, poignantly calls upon Lycidas' spirit to take
pity on him and his fellow mourners, whose presence has been
finally made explicit by 'our moist vows', as Alpers has plausibly
suggested (pp. 488–89). 'Angel' suggests a minister who will
preach the word, and pastoral elegy and the consolatory tradition
provide the precedents for Lycidas' speech. In *Eclogue* 10, as we
have seen, the major model for 'Lycidas', and Theocritus *Idyll* 1,
the love-torn Gallus and the dying Daphnis are the final speakers
after the procession of consolers and taunters. Lycidas, Daphnis,
and Gallus all have the final word – except for the singers of
their laments. Milton has defied convention once again. He
begins the procession with unprecedented abruptness and closes
it with unprecedented indirection. But once again the

119

convention is indispensable, for it prepares the reader for a speech by the subject of the lament.[27]

Moreover, Milton is also relying on the reader's familiarity with a second tradition, that of consolation in general. We saw in chapter 1 that the imagined speech of Suketus' dead son was the climax of Erasmus' model letter of consolation. Erasmus had many precedents, one in a favorite author, Lucian, whose fiercely sarcastic *De luctu* contains a similar prosopopoeia near its end. Burton quotes from this speech in his *Anatomy of Melancholy* (second partition, p. 184). Jerome uses the topos near the end of a consolatory letter (39.7). A prosopopoeia of Drusus forms the climax of the pseudo-Ovidian *Consolatio ad Liviam*.[28] Milton himself uses the convention at the end of the elegy for the Bishop of Ely, and it is interesting to note that, according to MacKellar (*Variorum*, I 205), editors before Masson did not realize that the bishop is the speaker of lines 27–68, although Cowper did in his translation. By way of introduction Milton only says, 'Audisse tales videor attonitus sonos' (25: 'astonished, I seemed to hear these sounds'), and it is not apparent until line 45 that the bishop is describing his own ascent to heaven.

The major difference between these consolatory precedents and 'Lycidas' is not that the others are framed more explicitly (Milton's least explicitly of all) and that the dead speak of themselves in the first person. The major difference is one of tone. Whereas all of the precedents I have just mentioned are squarely within the tradition of angry consolation and berate and threaten the bereaved, Lycidas' speech is astonishingly mild and sympathetic to the angry protests and sorrow which have constituted the poet's lament. As we have seen, this is even true of Milton's bishop, the one exception to sympathy for bereavement in all of Milton's elegy. In earlier poems one would expect words like the bishop's already quoted

> Caecos furores pone, pone vitream
> Bilemque et irritas minas.
> Quid temerè violas non nocenda numina
> Subitoque ad iras percita?

if not something still more severe, like the devastating speech in Lucian. In 'Lycidas' one hears soothing words of consolation and not a hint of reproach, not a memory of rigorism.

> Weep no more, wofull shepherds weep no more,
> For *Lycidas* your sorrow is not dead,
> Sunk though he be beneath the watry floar,
> So sinks the day star in the Ocean bed.... (165–68)

As a good minister, Lycidas suits his speech to his audience, the poet and his fellow shepherds, and thus remains true to his former shepherd self. He answers the question implicit in the invocation and tells them *where* he is, not in the Irish seas with his corpse, but in heaven with the saints. He adopts the repetition used at some of the most poignant, even despairing moments of the lament, for his gentle urging that they give over their tears.

> For *Lycidas* is dead, dead ere his prime
> Young *Lycidas*.... (8–9)

> But O the heavy change now thou art gone,
> Now thou art gon, and never must return! (37–38)

> What could the Muse her self that Orpheus bore,
> The Muse her self for her inchanting son.... (57–58)

'Weep no more, wofull shepherds weep no more' implies sympathetic understanding and approval of the weeping that has gone before, and the next line momentarily hints that the sorrow has moved Lycidas himself. Until the third line one might easily take the second as 'Your sorrow is not dead to Lycidas'. The second line remains confusing unless one recognizes Milton's bold imitation of Virgil's interjection 'tua cura' (*Eclogue* 1.57), and even if one does, the second meaning echoes in the background.

But the major way in which Lycidas, the good minister, suits his speech to his audience is his dazzling transformation of another pastoral convention, the disjunction between natural and human cycles. From 'Moschus' on, the cycles of the natural world, especially the return of flowers in the spring and the rising and setting of the sun, are emblems in pastoral elegy of man's mortality and exclusion from nature. The most famous example comes from outside of the pastoral, a much-imitated passage from Catullus.

> soles occidere et redire possunt:
> nobis cum semel occidit breuis lux,
> nox est perpetua una dormienda. (5.4–6)

> Sunnes, that set, may rise againe:
> But if once we loose this light,
> 'Tis, with vs, perpetuall night.[29]

121

There is, however, an inconsistency in using this topos in a pastoral elegy that places the dead in heaven, for the rising and setting of the sun are such common symbols of Christ's death and resurrection. For the Christian the sun no longer mocks man with its perpetual recurrence but provides a natural reassurance of immortality.[30] Milton's 'day star' stands as a silent rebuke to earlier elegies, Castiglione's and Drummond's for example, which fall into the contradiction of suggesting their subjects are in heaven while using a sun analogy to dramatize the finality of human death. By using a natural analogy suited to the experience of his listeners, Lycidas can remain within the pastoral even as he transcends it with the good news of his resurrection. He answers the expression of loss, 'As killing as the canker to the rose', with another pastoral analogy.

The words of explanation and comfort the poet has been longing to hear are consoling because, being spoken by Lycidas, they prove that he is not dead. Once the shepherds know that he lives and that the tears have been wiped from his eyes for ever, they too stop crying, as the poet, firmly the spokesman for the pastoral community disrupted by the death, assures Lycidas.

> Now *Lycidas*, the shepherds weep no more;
> Henceforth thou art the Genius of the shoar
> In thy large recompence, and shalt be good
> To all that wander in that perilous flood. (182–85)

The poet is answering Lycidas' gentle urging by repeating Lycidas' own phrase: the 'shepherds weep no more'. He expresses his gratitude for the soothing speech by calling Lycidas the 'Genius of the shoar'. Lycidas has just shown that he still cares for the shepherds whom he has left. Unlike Menalcas in Virgil's *Eclogue* 5, the poet does not pray to Lycidas that he be good and promise him *quid pro quo* worship. 'Sis bonus o felixque tuis!' (65: 'O may you be good and propitious to your people') becomes 'shalt be good'. Lycidas, in comforting his friends, has already been good to them, and thus the poet speaks confidently, not supplicatingly. 'Genius of the shoar' is a masterly touch and a splendid indication of Milton's sympathy for bereavement. The phrase satisfies the pastoral longing for a protective presence on earth. Unlike 'Epitaphium Damonis', 'Lycidas' does not end with the bliss of the dead shepherd in heaven, but rather with the continuity of his relationship with the survivors. Lycidas has not abandoned the shepherds when they most need him; his presence remains to protect them as they wander through the world. Milton has muted the common contrast, so prominent in Spenser, between the wretchedness of the survivors and the joy of the dead in heaven. Lycidas, although dead and in heaven, is still attached to his living friends.

The lines which conclude the poem suggest that Lycidas' words have been more than temporarily comforting.

> Thus sang the uncouth swain to th' oaks and rills,
> While the still morn went out with sandals gray;
> He toucht the tender stops of various quills,
> With eager thought warbling his *Dorick* lay:
> And now the Sun had stretcht out all the hills,
> And now was dropt into the western bay;
> At last he rose and twitcht his mantle blew:
> To morrow to fresh woods and pastures new. (186–93)

Just as Lycidas speaks of himself in the third person to indicate the great change in his condition, the poet uses third person to show that the singing of his song has brought the process of mourning to a close and made him a new person, ready to turn to other occupations.[31] Lycidas' resurrection is presented by analogy with the sun, and here the swain is also associated with it, since 'he' in line 192 looks as if it refers to the sun, which has just dropped and might at last be rising.[32] The poet is made new by Lycidas' resurrection through the Son/sun, and this renovation marks the final difference between 'Lycidas' and the pastoral. For the coda, not at all an unfocused 'collection of pastoral commonplaces', as Fish would have it (p. 17), is the poem's final challenge to its tradition. Immediately after Gallus' speech *Eclogue* 10 also ends with an eight-line coda, in which Virgil at first refers to himself in the third person.

> Haec sat erit, diuae, uestrum cecinisse poetam,
> dum sedet et gracili fiscellam texit hibisco,
> Pierides: uos haec facietis maxima Gallo,
> Gallo, cuius amor tantum mihi crescit in horas
> quantum uere nouo uiridis se subicit alnus.
> surgamus: solet esse grauis cantantibus umbra,
> iuniperi grauis umbra; nocent et frugibus umbrae.
> ite domum saturae, uenit Hesperus, ite capellae. (70–77)

This will be enough, goddesses, for your poet to sing, while he sits and weaves a basket with slender marsh-mallow. You, Muses, will make it very valuable to Gallus – Gallus, for whom love grows in me hourly as the green alder shoots up in early spring. Let us get up. Shade is wont to oppress singers; the shade of the juniper is oppressive; shades even harm crops. Go home, goats, now that you're full; go. Hesperus is coming.

Virgil ends this poem – and hence the *Eclogues* as a whole – on a despondent note. Love has just conquered Gallus and made both of them see the futility of pastoral as *remedium amoris*, and now the shades, which have provided a pleasant and protective site for singing since the opening of *Eclogue* 1, are sinister with the coming of evening.[33] As we saw, Virgil begins his poem reluctantly; these last lines are unsettling – anything but triumphant. The close of day is ominous. Milton's lines look towards the future with a vigor and confidence that have been hitherto absent from the poem. Milton has questioned the efficacy of pastoral, its assumptions and values, even more than Virgil, but rather than abandoning it despondently, Milton transcends it.

CONCLUSION

It is a long way from Erasmus' or Wilson's efforts to suppress grief with shame or guilt to the letter of condolence, a long way from Becon's complete condemnation of sorrow to Cole's sympathy for the process of mourning. It is a long way from Grimald's anxious attempt to justify a grief which he hardly expresses to the intimate sorrow of King's 'Exequy' or the angry protests and gentle consolation of 'Lycidas'. It is even a long way from Spenser's 'November', to take a major poem by a major precursor in the same genre, to 'Lycidas', once one recalls how Colin's consoling vision of Dido in heaven leads him to reflect on human wretchedness and folly. Nevertheless, the striking differences between Grimald and King or between Spenser and Milton should not be taken to imply that by the time of Milton all English elegists are free from anxiety about grief and pour out heartfelt expressions of sorrow. One need only recall Thomas Farnaby's poem in the collection in which 'Lycidas' first appeared.

> Lessus inanes mittite ergò & naenias:
> Virtute cassos impii & stulti fleant;
> Lugere felices nefas est & furor.

So stop your empty laments and dirges. Let the impious and foolish weep for those lacking in virtue. It is sacrilege and madness to mourn for the blessed.

Farnaby condemns grief and its expression in elegy as sternly as any sixteenth-century rigorist, and we have seen that the letter of condolence does not replace the bullying letter of consolation and that seventeenth-century theologians do not all embrace the process of mourning with Cole's wise acceptance.

Nevertheless, attitudes towards mourning are changing during the last decades of the sixteenth and the first decades of the seventeenth century. A play from the turn of the century, John Marston's *Antonio's Revenge*, may stand as an emblem of the

125

change. This play thematizes the problem of grief even more explicitly than *Hamlet*, which contains a much subtler and more complicated presentation of grief and revenge.[1] When Antonio hears of his father's death and Pandulpho of his son's, Antonio angrily rejects all comfort, while Pandulpho laughs his misfortune to scorn and defends his laughter with Stoic commonplaces. Marston is obviously contrasting their reactions, but it is very difficult to say whether Pandulpho's self-restraint is meant to be more admirable than Antonio's passionate outbursts of defiance and self-pity. The juxtaposition of such extremes may suggest the wisdom of a middle course of moderation.

In any event, what makes the play emblematic is its vehement rejection of Stoicism. It is to be expected that Antonio will deride *apatheia*,[2] but Pandulpho's recantation comes as a shock. Pandulpho has just been exploiting Stoic consolatory arguments and even claiming exemption from the blows of fortune, when he is overcome with grief for his son.

> Man will break out, despite philosophy.
> Why, all this while I ha' but play'd a part,
> Like to some boy that acts a tragedy,
> Speaks burly words and raves out passion;
> But when he thinks upon his infant weakness,
> He droops his eye. I spake more than a god,
> Yet am less than a man.
> I am the miserablest soul that breathes. (4.2.69–76)

As the Stoic gives up his defenses, the early sixteenth-century ideal of rational self-sufficiency is exposed as impossible and inhuman.

In addition, the changes in elegy between Surrey and Milton should not be taken to imply that simple expression of grief or greater tolerance for the process of mourning necessarily makes for more moving or better poetry. Narratives which trace a development, as this book has done, often present their final stage as if it were superior to the earlier ones. Although an ability to confront and accept feelings of loss is psychologically healthier than disavowal or repression or anxiety at having the feelings, it does not follow that poetry of suppressed grief is less moving than simple expression of sorrow.

In fact, the contrary can be the case. Who is to say that 'An Exequy' is more moving or more beautiful than Jonson's 'On My First Sonne'? Jonson is struggling to overcome feelings which his reason tells him he should not have; King voices his sorrow and affection without inhibition and does not oppose grief and reason. Jonson is trying to say farewell to his son forever, to rid himself of pain by swearing off future attachments; King focuses on reunion with his wife as his reason to live with 'Hope and Comfort'. Jonson pays back the loan of his son; King gives his wife into the care of the earth without giving up his grief and with the confidence that the earth will have to repay its loan. Although King's direct expression of his grief is extraordinarily moving, it is not, at least to me, as moving as Jonson's simultaneous longing to deny and to give way to his paternal loss, the conflict arising from his suppressed mourning.

NOTES

Introduction

1 Some useful information on the feelings of the bereaved and on funeral rites can be gleaned from Philippe Ariès, *The Hour of Our
Death*, trans. Helen Weaver (New York, 1981), but one must
approach this book with caution: Ariès builds sweeping generaliza-
tions out of a few anecdotes. It is staggering to read: 'It was not until
after the seventeenth century that it became important for the male
to master his emotions' (p. 6). As we shall see in the first chapter,
mastering the emotions is an obsession in sixteenth-century consolation. On English funeral rites and formal mourning behavior see
Myra Rifkin, 'Burial, Funeral and Mourning Customs in England
1558–1662', diss. Bryn Mawr, 1977; Paul S. Fritz, 'From "Public"
to "Private": The Royal Funerals in England, 1500–1830', in *Mirrors of Mortality: Studies in the Social History of Death*, ed.
Joachim Whaley (New York, 1981); Richard L. Greaves, *Society
and Religion in Elizabethan England* (Minneapolis, 1981), pp.
695–736; and Roland Mushat Frye, '"Looking Before and After":
The Use of Visual Evidence and Symbolism for Interpreting Hamlet', *Huntington Library Quarterly* 45 (1982) 1–19.

2 Lawrence Stone's contention that 'in the sixteenth and seventeenth
centuries interpersonal relations were at best cold and at worst hos-
tile' (*The Family, Sex and Marriage in England 1500–1800* [New
York, 1977], p. 99) has been severely criticized by reviewers (Keith
Thomas, *TLS*, 21 October 1977, p. 1227; Christopher Hill,
Economic History Review 31 [1978] 462; David S. Berkowitz,
Renaissance Quarterly 32 [1979] 399). Alan Macfarlane, the editor
of Josselin's diary, shows that Stone misinterprets Josselin's grief at
his daughter's death (*History and Theory* 18 [1979] 116), and
Michael MacDonald shows that bereavement was the third commonest cause of mental distress among Napier's patients and cites
several cases of spouses shattered by grief (*Mystical Bedlam: Madness, Anxiety, and Healing in Seventeenth-Century England* [Cam-
bridge, 1981], pp. 77–78, 103–4). (Stone has recently misinterpreted
MacDonald's findings as evidence that bereavement 'did not loom
large as a cause of anguish' by suggesting, 'It was the cumulation of
misfortunes that was too much' [*The New York Review of Books* 16
December 1982, p. 34].) Stone tells the story of Boswell's meeting
David Ross on a London Street in 1778: 'Ross broke down in the

street and "cried for the death of his wife", a response for which one can find no parallel in the sixteenth or early seventeenth centuries, when death was accepted as God's will' (*Family*, p. 250). This may be the most outrageous assertion in a provocative book. Stone does provide much useful information. In particular, one must not forget what Stone has called the most striking feature of the early modern family: 'the constant presence of death' (p. 66). Stone contends that in the early modern period fewer than half of the children who reached adulthood did so with both parents alive, that between a fourth and a third of the children born to English peers and peasants died before age fifteen, and that there was a 50 percent chance that death would claim one spouse after less than seventeen years of marriage (pp. 58–68). (See the table for life expectancy at birth in E. A. Wrigley and R. S. Schofield, *The Population History of England 1541–1871* [Cambridge, 1981], p. 230, and MacDonald, *Mystical Bedlam*, p. 76, with the references cited in his notes.) The incidence of major bereavements – the loss of a child, parent, sibling, or spouse – was thus very high. Given the constant presence of death, it is hardly surprising that there were so many attempts to control mourning and such anxiety about it. When Renaissance writers insist that the time of death is every moment, they are not exaggerating.

3 Anne Ferry has recently claimed, 'Both the nature of poetry about inward experience and the notion of what is in the heart rendered by it changed radically between Wyatt's lifetime and about 1600' (*The "Inward" Language: Sonnets of Wyatt, Sidney, Shakespeare, Donne* [Chicago, 1983], p. 4). The development Ferry traces in love poetry parallels the development of more direct and less conflicted expression of sorrow in elegy.

4 There are several surveys of the psychological literature on mourning: John Bowlby, 'Processes of Mourning', *International Journal of Psycho-Analysis* 42 (1961) 317–40; Geoffrey Gorer, *Death, Grief, and Mourning* (New York, 1965), pp. 136–52; Lorraine D. Siggins, 'Mourning: A Critical Survey of the Literature', *International Journal of Psycho-Analysis* 47 (1966) 14–25; Erna Furman, *A Child's Parent Dies: Studies in Childhood Bereavement* (New Haven, 1974), pp. 233–96. Bowlby, the most important and influential writer on mourning, has presented the fruits of many years of research in three long volumes, *Attachment and Loss* (New York, 1969–80). For the most part I follow his formulations; unless otherwise indicated, all references to Bowlby are to the third volume, *Loss: Sadness and Depression*.

5 One major controversy concerns the relationship between mourning and other reactions to loss. Everyone agrees in using 'mourning' to describe reactions to death, but are reactions to other kinds of loss forms of mourning? Freud includes in his definition of mourning losses of abstractions which have taken the place of a person (*The Standard Edition of the Complete Psychological Works of Sigmund Freud*, vol. 14 [London, 1957], p. 243). Karl Abraham regards

depression as 'an archaic form of mourning' (*Selected Papers*, trans. Douglas Bryan and Alix Strachey [New York, 1953], p. 437), while Max Schur thinks 'depression' a broad enough term to describe all responses to object loss, and mourning a not 'especially severe type of depression' ('Discussion of Dr. John Bowlby's Paper', *The Psychoanalytic Study of the Child* 15 [1960] 81). Erich Lindemann maintains that 'grief reactions are just one form of separation reactions' ('Symptomatology and Management of Acute Grief', in *Death and Identity*, ed. Robert Fulton [Bowie, Maryland, 1976], p. 220). Bowlby uses 'mourning' 'to cover a variety of reactions to loss, including those that lead to a pathological outcome' and argues that infant and childhood separation from the mothering figure is a form of mourning (pp. 16, 9–14). George H. Pollock remarks that the usual assumption that mourning and the reaction to permanent loss are equivalent requires further demonstration ('Mourning and Adaptation', *International Journal of Psycho-Analysis* 42 [1961] 343). Furman restricts 'mourning' to losses of love objects through death (pp. 34–49). Since this study is only concerned with reactions to deaths, I define mourning narrowly, even though I am convinced that the larger use of the term is not only legitimate but preferable.

6 Lindemann, passim, James R. Averill, 'Grief: Its Nature and Significance', *Psychological Bulletin* 70 (1968) 721–48, and Colin Murray Parkes, *Bereavement: Studies of Grief in Adult Life* (New York, 1972), prefer 'grief'. Pollock, p. 345, Furman, p. 34, and Bowlby, pp. 17–18, distinguish between 'grief' and 'mourning'.

7 'Absence of Grief', *Psychoanalytic Quarterly* 6 (1937) 12–22.

8 For full discussions of denial as part of mourning see Freud, p. 244; Lindemann, p. 211; Siggins, pp. 20–21; Parkes, p. 65; and Furman, pp. 248–50. Bowlby prefers to call 'denial' 'disbelief' because 'denial' carries with it a sense of active contradiction and because immediately after a death 'the cause of disbelief is often inadequate information' (p. 87).

9 'How Is Mourning Possible?', *The Psychoanalytic Study of the Child* 21 (1966) 93.

10 Otto Fenichel, in fact, regards the whole process of mourning as 'a postponed and apportioned neutralization of a wild and self-destructive kind of affect which can still be observed in a child's panic upon the disappearance of his mother or in the uninhibited mourning reactions of primitives' (*The Psychoanalytic Theory of Neurosis* [New York, 1945], p. 162). For examples of the extremes of self-abuse some cultures allow see Richard Huntington and Peter Metcalf, *Celebrations of Death: The Anthropology of Mortuary Ritual* (Cambridge, 1979), pp. 29–30.

11 Wolfenstein, p. 103.

12 A few cultures sanction expressions of anger against the dead for desertion; see Huntington and Metcalf, p. 74.

13 Although all writers on the subject agree that depression, despair, despondency, and apathy are part of mourning, they do not all agree that they constitute a stage of their own. Averill (p. 723), Bowlby

(p. 84), and Pollock (p. 346) think they do, but Parkes, in a rare difference of opinion with Bowlby, says that 'the suggestion that a phase of yearning and protest is normally followed by a phase of depression and submission has proved difficult to establish' (p. 87). Parkes points to the alternation of outbursts of grief with depression and observes that anger and yearning become less frequent with the passing of time while episodes of apathy and depression remain. Since the boundaries between stages are hardly inflexible, Parkes's observation confirms rather than questions the existence of a third stage of despair and disorganization.

14 *Letters of Sigmund Freud,* ed. E. L. Freud, trans. Tana and James Stern (New York, 1960) p. 386.

Chapter 1
The Angry Consoler

1 The best discussions of *consolatio* are by Rudolf Kassel, *Untersuchungen zur griechischen und römischen Konsolationsliteratur* (Munich, 1958), and Peter von Moos, *Consolatio: Studien zur mittellateinischen Trostliteratur über den Tod und zum Problem der christlichen Trauer,* 4 vols. (Munich, 1971–72). See also Charles Favez, *La consolation latine chrétienne* (Paris, 1937), and Horst-Theodor Johann, *Trauer und Trost: Eine quellen- und strukturanalytische Untersuchung der philosophischen Trostschriften über den Tod* (Munich, 1968). Unless otherwise indicated all translations are my own.

2 See Erich Auerbach, 'Passio als Leidenschaft', in *Gesammelte Aufsätze zur romanischen Philologie* (Bern, 1967), pp. 161–75, for an excellent discussion of the history of *passio,* especially the pejorative connotation which the word and its descendants acquired from the Stoics.

3 The treatise went through approximately 55 editions during Erasmus' lifetime and continued to be frequently reprinted for the rest of the century (*Opera Omnia Desiderii Erasmi Roterodami,* vol. 1, part 2, ed. Jean-Claude Margolin [Amsterdam, 1971], pp. 175–79.) Its primary example of a letter of consolation had originally been published as the *Declamatio de morte* in 1517 with some other works, including Erasmus' translation of Lucian's *De luctu,* which probably provided the model for the prosopopoeia of the dead son at the end of the *Declamatio.* All quotations from the letter are from the first edition of an anonymous sixteenth-century translation, published by Thomas Berthelet around 1531, *A treatise perswadynge a man patientlye to suffre the deth of his frende* (London, n.d.). (See E. J. Devereux, *Renaissance English Translations of Erasmus: A Bibliography to 1700* [Toronto, 1983], pp. 86–87, for the other three editions.) My translations of Erasmus' precepts for consolation are from Margolin's text. The *De conscribendis* was used as a school-text in sixteenth-century England; see Helmuth Exner, *Der Einfluss des Erasmus auf die englische Bildungsidee* (Berlin,

1939), p. 129, and T. W. Baldwin, *William Shakspere's Small Latine and Lesse Greeke* (Urbana, 1944), II 239, 265–69. Erasmus' work was still being recommended in 1659; see Charles Hoole, *The Masters Method*, in *A New Discovery of the old Art of Teaching Schoole*, ed. E. T. Campagnac (Liverpool, 1913), p. 155. Jean Robertson, *The Art of Letter Writing: An Essay on the Handbooks Published in England During the Sixteenth and Seventeenth Centuries* (London, 1942), p. 11, observes that F. B.'s *Clavis Grammatica* (1678) 'has the semblance of a direct descendant' from Erasmus.

4 The argument is a general favorite from antiquity through the Renaissance and beyond; for its early history see Hermann Wankel, '"Alle Menschen Müssen Sterben": Variationen eines Topos der griechischen Literatur', *Hermes* 111 (1983) 129–54.

5 *The Arte of Rhetorique (1553)*, facsimile ed. Robert Hood Bowers (Gainesville, 1962), p. 10.

6 Earlier in the letter Wilson announces, 'I can not blame your naturall sorowe, if that nowe after declaration of the same, you woulde moderate all youre griefe hereafter, and call backe your pensifenes, to the prescripte order of reason' (p. 85). In the poem which Wilson wrote to close the section of Cambridge tributes to the Brandons he adopts the moderate position and equates moderation with brevity (*Vita et obitus duorum fratrum Suffolciensium, Henrici et Caroli Brandoni* [London, 1551], sig. D2^r). In the Latin funeral oration which he delivered for the Earl of Devon in 1556, Wilson is not torn over the status of mourning and makes no reference to Christian repression of grief (John Strype, ed., *Ecclesiastical Memorials*, vol. 3 [Oxford, 1822], 2.420–7).

7 Wilson was not tutor to both brothers, as is frequently alleged. In *Vita et obitus*, sig. B1^v, he refers to himself as only Charles' tutor, and in the deposition which he made on behalf of Nicholas Udall in Chancery, 29 January 1553, Wilson says 'that he was servant and scolem^r to the lorde Charles brother to the dukes Grace of Suffolk that dyed at the tyme of his decesse and 5 years before' (A. W. Reed, 'Nicholas Udall and Thomas Wilson', *Review of English Studies* 1 [1925] 280).

8 'Thomas Wilson and the Tudor Commonwealth: An Essay in Civic Humanism', *Huntington Library Quarterly* 23 (1959) 50.

9 A. F. Pollard, 'Thomas Wilson', in *Dictionary of National Biography*, vol. 62 (London, 1900), p. 134.

10 Schmidt, p. 59.

11 A. J. Schmidt, 'Thomas Wilson, Tudor Scholar-Statesman', *Huntington Library Quarterly* 20 (1957) 211.

12 Robertson, pp. 10–11, 14. Robertson's is the best work on the subject, but Katherine Gee Hornbeak, 'The Complete Letter Writer in English, 1568–1800', *Smith College Studies in Modern Languages* vol. 15, nos. 3–4 (1934), is also important. The subtitle of one anonymous work gives a good idea of the audience for which the English formularies were composed: *The Prompters Packet of Private and Familiar Letters ... Not unworthy Imitation of the most:*

But most necessarie for such as want either facultie or facilitie to endight (London, 1612). Besides Erasmus', only one Latin treatise both enjoyed a large audience in England and had a section on consolation, Georgius Macropedius' *Methodus de conscribendis epistolis* (1543). Macropedius' treatment strongly recalls Erasmus, especially the attempts to shame the bereaved out of grief. In some instances Macropedius explicitly recommends reproaching the bereaved, and this is what he does in the model letter. He combines social pressure with religious arguments against immoderate mourning, and the social pressure is just as strong as the religious:

Denique patri non commodas, tibi incommodas, coniugi, liberis, & omnibus qui te amant molestus es, omnesque moeroribus efficis. Tibi à fletu cessandum est, si nos omnes lachrymis, quibus te iustiùs, quàm tu parentem, plangimus, moderari desideras. A modò ne sinas nos quaeso maleuolorum exponi ludibrio, qui tuas lachrymas tanquam muliebriter profusas rident. (London, 1609 ed., p. 26)

Finally, you do your father no good, you do yourself harm, and you disturb your wife, your children, and all who love you; you cause everyone to grieve. You must cease weeping, if you desire us all, who bewail you more justly than you bewail your father, to control our tears. Don't, I pray, let us be exposed to the ridicule of ill-wishers who laugh at your tears, which have flown like a woman's.

The influential works by Juan Vives, Conrad Celtis, and Justus Lipsius do not discuss consolation. Christopher Hegendorff only reproduces Sulpicius to Cicero (*Epistulae ad familiares* 4.5) without comment (*Methodus conscribendi epistolas*, in *D. Erasmi Roterodami opus de conscribendis epistolis* [Antwerp, 1565], pp. 64^v–66^r). (Sulpicius to Cicero with Cicero's reply serves as a model in Abraham Flemming, *A Panoplie of Epistles* [London, 1576], pp. 21–29, and Johann Buchler, *Thesaurus conscribendarum epistolarum* [Antwerp, 1653], pp. 52–55, 67–68. Simon Verepaeus, *De epistolis Latine conscribendis* [Wittenberg, 1599], p. 128, asserts that Sulpicius 'consolatur tanta auctoritate, prudentia, humanitate, et orationis suauitate, ut nihil in eo genere putetur exstare perfectius' ['consoles with such authority, prudence, humanity, and such a pleasing style that nothing more perfect exists in this genre']. Buchler steals this assertion, p. 51.) A fifteenth-century treatise by Lippo Brandolini was reprinted in London in 1573 along with Macropedius. Brandolini recommends exordial condolence and marshals the standard commonplaces of shame, but provides no model letters (*De ratione scribendi* [Basel, 1549], pp. 207–21.) In 1659 Hoole, p. 155, recommends Verepaeus' treatise, which was published in London in 1592, and Buchler's, which first appeared at Cologne in 1605, as texts for schoolboys. Verepaeus offers no model letter; his discussion adds nothing to Erasmus or Macropedius. Buchler has a mechanical section on consolation, largely compiled from the work of his predecessors.

13 The first English letter writer, William Fulwood's *The Enimie of Idlenesse* (London, 1568), a translation of a French work which

appeared in Lyons in 1566, shares Wilson's faith that the main reason not to grieve is that one should respect the rule of reason (p. 42). Flemming's collection of Latin letters in translation contains, in addition to Sulpicius to Cicero and Cicero's reply, Cicero to Titius (*Fam.* 5.16), as well as letters of consolation by Paulus Manutius, Conrad Celtis, and Walter Haddon. The modern letters do not depart from the Ciceronian pattern of introductory condolence followed by reasons for moderation. H. C., *The Forrest of Fancy* (London, 1579), turns the commonplaces of consolation to courtship by offering a letter to a young widow who just lost her old, crabby husband (sigs. C3ʳ–4ᵛ). W. Phist. (trans.), *The Welspring of wittie Conceites* (London, 1584), collects several topoi and excerpts from Cicero's letters of consolation (pp. 53–70). Angel Day's *The English Secretary* (1586) follows Erasmus so closely that its precepts are almost translations from *De conscribendis epistolis*, but Day, who calls consolation 'this sweet and gentle remedie to anie troubled conceit' (facsimile of 1599 edition, ed. Robert O. Evans [Gainesville, 1967], p. 112), is somewhat gentler than his model. Nicholas Breton's *A Poste with a madde Packet of Letters* (London, 1602), an immensely popular work, has the standard exordial condolence and insists upon the futility and unreasonableness of grief. M. R.'s *A President for Young Pen-Men* (London, 1615) avoids any gesture towards condolence, and Gervase Markham's *Hobsons Horse-load of Letters* (London, 1617) has a stern letter 'consolatory to a friend for the death of his Sonne'. Markham works several of the familiar commonplaces into a splendid first sentence:

> Though you may seeme (vertuous) to haue worthy cause of much lamentation and teares, hauing lost such a Sonne, of whom al men conceiued great hope, and his owne towardnesse promised with an assurance they should not be deceiued; yet, if with iudgement and truth taking away the veile of passion which blindeth our reason, we looke neuer [sic: for 'nearer'] into it, there will small or no cause appeare of such immoderate grieuing: a few drops are timely and well becomming a friendly Hearse; but, continuall languishment, as if you would dissolue into tears, like Niobe, shew either much weaknesse of man in you, or else bewray feare and ielousie, of your Sonnes vndoubted and happie deliuerie from this earthly prison, into a place of euerlasting ioy and delight. (sig. K3ᵛ)

Jacques Du Bosque's *The Secretary of Ladies*, trans. Jerome Hainhofer (London, 1638), is unmitigatedly harsh and does not even gesture towards condolence, but another contemporary French work, Puget de la Serre, *The Secretary in Fashion*, trans. John Massinger (London, 1640), follows the trend away from harshness. Two later formularies, Thomas Blount's *The Academie of Eloquence* (London, 1654) and John Hill's *The Young Secretary's Guide*, which seems to have first appeared in 1687, also follow the trend towards greater tolerance of grief.

14 I quote from the second edition, published in 1629.
15 One consoler excuses himself after declaring 'that unavoydable evils, are to be endured with constancy': 'I speak not this to condemne your Sighes and Teares, for I doe willingly approve of them, yea,

even in excesse' (de la Serre, p. 77). Another of de la Serre's consolers also defends immoderate mourning: 'If it be lawfull to love
perfectly, no man wil hinder us to lament without cease, since con-
tinuall tears are the Testimony of a Perfect Love' (p. 97).

16 Cf. Wilson, p. 83, and Day, p. 112.

17 In 1621, before launching into his catalogue of 'a few remedies and
comfortable speeches', Robert Burton expresses his own doubts
about the efficacy of consolation by collecting authorities who feel
consolation does little or no good. Among others, he quotes Girolamo Cardano on his *De consolatione*: 'I know beforehand, this tract
of mine many will contemn and reject; they that are fortunate,
happy, and in flourishing estate have no need of such consolatory
speeches; they that are miserable and unhappy think them
unsufficient to ease their grieved minds and comfort misery' (*The
Anatomy of Melancholy*, ed. Holbrook Jackson [Totowa, 1975], partition 2, pp. 126–27; this is Burton's translation from Cardano's *De
libris propriis*). Burton does not really meet the objection and concludes his doubts with the hope that his epitome may do some good,
for himself if for no one else.

18 'Mourning and Melancholia', *The Standard Edition of the Complete
Psychological Works of Sigmund Freud*, vol. 14 (London, 1957), p.
246.

19 The continuing, though invisible, presence and love of the deceased
and the promise of reunion in heaven soothe the bereaved's desire to
recover and could, at an appropriate time, be more comforting than
the other consolatory drugs; often, however, as in Erasmus, continuing presence becomes bitter because the deceased shows his love by
rebuking the bereaved.

20 As Malcolm advises Macduff after the murder of Macduff's wife and
children, 'Let grief / Convert to anger; blunt not the heart, enrage it'
(*Macbeth* 4.3.228–29).

Chapter 2
The Emergence of Compassionate Moderation

1 Strictly speaking, *apatheia* is freedom from excessive and irrational
emotions; total impassivity is a misinterpretation, but is the way in
which it was generally understood by opponents of Stoicism. Consequently, Renaissance defenders of moderate mourning often use
the Stoics as whipping boys, and Stoic 'stocks' or 'stones' become
opprobrious shorthands for inhumanity. J. M. Rist, *Stoic Philosophy* (Cambridge, 1969), pp. 25–27, offers the most cogent defense of
apatheia and argues forcefully that one should not confuse it with
insensibility. See also Pierre de Labriolle, 'Apatheia', in *Mélanges de
philologie, de littérature et d'histoire anciennes offerts à Alfred
Ernout* (Paris, 1940), pp. 215–23; Theodor Ruether, *Die sittliche
Forderung der Apatheia in den beiden ersten christlichen Jahrhunderten und bei Klemens von Alexandrien: Ein Beitrag zur Geschichte
des christlichen Vollkommenheitsbegriffes* (Freiburg im Breisgau,

1949); and A. A. Long, *Hellenistic Philosophy: Stoics, Epicureans, and Sceptics* (New York, 1974), pp. 175–78, 206–7. On *apatheia* in consolation see Kassel, pp. 56–59, von Moos, III 88–93, and Johann, pp. 41–43.

2 Tertullian, *De patientia* 9; Cyprian, *De mortalitate* 7, 20–21; *Epistula ad Turasium*, in *S. Thasci Caecili Cypriani Opera Omnia*, ed. G. Hartel (Vienna, 1871), III 274–82; *Sermones de consolatione mortuorum*, in *Patrologiae Cursus Completus, Series Latina* (Paris, 1887), XL 1159–68. *De mortalitate* was translated into English by Sir Thomas Elyot in 1534 and by John Scory in 1556. Cyprian is cited more often than any other patristic authority on mourning, although some of the people who cite him reject rigorism: Polydore Vergil, *Adagiorum Liber. Eiusdem de inuentoribus rerum libri octo* (Basel, 1521), p. 70ᵛ; Thomas Becon, *The Sicke mannes Salue*, in *The Worckes*, part 2 (London, 1560), fol. 238ʳᵛ; Thomas Cartwright, *A Replye to an answere made of M. Doctor Whitgifte againste the Admonition to Parliament* (London, 1574), p. 161; John Whitgift, *The Defense of the Aunswere to the Admonition, against the Replie of T. C.* (London, 1574), p. 732; Gervase Babington, *A briefe conference, betwixt mans Frailtie and Faith* (London, 1596), pp. 73–74 (excerpts in translation under the title 'Ciprians Sermon of Mortalitie'); Christopher Sutton, *Disce Mori. Learne to Die* (London, 1600), p. 276; Richard Stock, *The Churches Lamentation for the losse of the Godly* (London, 1614), pp. 58–59; William Sclater, *An Exposition with Notes vpon the first Epistle to the Thessalonians* (London, 1619), pp. 319–21; Daniel Featley et al., ΘΡΗΝΟΙΚΟΣ. *The House of Mourning* (London, 1640) pp. 818, 878, 888–89; Matthew Poole, *Annotations upon the Holy Bible ... Vol. II. Being a Continuation of Mr. 'Pool's' Work by certain Judicious and Learned Divines* (London, 1685), ad 1 Thessalonians 4.13. For a French translation of the *Epistula ad Turasium* and an attempt to identify the author and thus date the letter to the early fifth century, see J. Duhr, 'Une lettre de condoléance de Bachiarius (?)', *Revue d'histoire ecclésiastique* 47 (1952) 530–85. See also von Moos's criticisms of Duhr, I 26–27, and E. Dekkers, *Clavis Patrum Latinorum*, 2nd ed. (Steenbrugge, 1961), pp. 13, 173, who rejects Duhr's suggestion and proposes Caelestius, a fifth-century disciple of Pelagius, as the author. Erasmus, in his edition of Jerome's *Opera*, prints the letter after this scathing introduction, which nevertheless shows that several people took the letter seriously:

Animaduerte queso lector, quod totus sermo iaceat, adeo non facundus, ut nec semilatinus. Deinde quod nulla felix inuentio. Tum quod rara frigidaque sacrarum testimonia scripturarum. Sentias impudentissimum aliquem rabulam effutientem non proloquentem, & quicquid in buccam uenerit eblaterantem. Et tamen ausus est homo suauissimus, addito suis nugis Hieronymi nomine, sperare futurum, ut pro Hieronymianis legerentur. Ac uerissime quidem dictum est, nihil tam absurde fieri, quod non reperiat admiratorem. Non solum leguntur haec a magnis, ut sibi uidentur Theologis, uerum etiam in grauissimis quaestionibus, uelut oracula citantur. (*Omnium Operum Divi Hieronymi Stridonensis Tomus Secundus* [Basel, 1516], fols. 191ᵛ–92ᵛ)

Reader, notice, I pray, that the whole style is inert – much less eloquent, as not even half-Latin. Next, the divising of the subject is not at all happy. Then, the evidence from sacred scripture is infrequent and feeble. You will recognize some most impudent ranter who babbles rather than speaks, who blurts out whatever rises to his lips. And notwithstanding, this most charming man has dared, by adding Jerome's name to his rubbish, to hope it will be read as Jerome's. And it has indeed been said most truthfully that there is nothing so absurd as not to find an admirer. This rubbish is not only read by great (as they appear to themselves) theologians but is even cited as an oracle in the most serious disputes.

The *Sermones de consolatione mortuorum* were taken as genuine works of Augustine during the Renaissance; see, for example, Cartwright, p. 161, and Whitgift, p. 732.

3 Qui hoc testimonio abutuntur, vt Stoicam indolentiam, hoc est, ferream duritiem statuant inter Christianos, nihil tale reperient in Pauli verbis. Quod obiiciunt dolendum non esse in morte nostrorum, ne Deo resistamus, id in omnibus rebus aduersis valeret: sed aliud est, fraenare dolorem nostrum vt subiiciatur Deo: aliud abiecto humano sensu, instar lapidum obdurescere.
   (*Ioannis Calvini in omnes D. Pauli epistolas* [Geneva, 1551], pp. 481–82)

They who misuse this testimony to establish Stoic *apatheia*, that is, an iron insensibility, among Christians find nothing of the kind in Paul's words. What they raise as an objection, that we must not mourn at the death of our friends and relations lest we oppose God, would hold good in all instances of adversity. But it is one thing to bridle our grief to submit it to God and another to harden like a stone after throwing off human sensibility.

Calvin's invective should not lead one to expect a gentle conception of moderation, since Calvin says no more than that Paul requires moderation in grief, and since similar attacks elsewhere give way to stringent measures. Another influential continental theologian, Heinrich Bullinger, argues that Paul does not condemn the duties of humanity, but goes on to stress that Paul does condemn immoderate grief; Bullinger's word of praise for Lucian's sardonic *De luctu* is a sure indication that he holds immoderate grief in contempt and suggests that his conception of moderation is not mild (*In omnes apostolicas epistolas, divi videlicet Pauli XIIII. et VII. canonicas, commentarii* [Zurich, 1537], p. 515). John Colet, in a treatise composed around 1500, asserts that nothing is less worthy of a Christian than mourning the deaths of the just and argues that this is only the custom of those who live lives unlike Christ's and fear damnation. Colet quotes Thessalonians in support of his position, although he does not go so far as to say that all mourning is sinful. Like his friend Erasmus, he dwells on the shame of mourning (*Two Treatises on the Hierarchies of Dionysius*, ed. J. H. Lupton [London, 1867], pp. 255–60).

4 Wilson's poem appears in *De obitu ... Martini Buceri ... Epistolae duae* (1551), sig. 11[v].

5 *A Funeral Sermon ... Preached at S. Maries in Cambridge, Anno 1551, at the buriall of ... Martin Bucer*, trans. Thomas Newton (London, 1587), sig. A4[v].

6 Derrick Sherwin Bailey, *Thomas Becon and the Reformation of the Church in England* (Edinburgh, 1952), p. 144. Louis B. Wright, *Middle-Class Culture in Elizabethan England* (Chapel Hill, 1935), p. 242, comments on the popularity of *The Sicke mannes Salue*, and Helen C. White, *English Devotional Literature [Prose] 1600–1640* (Madison, 1931), p. 69, quotes Edmund Bunny, who mentions the tract in 1589 as evidence that the English are producing instructive works of devotion, piety, and contemplation. In Becon's *Worckes*, vol. I, sig. A2^r, a note asserts that all newly published works are marked by a hand in the table; *The Sicke mannes Salue* is not. Part II, in which the work appears (and which I cite), bears the date 1560; the first recorded separate edition is from 1561. For a summary and discussion of the work, see Nancy Lee Beaty, *The Craft of Dying: A Study in the Literary Tradition of the Ars Moriendi in England* (New Haven, 1970), pp. 108–56.

7 See the passage from Latimer quoted in the next paragraph; Paulinus, *Epistula* 13.1; Macropedius, p. 24^v; George Gascoigne, *The Complete Works*, ed. John W. Cunliffe (Cambridge, 1910), II 233; Verepaeus, p. 126; Sclater, p. 320; and Zacharie Boyd, *The Last Battell of the Soule in Death* (Edinburgh, 1628), II *7^r.

8 In 1517 Polydore Vergil mentions the custom of ancient Marseilles of celebrating funerals without lamentation and proceeds to approve the restraint at English funerals:

> Id quod Angli hodie rite seruant, animaduertentes, credo, nihil ad rem attinere, humano indulgere dolori, ceu stulte conquerendo, quod deus immortalitatem suam noluerit nobiscum partiri, cum praesertim moriendo relinquamus labores, et pericula, quae statim nascendo subimus. Quapropter Thraces huius rei memores natales hominum (prout in tertio huius operis uolumine diximus) flebiliter, exequias cum hilaritate merito celebrabant. (fol. 70^v)

> [A custom which] the English correctly preserve today; they realize, I believe, that indulgence in human sorrow or foolish complaining because God did not wish to share his immortality with us is beside the point, especially since by dying we leave behind the hardships and dangers which we endure from the moment of birth. For this reason, the Thracians, mindful of this, rightly used to celebrate human birthdays (as we said in the third volume of this work) tearfully and funerals joyfully.

The Utopians do not lament the deaths of those who die full of hope but celebrate their funerals with song (Thomas More, *Utopia*, ed. Edward Surtz and J. H. Hexter [New Haven, 1965], p. 222).

9 *Certayn Godly Sermons, made vppon the lords Prayer* (1562), fol. 105^v.

10 *A moste fruitefull, pithie, and learned treatise, how a Christian man ought to behaue himselfe in the daunger of death* (c. 1574), pp. 230–31.

11 *Of the Laws of Ecclesiastical Polity Book V*, ed. W. Speed Hill (Cambridge, 1977), p. 410.

12 *An Exposition vpon the two Epistles of the Apostle Sainct Paule to the Thessalonians* (1583), p. 160.

13 James Pilkington, *A Godlie Exposition upon certaine chapters of Nehemiah* (Cambridge, 1842), p. 319; Robert Southwell, *The Triumphs ouer Death* (1595), sig. B2ʳ.

14 *Lectures Vpon the First and Second Epistles of Paul to the Thessalonians* (Edinburgh, 1606), p. 205. Rollock's Latin commentary, which he published before his death, is not as expansive on the legitimacy of sorrow (*In epistolam Pauli apostoli ad Thessalonices priorem Commentarius* [Edinburgh, 1598], p. 111).

15 I have silently corrected three misprints in this passage. The whole work is full of misprints and other errors which show haste in composition and publication. In this passage, for instance, 'powring out' would make better sense than 'powre out'.

16 A collection of funeral sermons by Featley et al. published in 1640, shows no advance in sympathy over Cole – a slight retreat, if anything. As with Donne's sermons, one is struck by the lack of concern with mourning, although it is generally true that funeral sermons throughout the sixteenth and seventeenth centuries are surprisingly unconcerned with mourning, despite the fact some preaching manuals do recommend moderation in mourning as a theme (Andreas Hyperius, *The Practis of Preaching*, trans. John Ludham [1577], fol. 155ʳ). Only seven of the 47 sermons in ΘΡΗΝΟΙΚΟΣ treat mourning more than in passing, and only two dwell on the subject. One of these, 'The Praise of Mourning; or, Mourning preferred before Mirth', follows Sclater's defense of the affections, justifies moderate mourning, and even insists a bit more than Sclater that the Holy Ghost is not speaking according to the custom 'of naturall and wordly men; but with respect to the naturall disposition, and affection, that is in the heart of man' (p. 32). The second sermon which treats mourning at length, 'A restraint of exorbitant Passion; or, Grounds against unseasonable Mourning', is milder than the first because it does not inveigh against immoderate mourning or threaten punishment. One of Featley's sermons is the most compassionate in the collection. This is the opening:

> I feare lest some here present, that are of a more melting disposition, stung with the sense of their present losse, and overcome with griefe and sorrow for it, may frame an answer with a deep sigh to the interrogations in my Text saying: here is Deaths sting, here is the Graves victorie. (p. 847)

This is a perfect opportunity to warn against immoderation, but Featley neither chides nor threatens: he promises to show that the dead is not dead. This he does with a tedious and ostentatious display of learning. One of the few direct passages is a simple appeal for moderation:

> Neither doth Christian religion plucke out these affections by the roote, but only prunes them. All that my exhortation driveth unto, is but to moderate passion by reason, feare by hope, griefe by faith, and nature by grace: Let love expresse it selfe, yet so that in affection to the dead, we hurt not the living: Let the *naturall springs* of teares *swell*, but not too much *overflow* their *bankes*: let not our eye be all upon our losse on earth, but our brothers gaine also in heaven, and let the one *counter-ballance* at least, the other. (p. 857)

The moderation of this exhortation to moderation is, I hope, sufficiently apparent after the long journey we have traced from the early sixteenth century.

Chapter 3
Praise and Mourning

1 I follow the modern convention of calling funeral poetry 'elegy', even though it was not the most common designation in the Renaissance and often referred to other types of poetry; see John W. Draper, *The Funeral Elegy and the Rise of English Romanticism* (New York, 1929), and Francis White Weitzmann, 'Notes on the Elizabethan *Elegie*', *PMLA* 50 (1935) 435–43.

2 *The Enduring Monument: A Study of the Idea of Praise in Renaissance Literary Theory and Practice* (Chapel Hill, 1962), pp. 114–15. Cf. the more cautious remark by A. L. Bennett, 'The Principal Rhetorical Conventions in the Renaissance Personal Elegy', *Studies in Philology* 51 (1954) 108, 'Often the grief is so effectively subordinated that praise becomes the chief feature of the elegy; sometimes the title frankly indicates that the poet is attempting chiefly a panegyric rather than a lament.' Avon Jack Murphy, 'The Critical Elegy of Earlier Seventeenth-Century England', *Genre* 5 (1972) 75–105, accepts Hardison's thesis, and C. W. Jentoft, 'Surrey's Five Elegies: Rhetoric, Structure, and the Poetry of Praise' *PMLA* 91 (1976) 23–32, agrees that praise dominates lament in the funeral elegy, but asserts that lament is more prominent in pastoral elegy.

3 *Dionysii Halicarnasei quae fertur Ars Rhetorica*, ed. H. Usener (Leipzig, 1895), p. 29.

4 One must not forget the context of this observation. Wilson is advising his speaker to structure an encomium by going through the stages of the bereaved's life (one of the traditional patterns of praise). He is not implying, as Hardison, p. 116, asserts, that he is stating the major function of lament.

5 *Menander Rhetor*, ed. D. A. Russell and N. G. Wilson (Oxford, 1981), p. 202.

6 *Poetices Libri Septem: Faksimile-Neudruck der Ausgabe von Lyon 1561*, ed. August Buck (Stuttgart, 1964), p. 168. Cf. Johann Buchler, *Institutio Poetica, ex R. P. Pontani ... potissimum libris concinnata* (Schleusingen, 1630), pp. 161–63, and the summary of Buchler by Ruth Wallerstein, *Studies in Seventeenth-Century Poetic* (Madison, 1950), p. 25.

7 A late example is particularly instructive because of its codified recipes for epitaph, see F. B., *Clavis Grammatica: Or, The Ready Way to the Latin Tongue*, 4th ed. (London, 1708), pp. 105–07.

8 *A Speedie Post*, sig. G2ᵛ. Cf. the remark of the seventeenth-century scholar Ménage, as translated by Hoyt Hopewell Hudson, *The Epigram in the English Renaissance* (Princeton, 1947), p. 81, 'Whenever some celebrated person dies I am accustomed to remark: "He will not pass *unepitaphed*."'

9 *Exequiae Illustrissimi Equitis, D. Philippi Sidnaei* (Oxford, 1587), sig. A3ʳ, in A. J. Colaianne and W. L. Godshalk, eds. *Elegies for Sir Philip Sidney (1587)* (Delmar, 1980). Contrast Alexander Nevill in the preface to *Academiae Cantabrigiensis Lachrymae Tumulo Nobilissimi Equitis, D. Philippi Sidneij Sacratae* (Cambridge, 1587), sig. bʳᵛ; in a classic example of protesting too much, Nevill takes pains to assure Leicester that there is nothing mercenary about his motives. See also the letter which Donne sent the Countess of Bedford, which hints at reward very strongly indeed, and a letter he later sent to Goodyer which 'makes clear his bitter disappointment at the scale of his reward' (*The Epithalamions, Anniversaries and Epicedes*, ed. W. Milgate [Oxford, 1978], pp. 196–97).

10 *Death Repeal'd by a Thankfull Memorial Sent from Christ-Church in Oxford* (Oxford, 1638), p. 42. One thinks of Grierson's disapproving quip, 'Elegies like this, and I fear Donne's among them, were frankly addressed not so much to the memory of the dead as to the pocket of the living' (*The Poems of John Donne*, ed. Herbert J. C. Grierson [Oxford, 1912], II 209).

11 George Whetstone asserts that Sidney was the best scholar at Cambridge during his time and the author of *The Shepheardes Calendar* (*Sir Phillip Sidney, his honorable life, his valiant death, and true vertues* [c. 1587], sig. B2ʳ); Sidney attended Christ Church, Oxford, and was, of course, the dedicatee, not the author of *The Shepheardes Calendar*. Carew thinks nothing odd about writing a fulsome elegy for a lady he never met: 'But who shall guide my artlesse Pen, to draw / Those blooming beauties, which I never saw?' (*The Poems of Thomas Carew with His Masque 'Coelum Britannicum'*, ed. Rhodes Dunlap [Oxford, 1949], p. 67). The Earl of Abingdon commissioned Dryden to write a panegyric for his dead wife, even though Dryden, as he tells us in his preface, had never seen her; Dryden compares himself to Donne writing on Anne Drury (*The Poems and Fables of John Dryden*, ed. James Kinsley [Oxford, 1962], p. 467). Preachers would deliver funeral or commemorative sermons, including the conventional bit of idealizing praise, for people they did not know; see Barbara Kiefer Lewalski, *Donne's 'Anniversaries' and the Poetry of Praise: The Creation of a Symbolic Mode* (Princeton, 1973), pp. 191–92.

12 Spenser's Red Cross Knight, for example, tells Fradubio,

> He oft finds med'cine, who his griefe imparts;
> But double griefs afflict concealing harts,
> As raging flames who striueth to suppresse. (*The Faerie Queene* 1.2.34)

Cf. Malcolm's advice to Macduff, *Macbeth* 4.3.209–10, and *Titus Andronicus* 4.2.36–37, 'Sorrow concealed, like an oven stopped, / Doth burn the heart to cinders where it is'.

13 George Puttenham, *The Arte of English Poesie*, ed. Gladys Doidge Willock and Alice Walker (Cambridge, 1939), p. 47. Puttenham is not, however, always representative of Renaissance rhetoric or poetics, as Daniel Javitch has shown in another context, *Poetry and Courtliness in Renaissance England* (Princeton, 1978), pp. 61–66.

Puttenham declares, 'Such of these greefs as might be refrained or holpen by wisedome, and the parties owne good endeuour, the Poet gaue none order to sorrow them.' In earlier writers this sentence would lead to the conclusion that one should not grieve for the dead, but it leads Puttenham to single out death as one of the three cases which call for lament.

14 Lodovick Bryskett puts the following speech in Stella's mouth.

> Alas if thou my trustie guide
> Were wont to be, how canst thou leaue me thus alone
> In darknesse and astray; weake, wearie, desolate,
> Plung'd in a world of woe, refusing for to take
> Me with thee, to the place of rest where thou art gone.
> > (Edmund Spenser, *Poetical Works*, ed. J. C. Smith and
> > E. de Selincourt [Oxford, 1912], p. 552)

Cowley expresses his sense of abandonment with greater simplicity.

> My sweet *Companion*, and my gentle *Peere*,
> Why hast thou left me thus unkindly here,
> Thy *end* for ever, and my *Life* to moan;
> > O thou hast left me all alone!
> > ('On the Death of Mr. William Hervey', in Richard S.
> > Sylvester, ed., *English Seventeenth-Century Verse*, vol. 2,
> > [New York, 1974], p. 584)

Cf. Donne's guarded reproach in 'Obsequies to the Lord Harrington'.

> So, though, triumphant soule, I dare to write,
> Mov'd with a reverentiall anger, thus,
> That thou so earely wouldst abandon us;
> Yet am I farre from daring to dispute
> With that great soveraigntie, whose absolute
> Prerogative hath thus dispens'd for thee.... (*Epithalamions*, pp. 73–74)

See also the first lines of *Memoriae Matris Sacrum* XV (*The Works of George Herbert*, ed. F. E. Hutchinson [Oxford, 1941], p. 429).

15 I discuss Surrey's elegies in detail in chapter 5. Herbert does express sorrow for his mother, but is more emotional in his exuberant attack on the Stoics (*Memoriae Matris Sacrum* XII, p. 429) or at the close of the second poem of the collection when he lashes out against an imagined detractor of a son who praises his mother (pp. 423–24).

16 This poem provides the only information we have about Grimald's early life or his mother, who seems to have died in 1555 when he was about 36. See L. R. Merrill, *The Life and Poems of Nicholas Grimald* (New Haven, 1925), pp. 6–7. Even if Grimald's mother is not the Agnes Grymbold whose death was recorded in 1555 in the parish register of Winwick, Huntingdonshire, his mother must have died after January 1552, when her son left Oxford; see the poem itself, in *Tottel's Miscellany (1557–1587)*, ed. Hyder Edward Rollins, rev. ed. (Cambridge, 1965), I 112.28–30, and Merrill, p. 14.

17 Plutarch says that Sertorius was particularly attached to his mother and almost died of grief when he learned of her death; even though

his Spanish friends were urging him to become their leader, he kept his tent in solitude for seven days and could hardly be persuaded to resume his military enterprises (*Sertorius* 23).

18 Thomas North's translation of 1579, in William Shakespeare, *Coriolanus*, ed. Philip Brockbank (London, 1976), p. 363. Plutarch is following Dionysius of Halicarnassus, *Roman Antiquities* 8.54; Livy records no such speech and prefers Fabius Pictor's account that Coriolanus died of old age rather than at the hands of the Volscians. For the different stories see R. M. Ogilvie, *A Commentary on Livy: Books 1–5* (Oxford, 1970), pp. 314–16.

19 Herodotus 1.31; Cicero, *Tusculanae disputationes* 1.113. See Margherita Guarducci, 'Due note su Kleobis e Biton', in *Studi in onore di Ugo Enrico Paoli* (Florence, 1956), pp. 365–76. Grimald draws heavily on Valerius Maximus 5.4, 'De pietate in parentes', which gives the examples of Coriolanus and the two pairs of brothers.

20 See Livy 1.4.7, and Ogilvie, pp. 49–50.

21 For full discussions of the commonplaces of praise see Theodore Burgess, 'Epideictic Literature', *University of Chicago Studies in Classical Philology* 3 (1902) 89–261; Verdun L. Saulnier, 'L'oraison funèbre au XVIᵉ siècle', *Bibliothèque d'Humanisme et de Renaissance* 10 (1948) 124–55; Bennett, pp. 110–15; Heinrich Lausberg, *Handbuch der literarischen Rhetorik: Eine Grundlegung der Literaturwissenschaft*, 2nd ed. (Munich, 1973), I 132–35, and *Menander Rhetor*, pp. xviii–xxxi.

22 See, for example, Menander, p. 174, and Richard Rainolde, *The Foundacion of Rhetorike*, facsimile ed. Francis Johnson (New York, 1945), fol. 40ʳ.

23 Priscian, *Praeexercitamina* 7. Prodigies connected with birth are a common feature in biographies of ancient poets, (e.g., *Vitae Vergilianae Antiquae*, ed. Colin Hardie, 2nd ed. [Oxford, 1967], p. 7).

Chapter 4
The Shift from Anxious Elegy

1 *The Poems of Henry King*, ed. Margaret Crum (Oxford, 1965), p. 68.

2 There is no bibliography of English Renaissance elegy. My information comes from four main sources: the chronological card catalogue of STC in the Huntington Library; STC itself under 'Oxford'; Arthur E. Case, *A Bibliography of English Poetical Miscellanies 1521–1750* (Oxford, 1935); and Leicester Bradner, *Musae Anglicanae: A History of Anglo-Latin Poetry 1500–1925* (New York, 1940), pp. 99, 346–58. One should note that the number of Oxford collections of poetry of all kinds increases markedly during the 1620s, although there are more collections of elegy than of all of the other kinds (epithalamia, genethliaca, etc.) put together. For the elegies on Prince Henry see John Philip Edmond, 'Elegies and Other Tracts Issued on the Death of Henry, Prince of Wales, 1612', *Publications of the Edinburgh Bibliographical Society* 6 (1906) 141–58;

Elkin Calhoun Wilson, *Prince Henry and English Literature* (Ithaca, 1946), pp. 128–76; Wallerstein, pp. 59–95; and Lewalski, pp. 312–26.

3 Wilson's 'De luctu Cantabrigiensium compescendo' is characteristic of the later collection's anxiety about the legitimacy of grief.

> Iam satis est, (clamant superi) modus esto dolori.
> Dum breuis est, satis est, displicet immodicus.
> Conticuere omnes, gemitus tamen occupat omnes.
> Singultusque fouent pectore, uoce tacent.
> Sed DEVS affectus cohibens, iubet esse quietos.
> Iussa tenent omnes, pectore nemo dolet. (sig. D2ʳ)

Enough, the gods cry out, let there be measure to sorrow. While it is short, it is enough; immoderate sorrow is offensive. Everyone became silent, yet groaning takes possession of everyone. They nurture sobs in their breast, but are silent. But God, checking the passions, orders them to be calm. Everyone keeps His commands; no one grieves in his breast.

4 On Bucer's life and death in England see Martin Bucer, *De regno Christi Libri Duo 1550*, ed. François Wendel (Paris, 1955), pp. ix–xxxv.

5 For similar emphasis on the sins which killed Bucer see John Goodricus, sig. 11ᵛ; Thomas Wilson, sig. 11ᵛ (quoted above); Henry Wright, sig. 13ʳ; John Semanus, sig. 13ᵛ; William Temple, sig. 14ʳ; and Nicholas Karuillus, sig. m2ʳ. A poem written two years later is the most insistent on the sins of the living as the cause for death; William Baldwin strikes this note throughout his *Funeralles of King Edward the sixt* (London, 1560), which ends with the following stanza.

> Wo wurth vs men, whose sins let run at rage
> Have murdered him: wo wurth vs wretches all,
> In whom the wreke of righteous bloud must fall,
> Wo wurth our sins, for they, alas, haue slayne,
> The noblest prince that dyd, or eft shall rayne. (sig. B4ᵛ])

This topos does not disappear as attitudes towards mourning become more sympathetic, but is rarely used except at the deaths of royalty. It is particularly popular after the death of Prince Henry; see Wilson, p. 157.

6 *A Booke of Epitaphes made vpon the death of the Right worshipfull Sir William Buttes Knight: Who deceased the third day of September, Anno 1583*, ed. Robert Dallington (London, n.d.), sig. B4ʳ. The poem is a translation of Francis Burleigh's Latin epigram by Thomas Butts, Sir William's brother: 'Plange fidele genus, Buttus tellure recessit, / At petijt coelos, Plaude fidele genus'.

7 *Peplus. Illustrissimi Viri D. Philippi Sidnaei Supremus Honoribus Dicatus* (Oxford, 1587), p. 10; *Exequiae*, sigs. Aʳ, A2ʳ, B3ʳ, B3ᵛ, B4ᵛ, I2ʳ. The topos recurs in the seventeenth century, for example, Francis Harington, 'Light sorrowes talk, great griefs are tongueless quite' (Stock, p. 107), or Donne, 'Elegie upon the death of Mistress Boulstred': 'Language thou art too narrow, and too weake / To ease us now; great sorrow cannot speake' (*Epithalamions*, p. 61).

8 *Academiae Cantabrigiensis Lachrymae*, p. 29. A shorter version of this poem, not attributed to anyone, appears, pp. 21–22; from it I take 'nimis' for the 'minus' on p. 29. A short poem on p. 32 approaches the consolatory use of the topos. Another poem begins with a question which earlier would have led to reasons not to grieve, but which instead ushers in lament and praise (p. 63).

9 A later imitation of Horace's poem goes to even greater lengths to defend immoderate mourning. It begins as follows.

> Quae desiderio detur mensura pudórve
> Tam chari capitis? Lugubres incipe questus
> *Melpomene*, sacraeque modum nescite Sorores.
>
> (Henry Molle in *Cantabrigiensium Dolor & Solamen*
> [Cambridge, 1625], sig. D1ʳ)

What measure or restraint should be given to the loss of so dear a person? Begin mournful plaints, Melpomene, and, sacred sisters, acknowledge no limit.

The Sidney collections are not entirely lacking in sterner poems. The title and form of one of these make it particularly interesting; it is an anonymous pastoral elegy called 'Lycidas' (*Peplus*, pp. 27–29). Damoetas makes Amyntas give over his grief as effeminate and futile. The only grief which Damoetas countenances is for the unrewarded state of poetry and the death of Sidney as patron of letters. (One cannot help recalling Milton's lines on 'the homely slighted shepherds trade'.) Here is another of the sterner poems.

> CANTIA quid luges? gemitus quid fundis inanes?
> O perijt *Sidney*: spes mea tanta perit.
> Vita breuis, Mors certa venit, rapit omnia tempus:
>   Mens volat ad superos, corpora claudit humus.
> Abstergas lachrymas, vestes depone lugubres.
>   In coelis *Sidney*, florea serta gerit.
>
> (*Academiae Cantabrigiensis Lachrymae*, p. 65)

'Kent, why do you grieve? why do you pour out vain groans?' 'O, Sidney has perished: my great hope has perished.' 'Life is short, death is sure to come, time seizes all; the mind flies to the heavens, the earth buries bodies. Wipe away your tears, put away your mourning clothes. In heaven Sidney wears garlands of flowers.'

See also the poem on p. 38 of the same collection, William Suaddon's, *Peplus*, p. 31, and the anonymous poem which borrows the opening of Catullus 61, *Peplus*, pp. 24–25. These poems are few and far between, however, and not nearly as severe as those in the Bucer and Brandon collections.

10 *Campion's Works*, ed. Percival Vivian (Oxford, 1909), pp. 373–74.

11 *Thomae Campioni Poemata* (London, 1595), sig. F5ʳ. I have adopted some of Vivian's punctuation (which is based on the 1619 edition).

12 See *Aeneid* 5.79 and 6.884, and *P. Vergili Maronis Aeneidos Liber Quintus*, ed. R. D. Williams (Oxford, 1960), p. 57.

13 Cf. the beginning of 'To the Most High and Mighty Prince Charles', one of Campion's poems on the death of Prince Henry.

> Fortune and Glory may be lost and woone,
> But when the worke of Nature is undone
> That losse flyes past returning;
> No helpe is left but mourning.
>> (*The Works of Thomas Campion: Complete Songs,*
>> *Masques, and Treatises with a Selection of the Latin*
>> *Verse,* ed. Walter R. Davis [Garden City, 1967], p. 122)

Mourning is no longer just a painful struggle but a positive help – the only help – to the bereaved.

14 Campion writes a number of poems to Mychelburne and his two brothers, including an epigram to Edward on the death of this sister (Vivian, p. 284). For a few details of Mychelburne's life see Vivian, pp. xlviii–xlix, and Davis, p. 419. Both Vivian and Davis repeat Anthony à Wood's praise of Edward as a poet and his assertion that his only published verse is a pair of prefatory poems to Peter Bales' *Art of Brachygraphy,* but I have run across a number of Mychelburne's poems: *Iusta Oxoniensium* (Oxford, 1612), sig. K2ᵛ (two poems, the first an attack on anyone who refuses to weep); *Epithalamia, sive Lusus Palatini* (Oxford, 1613), sigs. F1ᵛ–2ʳ (three poems); *Iusta Funebria Ptolemaei Oxoniensis Thomae Bodleii Equitis Aurati* (Oxford, 1613), pp. 28–31 (five poems); *Camdeni Insignia* (Oxford, 1624), sig. C1ʳᵛ (two poems). Doubtless a thorough search through the Oxford collections of the period would turn up some more.

15 The end of another of the songs for Prince Henry also refers positively to the healing power of time.

> Yet the most bitter storme to height encreased
>> By heav'n againe is ceased:
>> O time, that all things movest,
> In griefe and joy thou equall measure lovest:
> Such the condition is of humane life,
> Care must with pleasure mixe, and peace with strife:
>> Thoughts with the dayes must change; as tapers waste,
>> So must our griefes; day breakes when night is past. (Davis, p. 124)

These lines almost offer an apology for the passing away of grief and not an exhortation to moderation, as might appear from a hasty reading. Although his practice shows that excessive grief is not a cause of concern, Campion does recognize, at least in theory, that grief can be excessive: 'nimios nobis omni arte dolores / Est mollire animus' (Davis, p. 116: 'It is my intention to mitigate with all my art excessive sorrows').

16 *The Shorter Poems, and Songs from the Plays and Masques,* ed. A. M. Gibbs (Oxford, 1972), p. 272.

17 *Ben Jonson,* ed. C. H. Herford and Percy and Evelyn Simpson (Oxford, 1925–52), XI 484. The quotations from *Jonsonus Virbius* come from this volume.

18 *Justa Edouardo King: A Facsimile Edition of the Memorial Volume*

in which Milton's 'Lycidas' First Appeared, ed. Edward Le Comte (n.p., 1978), p. 30; *Obsequies to the memorie of M' Edward King* (since the English poems are separately paginated, I will preface references with the first word of the title if it is not obvious which section is being cited), pp. 9, 12. The poem on p. 9 is by Cleveland, who also exclaims against artificial elegy in lines on the death of Archbishop Laud in 1645; see *The Poems of John Cleveland*, ed. Brian Morris and Eleanor Withington, p. 38. Carew puts the theme to consolatory use in 'To the Countesse of Anglesie upon the immoderatly-by-her-lamented death of her Husband'.

> Forbeare your fruitlesse griefe then, and let those
> Whose love was doubted, gaine beliefe with showes
> To their suspected faith; you, whose whole life
> In every act crown'd you a constant Wife,
> May spare the practise of that vulgar trade,
> Which superstitious custome onely made;
> Rather a Widow now of wisedome prove
> The patterne, as a Wife you were of love. (p. 69)

19 David Masson, *The Life of John Milton: Narrated in Connexion with the Political, Ecclesiastical, and Literary History of His Time*, 2nd ed. (London, 1881), I 647: 'The gist of all the panegyrics, various as they were in style, was that English poetry had died with Ben. The panegyrics themselves went near to prove it.'

20 The scholar with small Latin, so condescendingly treated in Le Comte's preface, will be wise to place small trust in Le Comte's translations. Despite noting an earlier reference to Xerxes, Le Comte translates the first line as 'A fool carries three hundred nets for the sea'. He fails to grasp the structure of the first four lines and bungles the referent of 'qui' in line 8; the sense of the passage is completely lost. Some of the poems may be 'crude', as Le Comte says, but they are not nonsense. I cannot resist pointing out another howler. The *Justa* opens with a prose epitaph in capital letters imitating an inscription; above the epitaph appear the three letters 'P. M. S.' Here is part of Le Comte's note.

What these initials stand for is not known. I suppose 'S.' stands for 'Scripsit'. Warton, p. 38, conjectured: 'This I suspect to have been composed either by Milton or Henry More' ... We would then have 'Poeta Miltonus Scripsit' or 'Poeta Morus Scripsit'.... Parker, II, 811, attributed both preface and following poem to John Alsop, Fellow of Christ's College from 1623.... But what about the initials P. M.? I would complete Parker's conjecture by proposing that they stand for 'Mildmay Preacher' in Latin and in Latin word order: a post held from December 1636 to 1638. (p. 60)

'P. M. S.' stands for 'piis manibus sacrum' ('consecrated to the blessed dead'); see Adriano Capelli, *Lexicon Abbreviaturarum: Dizionario di abbreviature latine ed italiane*, 6th ed. (Milan, 1979), p. 490. The abbreviation appears in the title of a poem in *Death Repeal'd*, p. 25.

21 Herodotus 7.35. A couple of other contributors to the Latin section

allude to the story: now that the sea has killed King it deserves its lashes and fetters (pp. 7, 12). This is just the sort of thing Farnaby is objecting to, and it appears in several of the poems.

22 William More's poem is similar to Farnaby's, though not quite so severe.

> My grief is great, but sober; thought upon
> Long since; and Reason now, not Passion.
> Nor do I like their pietie, who to sound
> His depth of learning, where they feel no ground,
> Strain till they lose their own; then think to ease
> The losse of both, by cursing guiltless seas. (pp. 10–11)

And More is just as defensive about his stance: 'Tell me no more of Stoicks'. No other poem in the collection approaches rigorism, but there are examples of anxious self-restraint, particularly in one of the poems by Henry King, Edward's brother (not to be confused with the Bishop of Chichester), *Obsequies*, pp. 1–4.

23 The other defense of immoderate grief, R. Mason's, takes its cue from Statius, *Silvae* 2.6.

> Dure nimis, quisquis lacrymis discrimina ponis
> Lugendique modum: nullo te praefica lessu,
> Nemo tuum funus ferali crine solutus
> Plangat; & in vacua si quando naufragus ora
> Jactaris vento, nemo squalentia ripis
> Ossa legat; media jaceas neglectus arena.
> Quisnam hîc castiget luctus? In funera planctus
> Quos ego suscipiam? quem non causa una canendi,
> Non trahit unus amor? (p. 9)

You are too harsh, who place limits to tears and grieving. May no mourner with hair loosened for a funeral bewail your death with lamentation, and if, shipwrecked, you should ever be cast by the wind on deserted shores, may no one pick your squalid bones from the banks: may you lie neglected in the middle of the sand. Who here would reprove grief? What laments shall I raise for his funeral, I, whom not one cause for singing, not one love, impels?

Despite this diversion of his sorrow into anger against potential critics Mason is able to give some personal expression to his loss and recalls how King used to encourage his poetry before launching into another invective against the sea. At the end of the poem he pledges anniversary elegies to King. See also the more moderate defense of tears by Jo. Hoper, *Justa*, p. 21.

Chapter 5
Surrey and Spenser

1 See Edmond Bapst, *Deux gentilshommes-poètes de la cour de Henry VIII* (Paris, 1891), pp. 225–32, and Edwin Casady, *Henry Howard, Earl of Surrey* (New York, 1938), pp. 60–63. The event must have occurred between 12 July and 8 August, as Surrey was at Kenninghall on the first date, and on the second date Norfolk mentions that Surrey might lose his right hand. Unless otherwise indicated, I

cite Surrey's poetry from Richard S. Sylvester, ed., *The Anchor Anthology of Sixteenth-Century Verse* (New York, 1974), which relies on 'The Poetry of Henry Howard, Earl of Surrey', ed. Charles Willison Eckert, diss. Washington University, 1960. A critical edition of Surrey is sorely needed.

2 *Letters and Papers, Foreign and Domestic, of the Reign of Henry VIII*, vol. 12, part 2, ed. James Gairdner (London, 1891), p. 104. (I owe the reference to Casady, p. 57.) 'Very weak...' is the editor's paraphrase, not a quotation from Norfolk. One wonders whether Surrey was experiencing an 'anniversary reaction' as the anniversary of Richmond's death was only ten days away; the 'thought' might have been for Richmond the second time as well as the first.

3 *A History of English Poetry* (New York, 1897), II 185.

4 Douglas L. Peterson, *The English Lyric from Wyatt to Donne: A History of the Plain and Eloquent Styles* (Princeton, 1966), pp. 71–72, regards the 'turn to the diction and phraseology of the courtly love poets' as an indication of the inadequacy of the vernacular at this early date; Walter R. Davis, 'Contexts in Surrey's Poetry', *English Literary Renaissance* 4 (1974) 52–54, defends the language of love-lament because it intensifies 'the love between man and man by relating it to that between man and woman'.

5 For almost endless examples see *P. Vergili Maronis Aeneidos Liber Quartus*, ed. A. S. Pease (Cambridge, 1935), pp. 316–18. 'Each wall' is first found in *Nugae Antiquae: Being a Miscellaneous Collection of Original Papers in Prose and Verse ... by Sir John Harrington ... and others*, ed. Henry Harington (London, 1769), I 191. Eckert, pp. 79–82, argues convincingly that Surrey's poems in this work were set up from the now missing leaves of the Arundel manuscript. The 1557 and 1559 editions of Tottel read 'Eccho (alas)'; the 1565 and 1567 editions and the one manuscript containing the poem, 'Eche alas'; the 1574, 1585, and 1587 editions, 'Eche stone'. See *Tottel's Miscellany*, I 267, Eckert, pp. 166, 239, and Henry Howard, Earl of Surrey, *Poems*, ed. Emrys Jones (Oxford, 1964), p. 122. The repetition of 'wall' in lines 33, 47, and 49 reinforces the contrast between the happy, protected past of comradeship and Surrey's present lonely confinement in prison.

6 Alastair Fowler, *Conceitful Thought: The Interpretation of English Renaissance Poems* (Edinburgh, 1975), p. 32. Leonard Nathan, 'The Course of a Particular: Surrey's Epitaph on Thomas Clere and the Fifteenth-Century Lyric Tradition', *Studies in English Literature, 1500–1900* 17 (1977) 1–12, praises this poem for directing precise attention to an actual life. S. P. Zitner, 'Truth and Mourning in a Sonnet by Surrey', *ELH* 50 (1983) 509–29, reexamines Surrey's relation to Clere and severely challenges the legend that Clere rescued Surrey at the battle of Montreuil.

7 This 'Epitaffe' is the only poem of Surrey's printed in his lifetime; it appeared in an eight-page pamphlet, probably in 1542, the year of Wyatt's death. Frederic B. Tromley, 'Surrey's Fidelity to Wyatt in "Wyatt Resteth Here"', *Studies in Philology* 57 (1980) 376–87,

argues that Surrey's attempt to depict Wyatt accurately accounts for the 'severely impersonal voice'.

8 Surrey's translation (Jones, p. 86), which for some reason omits 'ulta uirum poenas inimico a fratre recepi' ('I avenged my husband and punished a hostile brother'). Surrey probably changes fortune to nature in the 'Epitaffe' in accordance with Servius' comment at *Aeneid* 4.653 that fortune, as opposed to nature and fate, indicates an accidental death due to chance.

9 *The Works of Henry Howard, Earl of Surrey, and of Sir Thomas Wyatt the Elder*, ed. Geo. Fred. Nott, vol. 1 (London, 1815), p. 341; cf. Jones, p. 125. Davis, 'Contexts', p. 54, tries to defend the couplet by arguing that Surrey is intensifying his love for Wyatt by relating it to love between man and woman. I agree that Surrey uses the diction of love-lament for this purpose, but do not see that this accounts for the gruesome irony of Pyramus' tears and suicide.

10 It is curious that the allusion to Dido's speech in the 'Epitaffe' is also an allusion to suicide – Dido says those words just before killing herself – and that Surrey's 'When Windesor walles' ends with a suicidal fantasy.

11 Frederick Morgan Padelford, ed., *The Poems of Henry Howard, Earl of Surrey*, revised ed. (Seattle, 1928), p. 227, comes closest to a correct paraphrase. Nott, pp. 342–47, believing the poem unfinished, offered some emendations in his effort to make sense of it. Rollins, *Tottel's Miscellany*, II 311, says that the text printed by Tottell is corrupt and offers a tentative paraphrase which misses the mark. Jones, p. 125, calls the poem a 'tangle' and introduces a red herring about Jove's birthplaces; his note misleads Sylvester, p. 187. Jentoft's interpretation, pp. 28–30, stands the poem on its head. I have modified Sylvester's punctuation in an effort to make the sense clearer. Jentoft consulted the one manuscript in which the poem is preserved, British Library, Additional 36529, and prints a text which omits 'so' in the first line and reads 'Momus' for 'monnis' in line 12. Eckert's apparatus, pp. 121–22, says that in this manuscript 'so' is lightly struck through with a different ink and that there are five minims, the last dotted, for 'monnis'. I have followed Eckert and Sylvester. 'Momus' would be the *difficilior lectio*, but does not make as good sense. Momus will find fault no matter what; Surrey's point is that mourners of Wyatt do not merit the blame of open-minded people.

12 On euhemerism see Jean Pépin, *Mythe et allégorie: Les origines grecques et les contestations judéo-chrétiennes*, nouvelle éd. (Paris, 1976), pp. 146–52.

13 Cf. Duncan Harris and Nancy L. Steffen, 'The Other Side of the Garden: An Interpretive Comparison of Chaucer's *Book of the Duchess* and Spenser's *Daphnaida*', *The Journal of Medieval and Renaissance Studies* 8 (1978) 20: Spenser 'creates in the grieving shepherd Alcyon an instructional example, a personification of excessive, blasphemous grief whose very extremity forces the poet's audience to recall the tenets of proportion'. William Oram,

'*Daphnaida* and Spenser's Later Poetry', *Spenser Studies* 2 (1981) 141–58, comes to a similar conclusion.

14 C. S. Lewis, *English Literature in the Sixteenth Century Excluding Drama* (Oxford, 1954), p. 370, is typical of earlier criticism of *Daphnaida* because he does recoil with horror; he calls one of Alcyon's commands to nature 'a shrill witch's or maniac's curse'.

15 See Abessa's and Corceca's reaction to Kirkrapine's death (1.3.22), Matilda's particularly violent display at 6.5.4, and *Astrophel* 151–62.

16 One should not perhaps make too much of the reference to Ambrosia, for its primary purpose may be to assert that she is not a 'forged child', a charge that her great-uncle was making after her mother's death, at the time Spenser was writing his poem, in order to wrest away the Howard estate (*The Poems of Sir Arthur Gorges*, ed. Helen Estabrook Sandison [Oxford, 1954], p. xviii). Spenser does insert a purely topical passage, the stanzas in praise of Queen Elizabeth, which nevertheless sound a typically Spenserian note (Hallet Smith, 'The Use of Conventions in Spenser's Minor Poetry', in *Form and Convention in the Poetry of Edmond Spenser: Selected Papers from the English Institute*, ed. William Nelson [New York, 1961], p. 135).

17 Cicero's statement, *De amicitia* 10, is the *locus classicus*: 'Nihil mali accidisse Scipioni puto; mihi accidit si quid accidit. Suis autem incommodis graviter angi non amicum, sed se ipsum amantis est' ('I think no ill has occurred to Scipio; if any has occurred, it has occurred to me. But to be gravely disturbed at one's own misfortunes shows a person who loves himself instead of his friend'). On this ancient topos see Kassel, pp. 85–86, von Moos, III 69–74, 204–6, and Johann, pp. 92–99. A few Renaissance examples: Erasmus, p. 454; Girolamo Cardano, *Cardanus Comforte*, trans. Thomas Bedingfeld (London, 1573), pp. 41–42; John Lyly, *The Complete Works*, ed. R. Warwick Bond (Oxford, 1902), I 311, and Southwell, sig. B2^{rv}.

18 *Daphnaida* is composed in seven-line stanzas. Alcyon's lament consists of seven sections of seven stanzas. The lament is framed by 28 stanzas at the beginning and four stanzas (=28 lines) at the end. Alastair Fowler, *Triumphal Forms: Structural Patterns in Elizabethan Poetry* (Cambridge, 1970), p. 188, n. 5, asserts that 28 is a common number in elegy, and points out (*Spenser and the Numbers of Time* [New York, 1964], p. 248, n. 2) that seven, a number of mutability, is appropriate for *Daphnaida*. Maren-Sofie Røstvig, *The Hidden Sense* (Oslo, 1963), pp. 83–87, unconvincingly argues that spiritual, as opposed to sensual, denunciation takes over in the center of the poem, that seven is, in the Old Testament, the number of lament, penance, and expiation, and that 28, the second number of perfection, represents the lunar month, which symbolizes mutability and sin. One of the authorities for these interpretations is Macrobius, *Commentarii in somnium Scipionis* 1.6.49, who points to a connection between seven and 28 (a lunar month has 28 [=4×7] days) and remarks a bit later that seven is the number which

presides over all stages of a person's life. On the importance of mid-points in Spenser see David Burchmore, 'The Image of the Center in *Colin Clouts Come Home Againe*', *The Review of English Studies* 28 (1977) 393–406.

19 In and of itself there is nothing wrong with Alcyon's view; Parker and Wilson, as mentioned earlier, offer it to explain the deaths of Bucer and the Brandons. Theologians disagree whether death is a punishment for sin or deliverance from punishment. Contrast Ambrose, *De excessu fratris* II 47, who argues that death is a 'remedium', a release from pain, and Augustine, *Sermo* 172, who states that death is the penalty for the fall and that man would have lived forever if he had not sinned.

20 'Loss, Rage, and Repetition', *The Psychoanalytic Study of the Child* 24 (1969) 433.

21 On the vexed problem of the date of the preface to *Daphnaida* and hence of its temporal relation to *Colin Clout* see *The Works of Edmond Spenser: A Variorum Edition*, vol. 7, ed. Charles Grosvenor Osgood and Henry Gibbons Lotspeich (Baltimore, 1943), part I, pp. 435–38.

22 Contemporary accounts indicate that Elizabeth's grief for her brother was very severe at the time of his death. She refused food for two days and did not cease to weep. See Elkin Calhoun Wilson, p. 128.

23 For arguments in support of Spenser's authorship of the 'lay' see *Variorum*, pp. 500–5; in support of the countess of Pembroke, *The Triumph of Death and Other Unpublished and Uncollected Poems by Mary Sidney, Countess of Pembroke (1561–1621)*, ed. G. F. Waller (Salzburg, 1977), pp. 53–61. There is one strong bit of neglected evidence for Spenser's authorship of the 'lay'. *Astrophel* has 216 lines (2×108), the 'lay' has 108, and there are 108 sonnets in *Astrophil and Stella*, one for each of the 108 suitors of Penelope in the *Odyssey*; see Fowler, *Triumphal Forms*, p. 175. Besides the Spenserian links before and after the 'lay', one thus finds an overarching numerological structure, which is missing in the other non-Spenserian poems in the collection.

24 Spenser is not, of course, the first to modify the ancient dilemma of self-love versus love for the deceased. Jerome is a major predecessor: 'sed desiderium absentiae eius ferre non possumus, non illius sed nostrum uicem dolentes. quanto ille felicior, tanto nos amplius in dolore, quod tali caremus bono' (*Sancti Eusebii Hieronymi Epistulae*, ed. I. Hilberg [Vienna, 1910–18], I 555: 'But we cannot bear the longing for him who is absent, mourning our own lot, not his. The happier he is, the deeper we are in sorrow because we lack such a good person'). Mourning for loss was Parker's solution to the dilemma of legitimate mourning and was adopted by many of the elegists for Bucer.

25 *Oeuvres lyriques*, ed. C. A. Mayer (London, 1964), p. 337. On this poem see Ellen Zetzel Lambert, *Placing Sorrow: A Study of the Pas-*

toral Elegy Convention from Theocritus to Milton (Chapel Hill, 1976), pp. 107–12.

26 Envy of the dead is a topos closely related to the dilemma of self-love versus love of the deceased. See Cicero, *De amicitia* 14; Seneca, *Consolatio ad Polybium* 9.3; Jerome, *Epistula* 39.7; and von Moos, III 206–7. Erasmus uses the topos, p. 454; see also Lippo Brandolini, *De ratione scribendi* (Basel, 1549), p. 216, and *The Prompters Packet*, sig. G1ᵛ: 'Howbeit if for mine owne particular I should grieue, wheras for his I am much to reioyce, I shal be thought rather enuious of his good, then a friend of his happines.'

Chapter 6
Jonson and King

1 For Selden's remark see *Ben Jonson*, I 250. In *Eastward Hoe*, which Jonson wrote with Marston and Chapman in 1605, the audience begins to learn of Quicksilver's repentance when the jailer says: 'Hee can tell you, almost all the Stories of the *Booke of Martyres*, and speake you all the *Sicke-Mans Salve* without Booke' (IV 604). Incredible as Quicksilver's conversion may appear, the play does nothing to suggest that it is a pretense, and one thus assumes that Becon's book is cited with approval. The Oxford editors assign this scene to Jonson (IX 645). In *Epicoene* (1609) Jonson seems to be making fun of *The Sicke mannes Salue* by associating it with the spurious learning of Lady Haughty and her college. A dispute arises on the best authors to cure Morose's insanity, the ancients (Seneca, Aristotle, Plutarch) or moderns (Indian fables translated by North out of Doni confused with *Reynard the Fox*). Lady Haughty resolves the question by appealing to her woman, Mrs. Trusty, one of whose parents was cured by reading Becon.

Haughty. And one of 'hem (I know not which) was cur'd with the *Sick-mans salve*; and the other with GREENES *groates-worth of wit.*
True-wit. A very cheape cure, madame. (V 232)

It is difficult to conclude from these passages what Jonson thought about Becon's book (much less the section on mourning) except that he expected the audience to be familiar with it.

2 *Iambi et Elegi Graeci*, ed. M. L. West (Oxford, 1971–72), I 6. For examples of the topos see Kassel, p. 59, and von Moos, III 53, 233–36. The self-destructive violence of Apicata's grief and her execration against the gods provide a frightening image of the excesses of female mourning and more generally of the dangers which Jonson attributes to giving way to the emotions (*Sejanus*, IV 469).

3 The opening of this poem gestures towards the convention of requesting the reader's tears.

> I could begin with that grave forme, *Here lies*,
> And pray thee *Reader*, bring thy weepinge Eyes
> To see....

Primarily Jonson is disassociating himself from hackneyed epitaph (the pun on 'grave' is typically scornful), but he is also avoiding the approval of grief implicit in the convention.

4 See Herford and Simpsons' note, XI 5, for Jonson's use of the topos, and for its history see von Moos, III 137–41, and Richmond Lattimore, *Themes in Greek and Latin Epigraphs* (Urbana, 1962), pp. 170–71.

5 The topos is as old as Euripides, *Alcestis* 463; see Lattimore, pp. 65–74.

6 Jonson told Drummond he was separated from his wife for five years, during which he stayed with Lord Aubigny (I 139); in the famous passage in which he describes the vision of his son, Jonson says he was away from London when he died (I 139–40). Herford and Simpson originally dated Jonson's stay with Aubigny to 1602–07, but later were in doubt; see XI 576–77 for the details. 'On My First Sonne' has received more critical attention than most of Jonson's poems: L. A. Beaurline, 'The Selective Principle in Jonson's Shorter Poems', *Criticism* 8 (1966) 65–70; E. Pearlman, 'Ben Jonson: An Anatomy', *English Literary Renaissance* 9 (1979) 389–90; Francis Fike, 'Ben Jonson's "On My First Sonne"', *The Gordon Review* 11 (1969) 205–20; W. David Kay, 'The Christian Wisdom of Ben Jonson's "On My First Sonne"', *Studies in English Literature, 1500–1900* 11 (1971) 125–36; Arthur F. Marotti, 'All About Jonson's Poetry', *ELH* 39 (1972) 227–28; J. Z. Kronenfeld, 'The Father Found: Consolation Achieved Through Love in Ben Jonson's "On My First Sonne"', *Studies in Philology* 75 (1978) 64–83; Wesley Trimpi, '*BEN. IONSON* his best piece of *poetrie*', *Classical Antiquity* 2 (1983) 145–55.

7 Sylvester, ed., *English Seventeenth-Century Verse*, pp. 193–94.

8 *Sancti Pontii Meropii Paulini Nolani Carmina*, ed. G. Hartel (Vienna, 1894), p. 308.

9 Paulinus' letter of consolation to Pammachius expresses a similar ambivalence about piety, but not as paradoxically or anxiously:

pium est contristari diuulsione carorum, sed sanctum laetificari spe et fide promissionum dei.... Salua igitur fide pietatis officia pendamus et salua pietate fidei gaudia praeferamus. esto, temporaliter fleat pietas, sed oportet, ut iugiter gaudeat fides; desideremus ut praemissos, sed non desperemus recipiendos. (*Sancti Pontii Meropii Paulini Nolani Epistulae*, ed. G. Hartel [Vienna, 1894], pp. 90–91)

It is pious to become sad when torn away from our dear ones, but it is holy to rejoice in hope and faith in God's promises.... Therefore, with faith intact let us perform the duties of piety, and with piety intact let us esteem the joys of faith more highly. Be it so: let piety weep for a time, but it is necessary that faith rejoice continually; we should miss them as ones who have gone ahead, but not despair of recovering them.

Here piety and faith can coexist, provided that the requirements of faith take precedence, and Paulinus has been at pains in section 4 to justify Pammachius' grief with the examples of Abraham, Jacob, Joseph, and Jesus. For more examples of 'impia pietas' see von Moos, III 279.

10 *Poems* (London, 1658), p. 36.

11 *Epistulae*, I 298–99. For other examples see von Moos, III 197–99.

12 One sees the intensity of Digby's grief in a despairing poem he wrote after his wife's death, *Poems from Sir Kenelm Digby's Papers, in the Possession of Henry A. Bright* (London, 1877), pp. 7–9.

13 Ronald Berman, *Henry King and the Seventeenth Century* (London, 1964), p. 12.

14 *Iusta Oxoniensium*, sig. G2ᵛ. Contrary to Sir Geoffrey Keynes, *A Bibliography of Henry King D. D. Bishop of Chichester* (London, 1977), p. 21, there are two poems by King in this collection; these lines are from the first. The section on King's Latin poems is not done with Keynes' customary bibliographical care and is marred by misprints and inaccuracies. King also has two poems, not just one, in the collection on King James, and the first is on sig. I3ᵛ, not 13ᵛ (*Oxoniensis Academiae Parentalia* [Oxford, 1625]).

15 *Iusta Funebria ... Bodleii*, p. 66.

16 T. S. Eliot's admiration was probably the most influential: 'And in one of the finest poems of the age (a poem which could not have been written in any other age), the *Exequy* of Bishop King, the extended comparison is used with perfect success' ('The Metaphysical Poets' [1921], in *Selected Essays*, new ed. [New York, 1950], p. 243).

17 Robert Gomersall's 'An Elegy upon the death of Mʳⁱˢ Anne King' varies the life-as-loan topos in a way that emphasizes King's mastery of his grief in giving up his 'interest' in his wife: '...but since that Heav'n / Has harshly snatch'd what it had kindly giv'n' (*Poems* [1633], p. 2).

18 This is a very puzzling poem because it appears to be impossible that these two children were King's; see Crum's introduction, pp. 9–10. 'Dowre' suggests that both children are girls and makes Percy Simpson's unlikely belief that one of the children is King's son Philip even unlikelier ('The Bodleian Manuscripts of Henry King', *Bodleian Quarterly Record* 5 [1926–29] 332).

19 A sermon eight years after the elegy for Lady Stanhope shows that King was not completely free from anxieties about the unmanliness of mourning.

> That I heartily Lov'd, and from the converse of many younger years Valued the Owner of that Dead Relick lying before me, is a real Truth: For that cause Ye therefore must not expect any large Panegyricks from me, lest happily Yee might think He needed them.... Indeed in any Mournfull Arguments, Invention is commonly most free, where with least interest and Concern it looks upon the Object. Passion or Affection mingling with them, render it too serious for any Rhetorick but Sorrow. This I profess to be my Case; And if it would not betray more of the weaker Sex then is fit for me to own, I could make good the words of St. *Augustine, Potius libet flere quàm aliquid dicere*, My Eyes could easily prove more fluent than my Tongue. (*A Sermon Preached at the Funeral of the Rᵗ Reverend Father in God, Bryan, Lord Bp. of Winchester* [London, 1662], p. 33)

The simple declaration of love and the refusal to avoid the fact of death are more striking than the fear of effeminacy. King is demonstrating his self-control while hinting at his depth of sorrow.

Chapter 7
Milton

1 Except for one key passage from 'Lycidas', I cite from *The Complete Poetry of John Milton*, ed. John T. Shawcross (New York, 1971). It should be noted that by the time of *De Doctrina Christiana* Milton subscribes to the moderate interpretation of 1 Thessalonians 4.13–14 (*Complete Prose Works of John Milton*, gen. ed. Don M. Wolfe [New Haven, 1953–] VI 744). From the scripture which he quotes it appears that by immoderate grief Milton means the self-destructive practices of tearing the hair and cutting the flesh. The passage, however, is too brief to throw much light on Milton's elegies, and one must remember that the ones which envision the dead in heaven contradict the mortalist position which Milton adopts in this later work. (See the editor's introduction, pp. 91–95; Norman T. Burns, *Christian Mortalism from Tyndale to Milton* (Cambridge, 1972); and William Kerrigan, 'The Heretical Milton: From Assumption to Mortalism', *English Literary Renaissance* 5 (1975) 125–66.)

2 For the history of the metaphor see Pierre Courcelle, 'Tradition platonicienne et traditions chrétiennes du corps-prison', *Revue des Etudes latines* 43 (1965) 406–43.

3 'On the Death of a Fair Infant Dying of a Cough' contains no reversal from sorrow because there is no mourning for the infant. Even while narrating how Aquilo took her for his bride, the poet cannot persuade himself she is dead (29). The consolatory turn in the final stanza to the mother is not harsh and uses standard topoi: life as loan and the promise of more children. The poems on Hobson, the university carrier, do not mourn or console.

4 Cf. Michael West, 'The *Consolatio* in Milton's Funeral Elegies', *Huntington Library Quarterly* 34 (1971) 241.

5 *The English Diodatis* (New Brunswick, 1950), p. 178.

6 This interpretation already occurs in the Horatian scholia; pseudo-Acron glosses 'sedibus' ('dwellings') as 'Elysian Fields' and 'levem' ('insubstantial') as 'peccatricem' ('sinful'). By this interpretation the final stanza of Horace's hymn suggests that Mercury guides souls to their rewards or punishments.

> tu pias laetis animas reponis
> sedibus virgaque levem coerces
> aurea turbam, superis deorum
> gratus et imis. (*Odes* 1.10.17–20)

You, who are pleasing to the gods above and below, place the pious souls in the joyful dwellings and control the unsubstantial crowd with your golden staff.

The possibility of rewards in heaven is strengthened by Servius' note on another famous description of Mercury.

tum virgam capit: hac animas ille evocat Orco
pallentis, alias sub Tartara tristia mittit,
dat somnos adimitque et lumina morte resignat. (*Aeneid* 4.240–42)

Then he takes the staff: with it he summons the pale souls from Orcus, sends others below to sad Tartarus, bestows and takes away sleep, and unseals the eyes in death.

Servius comments, 'Animas pro "umbras" secundum poeticum morem. animae enim in caelo sunt' ('[He uses] "souls" for "shades" following poetic custom, for the souls are in heaven'), and quotes part of 5.722 in support. Lelio Gregorio Giraldi refers to the Pythagorean doctrine of spiritual purgation (which some scholars still believe to lie behind Virgil's lines) when he remarks that Mercury conducts the purified souls 'in excelsum' (*De Deis Gentium: Basel 1548* [New York, 1976], p. 410: 'on high [to heaven]'). The upshot of these views of Mercury is that there is little difference between where Damon is imagined to be at the beginning and end of the poem. One should compare Hermes' separation of Damon from the 'ignavum pecus' (25: 'slothful herd') with the 'tenues animas, pectúsque ignobile vulgi' (193: 'lowly souls and the ignoble breast of the crowd') whom Amor does not strike. Thyrsis does not 'learn' anything more about Damon over the course of the poem. The images of Olympus are no more Christian than the description of Hermes, and the first part of the vision of Damon in heaven sounds more like *Aeneid* 6 than Christianity.

7 There is ample evidence that Diodati was Milton's close, probably closest friend, but aside from a remark by Edward Philips which sounds like an extrapolation from 'Lycidas', there is no evidence that Edward King and Milton were more than acquaintances (William Riley Parker, *Milton: A Biography* [Oxford, 1968], p. 811). Milton says next to nothing about his mother, but we know that she died (on 3 April 1637) seven months before the composition of 'Lycidas'. It is likely that some of the poem's powerful emotion has its source in the death of Sara Milton, not that of King, and it is suggestive that the poem is so critical of the traditions which nurture it. Joseph Anthony Wittreich, Jr., remarks that in 'Lycidas' Milton confronts 'in King's death both his mother's death and his own possible death' (*Visionary Poetics: Milton's Tradition and His Legacy* [San Marino, 1979], p. 81).

8 My favorite answer to Johnson is Anthony Trollope's, 'I had my strong enthusiasms, and remember throwing out of the window in Northumberland Street, where I lived, a volume of Johnson's *Lives of the Poets*, because he spoke sneeringly of *Lycidas*' (*An Autobiography* [Oxford, 1922], p. 49).

9 *Milton 1732–1802: The Critical Heritage*, ed. John T. Shawcross (London, 1972), pp. 407–8.

10 '*Lycidas*: A Poem Finally Anonymous', *Glyph* 8 (1981) 14. Jason P. Rosenblatt writes of 'a transformation that cannot have been anticipated' from depression to consolation ('The Angel and the Shepherd in *Lycidas*', *Philological Quarterly* 62 [1983] 252).

11 Thyer: *Paradise Regain'd ... To which is added Samson Agonistes: And Poems upon Several Occasions,* ed. Thomas Newton (London, 1752), p. 501; Paul Alpers, '*Lycidas* and Modern Criticism', *ELH* 49 (1982) 488; Donald M. Friedman, '*Lycidas*: The Swain's Paedeia', *Milton Studies* 3 (1971) 19; William Madsen, *From Shadowy Types to Truth: Studies in Milton's Symbolism* (New Haven, 1968), pp. 12–14. A few words should be said about Fish's provocative attempt to silence the swain and make the second half of the poem present a succession of ambiguous, anonymous, or choral voices. The attempt begins inauspiciously, for Fish is simply wrong when he asserts that the reader does not know when Phoebus begins to speak and refers to 'Milton's unpunctuated text' (p. 8). I presume that Fish means that there are no quotation marks in the Trinity College manuscript of 'Lycidas' and the three editions of the poem published in Milton's lifetime. The manuscript has very light punctuation, but this means that the punctuation it does contain is important. In the manuscript lines 76–78 read

> and slits the thin-spun life. But not the praise
> Phoebus repli'd, and touch't my trembling eares,
> Fame is no plant that grows on mortall soile

This is the only time a period occurs in the middle of a line (there are only two or three more periods in the entire poem, which has hardly any punctuation at the ends of lines), and the manuscript is very sparing of capitals. With a couple of exceptions capitals do not appear at the beginnings of lines or sentences unless a verse paragraph is also beginning; proper names, adjectives from proper names, some other nouns, and the word 'O' are capitalized. The period in line 76, the capital 'B' in 'But', and the comma after 'repli'd' show that Milton is marking off the beginning of Phoebus' speech as clearly as the quotation marks of any modern editor. In the 1638 *Justa Edovardo King* (its text of 'Lycidas' is full of errors) line 76 has a semicolon instead of a period, but the capital 'B' is still there. The 1645 and 1673 editions of Milton's *Poems* have a period and the capital. All three editions have a comma after 'praise'. 1638 has a period after 'eares'; 1645 and 1673, a semicolon. Thus the punctuation of the editions also makes it clear that 'But' begins a new sentence (the only sentence in the poem which begins in midline) and Phoebus' speech. Fish goes on to misinterpret the allusion to Virgil in this passage, as I shall show later, and fails to recognize the pastoral convention of the procession of speakers, all of whose speeches are set off with sufficient clarity. In order to mount his argument at all Fish has to ignore the headnote to the 1645 edition: 'In this Monody the *Author* bewails a learned Freind' (my emphasis).

12 Alpers' attempt 'to deny the sudden emergence of a new voice' (p. 488) is not persuasive because it fails to explain the serene and confident tone of authority in a speaker who has been so doubting and plaintive. Alpers confuses the way in which the speaker's locutions 'generate and direct the poem' with 'the strength hitherto

associated with the voices of Phoebus and St. Peter' (p. 490). Alpers is led astray by a determination to refute Fish's contention that the swain loses control of the poem once Phoebus speaks.

13 Shawcross in his edition of Milton says, 'Lines 165–81 are perhaps said by Michael' (p. 163), and Louis L. Martz, *Poet of Exile: A Study of Milton's Poetry* (New Haven, 1980), p. 320, calls Madsen's an 'interesting suggestion', but comments, 'I would not go so far, but the lines do seem to be a result of the speaker's appeal, "Look homeward Angel".' One of the curious things about Madsen's argument, aside from his refusal to hint how the reader is to know that Michael is speaking, is his tentativeness concerning lines 182–85: 'The voice of the swain perhaps returns with [these] lines' (p. 16).

14 One should not forget the poem's extraordinary use of periphrasis and allusion and the problems these techniques have posed interpreters. Leaving aside the vexed question of 'the two-handed engine', one still has to struggle with the identity of 'the Pilot of the *Galilean* lake'. Mother M. Christopher Pecheux, 'The Dread Voice in *Lycidas*', *Milton Studies* 9 (1976) 221–41, elaborates Ralph E. Hone's suggestion that the Pilot is Christ ('"The Pilot of the *Galilean* Lake"', *Studies in Philology* 56 [1959] 55–61) and argues that the Pilot is a composite of Peter, Moses, and Christ; Fish (p. 11) agrees with her.

15 On the importance of *Eclogue* 10 the earliest and most recent commentators I know are Newton, p. 480, and J. Martin Evans, 'Lycidas, Daphnis, and Gallus', in *English Renaissance Studies Presented to Dame Helen Gardner in honour of her Seventieth Birthday* (Oxford, 1980), p. 228. Since A. S. P. Woodhouse and Douglas Bush, *A Variorum Commentary on The Poems of John Milton*, vol. 2 (New York, 1972), p. 561, assert that there were 'relatively few pastoral elegies' in the 60 or 70 years before 'Lycidas', and one reads that 'Milton's choice of the genre must have appeared to his contemporaries an act of conscious archaism' (Friedman, p. 20), it is worthwhile to recall Bradner's observation that the university collections reveal the popularity of pastoral elegy in the first part of the seventeenth century (p. 101). I have made no systematic search, but have come across enough to accept Bradner's statement. (Alberta T. Turner, 'Milton and the Convention of the Academic Miscellanies', *Yearbook of English Studies* 5 [1975] 91–92, notes that pastoral elegies occur one or two to a volume in about one-seventh of the university miscellanies: in six volumes before 1626, then in *Justa* itself, then several more after 1640.) Aside from the nineteen pastoral elegies published in England between 1569 and 1638 listed by Watson Kirkconnell, *Awake the Courteous Echo: The Themes and Prosody of 'Comus', 'Lycidas', and 'Paradise Regained' in World Literature with Translations of the Major Analogues* (Toronto, 1973), I have seen: four on Sidney, a beautiful anonymous one in Francis Davison, *A Poetical Rhapsody 1602–1621*, ed. Hyder Edward Rollins, I 36–44, strongly reminiscent of Spenser's 'November', two in the *Exequiae* besides Gager's, sigs. E1ᵛ–E3ʳ

(anonymous), and G4ᵛ–H4ᵛ (Francis Mason), the 'Lycidas' in *Peplus* mentioned earlier (pp. 27–29); two on Queen Elizabeth in *Threno-thriambeuticon* (Cambridge, 1603), one by Albert Morton (pp. 22–24), the other by Willam Burton (pp. 67–73); one on King James by William de Insula in *Cantabrigiensium Dolor & Solamen*, pp. 51–54; and Joseph Rutter, 'Thyrsis. A Pastorall Elegie in the person of Sir *Kenelme Digby*, on the Death of his Noble Lady, the Lady *Venetia Digby*', in his *The Shepheards Holy-Day* (London, 1635), sigs. H1ʳ–H3ʳ. And in 1638, the year in which 'Lycidas' first appears, there is Falkland's pastoral elegy for Jonson (*Ben Jonson*, XI 430–37) in addition to Drummond's 'Alcon', canonized in *The Pastoral Elegy: An Anthology*, ed. Thomas Perrin Harrison, trans. Harry Joshua Leon (1939; rpt. New York, 1968), pp. 198–202. (William Bas's *Three Pastoral Elegies* [1602] are love poems, not funeral elegies.) Sidney's death set a fashion for pastoral elegy in England that was very much alive in 1638. What is unusual about 'Lycidas' is not that it is a pastoral elegy, but that Milton both imitates *Eclogue* 10, not at all a popular model, and departs from it so radically and critically. For the theoretical background of the revisionary imitation which Milton practices see my 'Versions of Imitation in the Renaissance', *Renaissance Quarterly* 33 (1980) 1–32.

16 *Milton 1732–1802*, p. 330.

17 On *recusatio* see Hans Lucas, 'Recusatio', in *Festschrift Johannes Vahlen zum siebzigsten Geburtstag* (Berlin, 1900), pp. 319–33, and Walter Wimmel, *Kallimachos im Rom: Die Nachfolge seines apologetischen Dichtens in der Augusteerzeit* (Wiesbaden, 1960), pp. 135–41. Milton could not have know the passage in Callimachus, as the papyrus which contains it was not published until this century, but he surely knew the convention, which Jacobus Pontanus identifies in his commentary on Virgil (*Symbolarum Libri XVII Virgili: Augsburg 1599* [New York, 1976], p. 124). On this passage in *Eclogue* 6 Pontanus remarks, 'Persimilia his, & eiusdem paene sensus memini legere apud multos' ('I recall I have read lines very similar to these with almost the same sense in many [authors]'), and proceeds to quote, among others, Horace, *Odes* 4.15.1–4; Ovid, *Amores* 1.1.1–2; and Propertius 3.3.1–18. Besides Ovid, *Ars amatoria* 2.493–508 (which Pontanus does not cite), these are the major *recusationes*.

18 Compare the passages by Nemesianus (pp. 53–54), Sannazaro (pp. 95, 98), and Ronsard (p. 156) in Harrison's anthology.

19 *Paradise Regain'd*, ed. Newton, p. 496.

20 *Poems of Mr. John Milton, Both English and Latin, Compos'd at several times* (London, 1645), pp. 63–64.

21 *Poems Upon Several Occasions, English, Italian, and Latin, with Translations, by John Milton*, 2nd ed. (London, 1791). This posthumously published edition strengthens and elaborates arguments made in the first (1785). Warton is responding to Thyer in Newton's 1752 edition. Thyer's whole note on 'Look homeward Angel now' reads as follows.

So the Pastory [sic] Elegy on Sir Philip Sidney.
> Philisides is dead. O happy Sprite,
> That now in Heav'n with blessed souls dost bide,
> Look down awhile from where thou sitst above &c. (p. 498)

Thyer is quoting from Lodovick Bryskett's elegy (Spenser, *Poetical Works*, p. 555). See the Milton *Variorum* for a brief history of the interpretation, although it should be noted that the *Variorum* is incorrect to say that Hughes accepted Jerram's 1874 interpretation of the angel as Lycidas in 1937. What Hughes really said was: 'If the thought in lines 161–2 is parenthetical, the *Angel* is Lycidas; but the play on *Looks–Look* suggests that Michael is meant' (*Paradise Regained, The Minor Poems, and Samson Agonistes*, ed. Merritt Y. Hughes [New York, 1937], p. 295). Christopher Grose, 'Lucky Words: Process of Speech in *Lycidas*', *Journal of English and Germanic Philology* 70 (1971) 384–91, also argues against Warton that the angel is Lycidas.

22 A supporting argument added to the 1791 edition is not particularly compelling. At line 177 Warton comments:

Even here, after Lycidas is received into heaven, Milton does not make him an *angel*. He makes him, indeed, a being of a higher order, the *Genius of the shore*, as at v. 183. If the poet in finally disclosing this great change of circumstances, and in this prolix and solemn description of his friend's new situation in the realms of bliss after so disastrous a death, had exalted him into an angel, he would not have forestalled that idea, according to Thyer's interpretation, at v. 163. (p. 32)

Warton does not specify in what hierarchy of beings a genius of the shore is superior to an angel and gives no reason why Milton would not have anticipated the description of the realms of bliss.

23 The *Variorum* editors agree with Warton that the identification of the angel as Michael requires the punctuation of 1638. This punctuation, however, is incorrect. 1638 is the most unreliable of the three editions of 'Lycidas' which appeared in Milton's lifetime. 1638 omits line 177, fails to indicate the beginnings of five of the verse paragraphs, and changes several manuscript readings which are restored in 1645 (see John T. Shawcross, 'Establishment of a Text of Milton's Poems Through a Study of *Lycidas*', *Papers of the Bibliographical Society of America* 56 [1962] 319–20). (One of the seven copies of 1638 examined by Fletcher has only five verse paragraphs; the others have six, whereas the manuscript, 1645, and 1673 have eleven; see *John Milton's Complete Poetical Works Reproduced in Photographic Facsimile*, ed. Harris Francis Fletcher, vol. 1 [Urbana, 1943], p. 347.) 1638 is very fond of semicolons; it contains 21, 13 of which are changed in the 1645 edition. This includes the incorrect semicolon at line 76, where the manuscript and the other editions have a period, and 1638 itself capitalizes the next word, 'But', to indicate the beginning of a new sentence. (Shawcross, p. 322, considers the semicolon at line 76 'unquestionably wrong'.) The textual authority of the semicolon in line 153 is very dubious indeed.

What about the punctuation of 1645? Shawcross believes that the copy for 1645 was a corrected copy of 1638, but that Milton himself was not the person who prepared the copy. I see no reason to posit a copyist even if one grants Shawcross that the spelling, punctuation, and capitalization do not represent Milton's personal preferences as witnessed by the manuscripts. There is no evidence that Milton was so devoted to his personal preferences in such matters – Shawcross admits that the preferences changed over time – as to resist the printing conventions of his day. With 1638 in print I see no reason why Milton himself would not correct its substantive errors, make any revisions he liked (including the bold assertion of prophecy in the headnote), change such accidentals as seemed important, hand it over to the 1645 printers, and go along with their modifications of spelling, punctuation, and capitalization. Why must one assume an adversary relationship between poet and printer rather than a cooperative one? Shawcross' hypothesis of a scribe with access to the Trinity manuscript and 'some knowledge of Milton's spelling preferences' (p. 324) seems to me unnecessarily complicated.

In the case of the punctuation of line 153 there is one aspect of the manuscript which suggests that Milton intended to begin a new sentence with 'Ay me' and hence that the 1645 period is correct. Milton does not capitalize the first word of a line unless that line begins a new verse paragraph. I count only five exceptions: 'I' (3), 'Fame' (78), 'Bring' (142), 'Ay' (154), and 'To morrow' (193). 'I' is no exception, since the manuscript capitalizes it everywhere in the poem. 'Bring' introduces the flower passage, an afterthought which is indicated in the margin; the capital looks as if it is calling attention to the insert. (The other passage to be inserted is indicated by a big star.) 'To morrow' is the last line of the poem. 'Fame' is curious, especially since one finds 'fame' at the beginning of line 70. This leaves 'Ay', which looks very much like an indication that a new sentence is beginning despite the absence of a period at line 153. At line 56 'ay' is also the first word of the line; there it is not capitalized. To this suggestive, though hardly conclusive, detail one can add another bit of evidence. Every exclamatory 'Ah', 'Ah me', 'Ay', and 'Ay me' in Milton's poetry comes at the beginning of an independent clause; nine of the eleven occurrences are also at the beginning of a sentence. It would thus violate a remarkable consistency of usage if the twelfth occurrence, the 'Ay me' of line 154, were a parenthetical exclamation separating a subordinate clause from the rest of its sentence. It seems clear to me that both 'Ay me's in 'Lycidas' introduce a new thought and that the 'whilst' clause has to depend on 'Look' in line 163. The flow of the sentence, as Warton saw would be the case, makes it more likely that the addressee does not change until the appeal to the dolphins (note the *And*) and thus that the angel is Lycidas.

24 Scaliger is quoting *Hymn* 49.4–7 (*Orphica*, ed. Eugenius Abel [Leipzig, 1885], p. 84); Hermann Kleinknecht notes that the 'whether ... or' construction is particularly common in Orphic Hymns (*Die Gebetsparodie in der Antike* [Stuttgart, 1937], p. 24). As is often the

case, Scaliger is heavily dependent on Menander (pp. 8–10). One example of the 'whether ... or' place construction occurs in the first of all pastoral elegies, Theocritus, *Idyll* 1.123–26. For more elaborate examples see Aristophanes, *Clouds* 279–74, Statius, *Thebaid* 1.696–702, and Apuleius, *Metamorphoses* 6.4. Virgil, *Georgics* 1.24–35, part of which Warton cites as Milton's original for the use of the topos in the 'Fair Infant' (p. 291), is an interesting example of the extension of the topos in his deification of Augustus. Statius, *Silvae* 2.7.107–22, is a more interesting extension because Statius is addressing the spirit of the dead Lucan and calling for his appearance on his birthday. The use of the convention in the first stanza of Dryden's 'To the Memory of Anne Killigrew' contributed to Johnson's judgment of the poem: 'undoubtedly the noblest ode that our language ever has produced'. It should now be apparent that the passage in Sannazaro's first piscatory eclogue, cited since Jerram and Hanford (most recently by Alpers, p. 491) as the source for 'Lycidas', is not Milton's source but just another instance of the convention. For Milton's use of other hymn conventions in 'At a solemn Musick', 'L'Allegro', and 'Il Penseroso' see Kurt Schlüter, *Die Englische Ode* (Bonn, 1964), pp. 59–77. Milton uses the commonest hymn convention at the end of 'Epitaphium Damonis' when he speculates on the proper name to call Damon:

> placidúsque fave quicúnque vocaris,
> Seu tu noster eris Damon, sive aequior audis
> Diodatus.... (208–10)

Be propitious and indulgent, whatever you are called, whether you will be our Damon or prefer to be addressed as Diodati.

For this convention see Eduard Norden's classic discussion, *Agnostos Theos: Untersuchungen zur Formengeschichte religiöser Rede*, 6th ed. (Stuttgart, 1974), pp. 143–63.

25 Milton is applying what Norden calls the 'Relativstil der Prädikation' to the places instead of the deity (pp. 168–76) and bears out Menander's remark that poets can linger over description when they mention more than one place (p. 10).

26 *Complete Prose*, I 713. Milton's reference to John the Baptist is to Matthew 11.10. See Revelation 2–3 for the angels of the seven churches of Asia and a passage in *Of Reformation Touching Church-Discipline in England* (I 606) for another comment on 'angel' for 'minister'.

27 It is worth recalling that in Boccaccio's pastoral elegy, 'Olympia', the dead daughter speaks with her grieving father.

28 Evidence for the familiarity of this poem in seventeenth-century England may be found in the appearance of lines 447–48 (the beginning of the prosopopoeia) without indication of source on the separate title page of Heywood's elegy on Prince Henry (Cyril Tourneur, John Webster, and Thomas Heywood, *Three Elegies on the most lamented death of Prince Henrie* [London, 1613]). One also finds whole poems which consist of addresses of the dead to the survivors, for example, to stay with the Prince Henry poems, Magdalen

College's *Luctus Posthumus* (Oxford, 1612), pp. 2–3 (two poems) and *Eidyllia*, sig. D3ʳ, an imitation of Horace, *Odes* 2.20.

29 *Ben Jonson*, VIII 102. For examples within the pastoral tradition see especially Castiglione and Drummond, and also 'Moschus', Sannazaro, Alamanni, and Marot (Harrison, pp. 114–15, 199, 39, 132, 141). See also the pastoral elegy on Sidney in Davison, p. 39. The elegists for Edward King often lament that their sun is set (*Justa*, pp. 9, 13; *Obsequies*, pp. 8, 19–20 [this last passage, by Norton, is quoted in chapter 4]). Of the elegists for King only Hall (p. 13) uses the sun analogy to speak of Lycidas' afterlife.

30 See *Variorum*, pp. 725–26, and Franz Joseph Dölger, *Sol Salutatis: Gebet und Gesang in christlichem Altertum* (Münster, 1925), pp. 364ff., for Christian sun symbolism. Further evidence that Milton understands this inconsistency is his modification of the 'Moschus' topos in 'Epitaphium Damonis'; Milton contrasts the ease with which animals find new companions if old ones die with human attachment to an individual (cf. Woodhouse, in *Variorum*, vol. 1, ed. Douglas Bush [1970], p. 290).

31 As I mentioned in the introduction, during the final stage of mourning the bereaved recovers and is able to resume life and move on to new things. This is, to my mind, the most striking fit between the structure of the poem and the process of mourning. For attempts to find closer correspondences see Barbara Currier Bell, '"Lycidas" and the Stages of Grief', *Literature and Psychology* 25 (1975) 166–74 (not at all persuasive) and Marcia Landy, 'Language and Mourning in "Lycidas"', *American Imago* 30 (1973) 294–312 (more plausible).

32 Cf. Edward W. Tayler, '*Lycidas* Yet Once More', *Huntington Library Quarterly* 41 (1978) 116–17.

33 Peter L. Smith comments, 'The concluding verses of the tenth *Eclogue* are, I feel, almost a renunciation or recantation; the symbolic mask is removed, and shade becomes a noxious evil that damns the pastoral profession' ('*Lentus in Umbra*: A Symbolic Pattern in Vergil's *Eclogues*', *Phoenix* 19 [1965] 303).

Conclusion

1 See Arthur Kirsch, 'Hamlet's Grief', *ELH* 48 (1982) 17–36, and Peter Sacks, 'Where Words Prevail Not: Grief, Revenge, and Language in Kyd and Shakespeare', *ELH* 49 (1982) 593–600, for recent discussions of the problem, and Roland Mushat Frye, '"Looking Before and After": The Use of Visual Evidence and Symbolism for Interpreting Hamlet', *Huntington Library Quarterly* 45 (1982) 1–6, for the intriguing suggestion that Hamlet, when he first appears on stage, is wearing 'the voluminous outer mourning garment' associated with funeral processions rather than the customary blacks of mourning. The relation between *Hamlet* and *Antonio's Revenge* is still disputed.

2 He has already lashed out at advice to be patient, 'Patience is slave to fools, a chain that's fix'd / Only to posts and senseless log-like

dolts' (1.2.270–72), and later he will read from Seneca's *De providentia* only to dispute its application to a truly afflicted individual (2.2.47–56). (My text is *Antonio's Revenge: The Second Part of Antonio and Mellida*, ed. G. K. Hunter [Lincoln, 1965].)

BIBLIOGRAPHY

Abel, Eugenius, ed. *Orphica*. Leipzig, 1885.

Abraham, Karl. 'A Short Study of the Development of the Libido, Viewed in the Light of Mental Disorders'. In *Selected Papers*. Trans. Douglas Bryan and Alix Strachey. New York, 1953. Pp. 418–501.

Alpers, Paul. '*Lycidas* and Modern Criticism'. *ELH* 49 (1982) 468–96.

Anon. *The Prompters Packet of Private and Familiar Letters ... Not unworthy Imitation of the most: But most necessarie for such as want either facultie or facilitie to endight*. London, 1612.

Cupids Messenger. London, 1629.

Sermones de consolatione mortuorum. In *Patrologiae Cursus Completus, Series Latina*. Vol. 40. Ed. J.-P. Migne. Paris, 1845. Pp. 1159–68.

Epistula ad Turasium Presbyterum. In *S. Thasci Caecili Cypriani Opera Omnia, Pars III*. Ed. G. Hartel. Vienna, 1871. Pp. 274–82.

Ariès, Philippe. *The Hour of Our Death*. Trans. Helen Weaver. New York, 1981.

Auerbach, Erich. 'Passio als Leidenschaft'. In *Gesammelte Aufsätze zur romanischen Philologie*. Bern, 1967. Pp. 161–75.

Augustine. *Sermones 172 and 173*. In *Patrologiae Cursus Completus, Series Latina*. Vol. 38. Ed. J.-P. Migne. Paris, 1845.

Averill, James R. 'Grief: Its Nature and Significance'. *Psychological Bulletin* 70 (1968) 721–48.

B., F. *Clavis Grammatica: Or, The Ready Way to the Latin Tongue*. 4th ed. London, 1708.

Babington, Gervase. *A briefe conference, betwixt mans Frailtie and Faith ... With a new addition of some comfort against the death of friends*. London, 1596.

Bailey, Derrick Sherwin. *Thomas Becon and the Reformation of the Church of England*. Edinburgh, 1952.

Baldwin, T. W. *William Shakspere's Small Latine and Lesse Greeke*. 2 vols. Urbana, 1944.

Baldwin, William. *Funeralles of King Edward the sixt*. London, 1560.

Bapst, Edmond. *Deux gentilshommes-poètes de la cour de Henry VIII*. Paris, 1891.

Bas, William. *Three Pastoral Elegies; of Anander, Anetor, and Muridelle*. London, 1602.

Beaty, Nancy Lee. *The Craft of Dying: A Study in the Literary Tradition of the Ars Moriendi in England.* New Haven, 1970.

Beaurline, L. A. 'The Selective Principle in Jonson's Shorter Poems'. *Criticism* 8 (1966) 64–74.

Becon, Thomas. *The Sicke mannes Salue.* In *The Worckes of Thomas Becon.* Part 2. London, 1560.

Bell, Barbara Currier. '"Lycidas" and the Stages of Grief'. *Literature and Psychology* 25 (1975) 166–74.

Bennett, A. L. 'The Principal Rhetorical Conventions in the Renaissance Personal Elegy'. *Studies in Philology* 51 (1954) 107–26.

Berkowitz, David S. Review of Stone. *Renaissance Quarterly* 32 (1979) 396–403.

Berman, Ronald. *Henry King and the Seventeenth Century.* London, 1964.

Blount, Thomas. *The Academie of Eloquence.* London, 1654.

Bowlby, John. 'Processes of Mourning'. *International Journal of Psycho-Analysis* 42 (1961) 317–40.

Attachment and Loss. New York, 1969–80.

Boyd, Zacharie. *The Last Battell of the Soule in Death.* Edinburgh, 1628.

Bradner, Leicester. *Musae Anglicanae: A History of Anglo-Latin Poetry 1500–1925.* New York, 1940.

Brandolini, Lippo. *De ratione scribendi.* Basel, 1549.

Breton, Nicholas. *A Poste with a madde Packet of Letters.* London, 1602.

Bucer, Martin. *De obitu ... Martini Buceri ... Epistolae duae.* London, 1551.

De Regno Christi Libri Duo 1550. Ed. François Wendel. Paris, 1955.

Buchler, Johann. *Institutio Poetica, ex R. P. Pontani ... potissimum libris concinnata.* Schleusingen, 1630.

Thesaurus conscribendarum epistolarum. Antwerp, 1653.

Bullinger, Heinrich. *In omnes apostolicas epistolas, divi videlicet Pauli XIIII. et VII. canonicas, commentarii.* Zurich, 1537.

Burchmore, David W. 'The Image of the Centre in *Colin Clouts Come Home Againe*'. *The Review of English Studies,* n.s., 28 (1977) 393–406.

Burgess, Theodore. 'Epideictic Literature'. *University of Chicago Studies in Classical Philology* 3 (1902) 89–261.

Burns, Norman T. *Christian Mortalism from Tyndale to Milton.* Cambridge, 1972.

Burton, Robert. *The Anatomy of Melancholy.* Ed. Holbrook Jackson. Totowa, 1975.

Bush, Douglas, et al., eds. *A Variorum Commentary on The Poems of John Milton.* Vol. 1. New York, 1970.

C., H. *The Forrest of Fancy.* London, 1579.

Calvin, John. *Ioannis Calvini in omnes D. Pauli epistolas.* Geneva, 1551.

Cambridge University. *Threno-thriambeuticon. Academiae Cantabri-*

giensis ob damnum lucrosum, & infoelicitatem foelicissimum, luctuosus triumphus. Cambridge, 1603.

Cantabrigiensium Dolor & Solamen: Seu Decessio Beatissimi Regis Jacobi: et Successio.... Cambridge, 1625.

Campion, Thomas. *Thomae Campioni Poemata.* London, 1595.

Campion's Works. Ed. Percival Vivian. Oxford, 1909.

The Works of Thomas Campion: Complete Songs, Masques, and Treatises with a Selection of the Latin Verse. Ed. Walter R. Davis. Garden City, 1967.

Cappelli, Adriano. *Lexicon abbreviaturarum: Dizionario di abbreviature latine ed italiane.* 6th ed. Milan, 1979.

Cardano, Girolamo. *Cardanus Comforte.* Trans. Thomas Bedingfeld. London, 1573.

Carew, Thomas. *The Poems of Thomas Carew with His Masque 'Coelum Britannicum'.* Ed. Rhodes Dunlap. Oxford, 1949.

Cartwright, Thomas. *A Replye to an anwere made of M. Doctor Whitgifte againste the Admonition to Parliament.* London, 1574.

Casady, Edwin. *Henry Howard, Earl of Surrey.* New York, 1938.

Case, Arthur E. *A Bibliography of English Poetical Miscellanies 1521–1750.* Oxford, 1935.

Christ Church College, Oxford. *Death Repeal'd by a Thankfull Memorial Sent from Christ-Church in Oxford.* Oxford, 1638.

Cleveland, John. *The Poems of John Cleveland.* Ed. Brian Morris and Eleanor Withington. Oxford, 1967.

Colaianne, A. J., and W. L. Godshalk, eds. *Elegies for Sir Philip Sidney (1587).* Delmar, 1980.

Cole, James. *Of Death a True Description: And against it A good Preparation: Together with A sweet Consolation, for the suruiuing Mourners.* London, 1629.

Colet, John. *Two Treatises on the Hierarchies of Dionysius.* Ed. J. H. Lupton. London, 1867.

Cotgrave, John. *Witts Interpreter.* London, 1655.

Courcelle, Pierre. 'Tradition platonicienne et traditions chrétiennes du corps-prison'. *Revue des Etudes latines.* 43 (1965) 406–43.

Courthope, W. J. *A History of English Poetry.* New York, 1897.

Cyprian. *A Swete and Devoute Sermon of Holy Saynt Ciprian of mortalitie of man.* Trans. Sir Thomas Elyot. London, 1534.

Certein Workes of blessed Cipriane the martyr. Trans. John Scory. N.p., 1556.

Sancti Cypriani Episcopi Opera, Pars II. Ed. M. Simonetti and C. Moreschini. Turnhout, 1976.

Dallington, Robert, ed. *A Booke Of Epitaphes made vpon the death of the Right worshipfull Sir William Buttes Knight: Who deceased the third day of September, Anno 1583.* London, [1584].

Davenant, Sir William. *The Shorter Poems, and Songs from the Plays and Masques.* Ed. A. M. Gibbs. Oxford, 1972.

Davis, Walter R. 'Contexts in Surrey's Poetry'. *English Literary Renaissance* 4 (1974) 40–56.

Bibliography

Davison, Francis, ed. *A Poetical Rhapsody 1602–1621.* Ed. Hyder Edward Rollins. Cambridge, 1931.

Day, Angel. *The English Secretary.* Facsimile of 1599 ed. Ed. Robert O. Evans. Gainesville, 1967.

Dekkers, E. *Clavis Patrum Latinorum.* 2nd ed. Steenbrugge, 1961.

Deutsch, Helene. 'Absence of Grief'. *Psychoanalytic Quarterly* 6 (1937) 12–22.

Devereux, E. J. *Renaissance English Translations of Erasmus: A Bibliography to 1700.* Toronto, 1983.

Digby, Sir Kenelm. *Poems from Sir Kenelm Digby's Papers, in the Possession of Henry A. Bright.* London, 1877.

'Dionysius of Halicarnassus'. *Dionysii Halicarnasei quae fertur Ars Rhetorica.* Ed. H. Usener. Leipzig, 1895.

Dölger, Franz Joseph. *Sol Salutatis: Gebet und Gesang in christlichem Altertum.* Münster, 1925.

Donne, John. *The Poems of John Donne.* Ed. Herbert J. C. Grierson. Oxford, 1912.

The Epithalamions, Anniversaries and Epicedes. Ed. W. Milgate. Oxford, 1978.

Dorian, Donald C. *The English Diodatis.* New Brunswick, 1950.

Draper, John W. *The Funeral Elegy and the Rise of English Romanticism.* New York, 1929.

Dryden, John. *The Poems and Fables.* Ed. James Kinsley. Oxford, 1962.

Du Bosque, Jacques. *The Secretary of Ladies.* Trans. Jerome Hainhofer. London, 1638.

Duhr, J. 'Une lettre de condoléance de Bachiarius (?)'. *Revue d'histoire ecclésiastique* 47 (1952) 530–85.

Edmond, John Philip. 'Elegies and Other Tracts Issued on the Death of Henry, Prince of Wales, 1612'. *Publications of the Edinburgh Bibliographical Society* 6 (1906) 141–58.

Eliot, John. *Poems.* London, 1658.

Eliot, T. S. *Selected Essays.* New ed. New York, 1950.

Erasmus, Desiderius. *A treatise perswadynge a man patientlye to suffre the deth of his frende.* London, [1531].

De conscribendis epistolis. Ed. Jean-Claude Margolin. In *Opera Omnia Desiderii Erasmi Roterodami.* Vol. 1, part 2. Amsterdam, 1971.

Evans, J. Martin. 'Lycidas, Daphnis, and Gallus'. In *English Renaissance Studies Presented to Dame Helen Gardner in Honour of Her Seventieth Birthday.* Oxford, 1980. Pp. 228–44.

Exner, Helmuth. *Der Einfluss des Erasmus auf die englische Bildungsidee.* Berlin, 1939.

Favez, Charles. *La consolation latine chrétienne.* Paris, 1937.

Featley, Daniel, et al. ΘΡΗΝΟΙΚΟΣ. *The House of Mourning.* London, 1640.

Fenichel, Otto. *The Psychoanalytic Theory of Neurosis.* New York, 1945.

Bibliography

Ferry, Anne. *The 'Inward' Language: Sonnets of Wyatt, Sidney, Shakespeare, Donne.* Chicago, 1983.

Fike, Francis. 'Ben Jonson's "On My First Sonne"'. *The Gordon Review* 11 (1969) 205–20.

Fish, Stanley. '*Lycidas*: A Poem Finally Anonymous'. *Glyph* 8 (1981) 1–18.

Flemming, Abraham, trans. *A Panoplie of Epistles.* London, 1576.

Fowler, Alastair. *Spenser and the Numbers of Time.* New York, 1964.
Triumphal Forms: Structural Patterns in Elizabethan Poetry. Cambridge, 1970.
Conceitful Thought: The Interpretation of English Renaissance Poems. Edinburgh, 1975.

Freud, Sigmund. 'Mourning and Melancholia'. *The Standard Edition of the Complete Psychological Works of Sigmund Freud.* Vol. 14. London, 1957.
Letters of Sigmund Freud. Ed. E. L. Freud. Trans. Tana and James Stern. New York, 1960.

Friedman, Donald M. '*Lycidas*: The Swain's Paideia'. *Milton Studies* 3 (1971) 3–34.

Fritz, Paul S. 'From "Public" to "Private": The Royal Funerals in England, 1500–1830'. In *Mirrors of Mortality: Studies in the Social History of Death.* Ed. Joachim Whaley. New York, 1981. Pp. 61–79.

Frye, Roland Mushat. '"Looking Before and After": The Use of Visual Evidence and Symbolism for Interpreting Hamlet'. *Huntington Library Quarterly* 45 (1982) 1–19.

Fulwood, William, trans. *The Enimie of Idlenesse.* London, 1568.

Furman, Erna. *A Child's Parent Dies: Studies in Childhood Bereavement.* New Haven, 1974.

Gairdner, James, ed. *Letters and Papers, Foreign and Domestic, of the Reign of Henry VIII.* Vol. 12, part 2. London, 1891.

Gascoigne, George. *The Droome of Doomes day.* In *The Complete Works.* Vol. 2. Ed. John W. Cunliffe. Cambridge, 1910.

Giraldi, Lilio Gregorio. *De Deis Gentium: Basel 1548.* New York, 1976.

Gomersall, Robert. *Poems.* London, 1633.

Gorer, Geoffrey. *Death, Grief, and Mourning.* New York, 1965.

Gorges, Sir Arthur. *The Poems of Sir Arthur Gorges.* Ed. Helen Estabrook Sandison. Oxford, 1954.

Greaves, Richard L. *Society and Religion in Elizabethan England.* Minneapolis, 1981.

Greenblatt, Stephen. *Renaissance Self-Fashioning: From More to Shakespeare.* Chicago, 1980.

Grose, Christopher. 'Lucky Words: Process of Speech in *Lycidas*'. *Journal of English and Germanic Philology* 70 (1971) 383–403.

Guarducci, Margherita. 'Due note su Kleobis e Biton'. In *Studi in onore di Ugo Enrico Paoli.* Florence, 1956. Pp. 365–76.

Hardie, Colin, ed. *Vitae Vergilianae Antiquae.* 2nd ed. Oxford, 1967.

Hardison, O. B., Jr. *The Enduring Monument: A Study of the Idea of*

Praise in Renaissance Literary Theory and Practice. Chapel Hill, 1962.

Harington, Henry, ed. *Nugae Antiquae: Being a Miscellaneous Collection of Original Papers in Prose and Verse ... by Sir John Harington ... and others.* London, 1769.

Harris, Duncan, and Nancy L. Steffen, 'The Other Side of the Garden: An Interpretive Comparison of Chaucer's *Book of the Duchess* and Spenser's *Daphnaida'. The Journal of Medieval and Renaissance Studies* 8 (1978) 17–36.

Harrison, Thomas Perrin, ed., and Leon, Harry Joshua, trans. *The Pastoral Elegy: An Anthology.* New York, 1968.

Hegendorff, Christopher. *Methodus conscribendi epistolas.* In *D. Erasmi Roterdami opus de conscribendis epistolis.* Antwerp, 1565.

Herbert, George. *The Works of George Herbert.* Ed. F. E. Hutchinson. Oxford, 1941.

Hill, Christopher. 'Sex, Marriage, and the Family in England'. *Economic History Review* 31 (1978) 450–63.

Hill, John. *The Young Secretary's Guide.* 8th ed. London, 1697.

Hone, Ralph E. '"The Pilot of the *Galilean* Lake"'. *Studies in Philology* 56 (1959) 55–61.

Hooker, Richard. *Of the Laws of Ecclesiastical Polity Book V.* Ed. W. Speed Hill. Cambridge, 1977.

Hoole, Charles. *The Masters Method.* In *A New Discovery of the old Art of Teaching Schoole.* Ed. E. T. Campagnac. Liverpool, 1913.

Hornbeak, Katherine Gee. 'The Complete Letter Writer in English, 1568–1800'. *Smith College Studies in Modern Languages* vol. 15, nos. 3–4 (1934).

Hoskins, John. *Directions for Speech and Style.* Ed. Hoyt H. Hudson. Princeton, 1935.

Howard, Henry, Earl of Surrey. *The Works of Henry Howard Earl of Surrey and of Sir Thomas Wyatt the Elder.* Vol. 1. Ed. Geo. Fred. Nott. London, 1815.

The Poems of Henry Howard, Earl of Surrey. Ed. Frederick Morgan Padelford. Rev. ed. Seattle, 1928.

'The Poetry of Henry Howard, Earl of Surrey'. Ed. Charles Ellison Wickert. Diss. Washington University, 1960.

Poems. Ed. Emrys Jones. Oxford, 1964.

Hudson, Hoyt Hopewell. *The Epigram in the English Renaissance.* Princeton, 1947.

Huntington, Richard, and Peter Metcalf. *Celebrations of Death: The Anthropology of Mortuary Ritual.* Cambridge, 1979.

Hyperius, Andreas. *The Practis of Preaching.* Trans. John Ludham. London, 1577.

Javitch, Daniel. *Poetry and Courtliness in Renaissance England.* Princeton, 1978.

Jayne, Sears. *Library Catalogues of the English Renaissance.* Berkeley, 1956.

Jentoft, C. W. 'Surrey's Five Elegies: Rhetoric, Structure, and the Poetry of Praise'. *PMLA* 91 (1976) 23–32.

Bibliography

Jerome. *Omnium Operum Divi Hieronymi Stridonensis Tomus Secundus.* Ed. Desiderius Erasmus. Basel, 1516.

Sancti Eusebii Hieronymi Epistulae. Ed. I. Hilberg. Vienna, 1910–18.

Jewel, John. *An Exposition vpon the two Epistles of the Apostle Sainct Paule to the Thessalonians.* London, 1583.

Johann, Horst-Theodor. *Trauer und Trost: Eine quellen- und strukturanalytische Untersuchung der philosophischen Trostschriften über den Tod.* Munich, 1968.

Jonson, Ben. *Ben Jonson.* 11 vols. Ed. C. H. Herford, Percy and Evelyn Simpson. Oxford, 1925–52.

Justa Edovardo King: A Facsimile Edition of the Memorial Volume in which Milton's 'Lycidas' First Appeared. Ed. Edward Le Comte. N.p., 1978.

Kassel, Rudolf. *Untersuchungen zur griechischen und römischen Konsolationsliteratur.* Munich, 1958.

Kay, W. David. 'The Christian Wisdom of Ben Jonson's "On My First Sonne"'. *Studies in English Literature 1500–1900* 11 (1971) 125–36.

Keynes, Sir Geoffrey. *A Bibliography of Henry King D. D. Bishop of Chichester.* London, 1977.

Kerrigan, William. 'The Heretical Milton: From Assumption to Mortalism'. *English Literary Renaissance* 5 (1975) 125–66.

King, Henry. *A Sermon Preached at the Funeral of the R' Reverend Father in God Bryan, Lord Bp. of Winchester.* London, 1662.

The Poems of Henry King. Ed. Margaret Crum. Oxford, 1965.

Kirkconnell, Watson. *Awake the Courteous Echo: The Themes and Prosody of 'Comus', 'Lycidas', and 'Paradise Regained' in World Literature with Translations of the Major Analogues.* Toronto, 1973.

Kirsch, Arthur. 'Hamlet's Grief'. *ELH* 48 (1982) 17–36.

Kleinknecht, Hermann. *Die Gebetsparodie in der Antike.* Stuttgart, 1937.

Kronenfeld, J. Z. 'The Father Found: Consolation Achieved Through Love in Ben Jonson's "On My First Sonne"'. *Studies in Philology* 75 (1978) 64–83.

Labriolle, Pierre de. 'Apatheia'. In *Mélanges de philologie, de littérature et d'histoire anciennes offerts à Alfred Ernout.* Paris, 1940. Pp. 215–23.

Lambert, Ellen Zetzel. *Placing Sorrow: A Study of the Pastoral Elegy Convention from Theocritus to Milton.* Chapel Hill, 1976.

Landy, Marcia. 'Language and Mourning in "Lycidas"'. *American Imago* 30 (1973) 294–312.

la Serre, Puget de. *The Secretary in Fashion.* Trans. John Massinger, London, 1640.

Latimer, Hugh. *Certayn Godly Sermons, made vppon the lords Prayer ... before ... Lady Katherine, Duches of Suffolke, in the yeare of our Lorde. 1553.* London, 1562.

Lattimore, Richmond. *Themes in Greek and Latin Epitaphs.* Urbana, 1962.

Bibliography

Lausberg, Heinrich. *Handbuch der literarischen Rhetorik: Eine Grundlegung der Literaturwissenschaft.* 2nd ed. Munich, 1973.

Lewalski, Barbara Kiefer. *Donne's 'Anniversaries' and the Poetry of Praise: The Creation of a Symbolic Mode.* Princeton, 1973.

Lewis, C. S. *English Literature in the Sixteenth Century Excluding Drama.* Oxford, 1954.

Lindemann, Erich. 'Symptomatology and Management of Acute Grief'. In *Death and Identity.* Rev. ed. Ed. Robert Fulton. Bowie, Maryland, 1976. Pp. 210–21.

Long, A. A. *Hellenistic Philosophy: Stoics, Epicureans, Sceptics.* New York, 1974.

Lucas, Hans. 'Recusatio'. In *Festschrift Johannes Vahlen zum siebenzigsten Geburtstag.* Berlin, 1900. Pp. 319–33.

Lyly, John. *The Complete Works.* Ed. R. Warwick Bond. Oxford, 1902.

MacDonald, Michael. *Mystical Bedlam: Madness, Anxiety, and Healing in Seventeenth-Century England.* Cambridge, 1981.

Macfarlane, Alan. Review of Stone. *History and Theory* 18 (1979) 103–26.

Macropedius, Georgius. *Methodus de conscribendis epistolis.* London, 1609.

Madsen, William. *From Shadowy Types to Truth: Studies in Milton's Symbolism.* New Haven, 1968.

Magdalen College, Oxford. *Luctus Posthumus sive erga Defunctum illustrissimum Henricem Walliae Principem.* Oxford, 1612.

Markham, Gervase. *Hobsons Horse-load of Letters.* 2nd ed. London, 1617.

Marot, Clément. *Oeuvres lyriques.* Ed. C. A. Mayer. London, 1964.

Marotti, Arthur F. 'All About Jonson's Poetry'. *ELH* 39 (1972) 208–37.

Marston, John. *Antonio's Revenge: The Second Part of Antonio and Mellida.* Ed. G. K. Hunter. Lincoln, 1965.

Martz, Louis L. *Poet of Exile: A Study of Milton's Poetry.* New Haven, 1980.

Masson, David. *The Life of John Milton: Narrated in Connexion with the Political, Ecclesiastical, and Literary History of His Time.* 2nd ed. London, 1881.

Menander. *Menander Rhetor.* Ed. D. A. Russell and N. G. Wilson. Oxford, 1981.

Merrill, L. R. *The Life and Poems of Nicholas Grimald.* New Haven, 1925.

Milton, John. *Poems of Mr. John Milton, Both English and Latin, Compos'd at several times.* London, 1645.

   Paradise Regain'd ... To which is added Samson Agonistes: And Poems upon Several Occasions. Ed. Thomas Newton. London, 1752.

   Poems Upon Several Occasions, English, Italian, and Latin. Ed. Thomas Warton. London, 1785. 2nd ed. London, 1791.

   Paradise Regained, The Minor Poems, and Samson Agonistes. Ed. Merritt Y. Hughes. New York, 1937.

Bibliography

John Milton's Complete Poetical Works Reproduced in Photographic Facsimile. Vol. 1. Ed. Harris Francis Fletcher. Urbana, 1943.

Complete Prose Works of John Milton. Gen. ed. Don M. Wolfe. New Haven, 1953– .

The Complete Poetry of John Milton. Rev. ed. Ed. John T. Shawcross. New York, 1971.

More, Thomas. *Utopia.* Ed. Edward Surtz and J. H. Hexter. New Haven, 1965.

Murphy, Avon Jack. 'The Critical Elegy of Earlier Seventeenth-Century England'. *Genre* 5 (1972) 75–105.

Nathan, Leonard. 'The Course of a Particular: Surrey's Epitaph on Thomas Clere and the Fifteenth-Century Lyric Tradition'. *Studies in English Literature, 1500–1900* 17 (1977) 1–12.

Nevill, Alexander, ed. *Academiae Cantabrigiensis Lachrymae Tumulo Nobilissimi Equitis, D. Philippi Sidneij Sacratae.* London, 1587. Facsimile in Colaianne and Godshalk.

New College, Oxford. *Peplus. Illustrissimi Viri D. Philippi Sidnaei Supremus Honoribus Dicatus.* Oxford. London, 1587. Facsimile in Colaianne and Godshalk.

Norden, Eduard. *Agnostos Theos: Untersuchungen zur Formengeschichte religiöser Rede.* 6th ed. Stuttgart, 1974.

Ogilvie, R. M. *A Commentary on Livy: Books 1–5.* Oxford, 1970.

Oram, William. '*Daphnaida* and Spenser's Later Poetry'. *Spenser Studies* 2 (1981) 141–58.

Oxford University. *Exequiae Illustrissimi Equitis, D. Philippi Sidnaei.* Oxford, 1587. Facsimile in Colaianne and Godshalk.

Eidyllia in obitum fulgentissimi Henrici. Oxford, 1612.

Iusta Oxoniensium. Oxford, 1612.

Epithalamia, sive Lusus Palatini. Oxford, 1613.

Iusta Funebria Ptolemaei Oxoniensis Thomae Bodleii Equitis Aurati. Oxford, 1613.

Camdeni Insignia. Oxford, 1624.

Oxoniensis Academiae Parentalia. Sacratissimae Memoriae potentissimi Monarchae Iacobi ... dicata. Oxford, 1625.

Parker, Matthew. *A Funerall Sermon ... Preached at S. Maries in Cambridge, Anno 1551, at the buriall of ... Martin Bucer.* Trans. Thomas Newton. London, 1587.

Parker, William Riley. *Milton: A Biography.* Oxford, 1968.

Parkes, Colin Murray. *Bereavement: Studies of Grief in Adult Life.* New York, 1972.

Paulinus. *Sancti Pontii Meropii Paulini Nolani Carmina.* Ed. G. Hartel. Vienna, 1894.

Sancti Pontii Meropii Paulini Nolani Epistulae. Ed. G. Hartel. Vienna, 1894.

Pearlman, E. 'Ben Jonson: An Anatomy'. *English Literary Renaissance* 9 (1979) 364–93.

Pecheux, Mother M. Christopher. 'The Dread Voice in *Lycidas*'. *Milton Studies* 9 (1976) 221–41.

Bibliography

Pépin, Jean. *Mythe et allégorie: Les origines greques et les contestations judéo-chrétiennes.* Nouvelle éd. Paris, 1976.

Peterson, Douglas L. *The English Lyric from Wyatt to Donne: A History of the Plain and Eloquent Styles.* Princeton, 1966.

Phist., W., trans. *The Welspring of wittie Conceites.* London, 1584.

Pigman, G. W., III. 'Versions of Imitation in the Renaissance'. *Renaissance Quarterly* 33 (1980) 1–32.

Pilkington, James. *A Godlie Exposition upon certaine chapters of Nehemiah.* Cambridge, 1842.

Pollock, George H. 'Mourning and Adaptation'. *International Journal of Psycho-Analysis* 42 (1961) 341–61.

Pontanus, Jacobus. *Symbolarum Libri XVII Virgilii: Augsburg 1599.* 3 vols. Facsimile ed. New York, 1976.

Poole, Matthew. *Annotations upon the Holy Bible ... Vol. II. Being a Continuation of Mr. 'Pool's' Work by certain Judicious and Learned Divines.* London, 1685.

Puttenham, George. *The Arte of English Poesie.* Ed. Gladys Doidge Willock and Alice Walker. Cambridge, 1939.

R., M. *A President for Young Pen-Men.* London, 1615.

Rainolde, Richard. *The Foundacion of Rhetorike.* Facsimile ed. Francis Johnson. New York, 1945.

Reed, A. W. 'Nicholas Udall and Thomas Wilson'. *Review of English Studies* 1 (1925) 275–83.

Rifkin, Myra. 'Burial, Funeral and Mourning Customs in England 1558–1662'. Diss. Bryn Mawr, 1977.

Rist, J. M. *Stoic Philosophy.* Cambridge, 1969.

Robertson, Jean. *The Art of Letter Writing: An Essay on the Handbooks Published in England During the Sixteenth and Seventeenth Centuries.* London, 1942.

Rollins, Hyder Edward, ed. *Tottel's Miscellany (1557–1587).* Rev. ed. Cambridge, 1965.

Rollock, Robert. *In epistolam Pauli apostoli ad Thessalonices priorem Commentarius.* Edinburgh, 1598.
Lectures Vpon the First and Second Epistles of Paul to the Thessalonians. Edinburgh, 1606.

Rosenblatt, Jason P. 'The Angel and the Shepherd in *Lycidas*'. *Philological Quarterly* 62 (1983) 252–58.

Røstvig, Maren-Sofie. *The Hidden Sense.* Oslo, 1963.

Ruether, Theodor. *Die sittliche Forderung der Apatheia in den beiden ersten christlichen Jahrhunderten und bei Klemens von Alexandrien: Ein Beitrag zur Geschichte des christlichen Vollkommenheitsbegriffes.* Freiburg im Breisgau, 1949.

Rutter, Joseph. *The Shepheards Holy-Day.* London, 1635.

Sacks, Peter. 'Where Words Prevail Not: Grief, Revenge, and Language in Kyd and Shakespeare'. *ELH* 49 (1982) 576–601.

Saulnier, Verdun L. 'L'oraison funèbre au XVIᵉ siècle'. *Bibliothèque d'Humanisme et de Renaissance* 10 (1948) 124–55.

Scaliger, Julius Caesar. *Poetices Libri Septem: Faksimile-Neudruck der Ausgabe von Lyon 1561.* Ed. August Buck. Stuttgart, 1964.

Schlüter, Kurt. *Die Englische Ode.* Bonn, 1964.

Schmidt, A. J. 'Thomas Wilson, Tudor Scholar-Statesman', *Huntington Library Quarterly* 20 (1957) 205–18.

'Thomas Wilson and the Tudor Commonwealth: An Essay in Civic Humanism'. *Huntington Library Quarterly* 23 (1959) 49–60.

Schur, Max. 'Discussion of Dr. John Bowlby's Paper'. *The Psychoanalytic Study of the Child* 15 (1960) 63–84.

Sclater, William. *An Exposition with Notes vpon the first Epistle to the Thessalonians.* London, 1619.

Shakespeare, William. *Coriolanus.* Ed. Philip Brockbank. London, 1976.

Shawcross, John T. 'Establishment of a Text of Milton's Poems Through a Study of *Lycidas*'. *Papers of the Bibliographical Society of America* 56 (1962) 317–31.

Milton 1732–1802: The Critical Heritage. London, 1972.

Sidney, Mary. *The Triumph of Death and Other Unpublished and Uncollected Poems by Mary Sidney, Countess of Pembroke (1561–1621).* Ed. G. F. Waller. Salzburg, 1977.

Siggins, Lorraine D. 'Mourning: A Critical Survey of the Literature'. *International Journal of Psycho-Analysis* 47 (1966) 14–25.

Simpson, Percy. 'The Bodleian Manuscripts of Henry King'. *Bodleian Quarterly Record* 5 (1926–29) 324–40.

Smith, Hallet. 'The Use of Conventions in Spenser's Minor Poems'. In *Form and Convention in the Poetry of Edmund Spenser: Selected Papers from the English Institute.* Ed. William Nelson. New York, 1961. Pp. 121–45.

Smith, Peter L. '*Lentus in Umbra*: A Symbolic Pattern in Vergil's *Eclogues*'. *Phoenix* 19 (1965) 298–304.

Southwell, Robert. *The Triumphs ouer Death.* London, 1595.

Spenser, Edmund. *Poetical Works.* Ed. J. C. Smith and E. de Selincourt. Oxford, 1912.

The Works of Edmund Spenser: A Variorum Edition. Vol. 7. Ed. Charles Grosvenor Osgood and Henry Gibbons Lotspeich. Baltimore, 1943.

Stock, Richard. *The Churches Lamentation for the losse of the Godly.* London, 1614.

Stone, Lawrence. *The Family, Sex and Marriage in England 1500–1800.* New York, 1977.

Review of MacDonald. *The New York Review of Books*, 16 December 1982.

Strype, John, ed. *Ecclesiastical Memorials.* Vol. 3. Oxford, 1822.

Sutton, Christopher. *Disce mori. Learne to Die.* London, 1600.

Sylvester, Richard S., ed. *English Seventeenth-Century Verse.* Vol. 2. New York, 1974.

The Anchor Anthology of Sixteenth Century Verse. New York, 1974.

Tayler, Edward W. '*Lycidas* Yet Once More'. *Huntington Library Quarterly* 41 (1978) 103–17.

Tertullian. *De patientia.* Ed. J. G. Ph. Borleffs. In *Quinti Septimi Florentis Tertulliani Opera, Pars I.* Turnhout, 1954.

Thomas, Keith. Review of Stone. *TLS*, 21 October 1977, 1226–27.

Tourneur, Cyril, John Webster, and Thomas Heywood. *Three Elegies on the most lamented death of Prince Henrie*. London, 1613.

Tromley, Frederic B. 'Surrey's Fidelity to Wyatt in "Wyatt Resteth Here"'. *Studies in Philology* 57 (1980) 376–87.

Trollope, Anthony. *An Autobiography*. Oxford, 1923.

Turner, Alberta T. 'Milton and the Convention of the Academic Miscellanies', *Yearbook of English Studies* 5 (1975) 86–93.

Verepaeus, Simon. *De epistolis Latine conscribendis libri V*. Wittenberg, 1599.

Vergil, Polydore. *Adagiorum Liber. Eiusdem de inuentoribus rerum libri octo*. Basel, 1521.

Virgil. *P. Vergili Maronis Aeneidos Liber Quartus*. Ed. A. S. Pease. Cambridge, 1935.

   P. Vergili Maronis Aeneidos Liber Quintus. Ed. R. D. Williams. Oxford, 1960.

von Moos, Peter. *Consolatio: Studien zur mittellateinischen Trostliteratur über den Tod und zum Problem der christlichen Trauer*. 4 vols. Munich, 1971–72.

W., I., Gent. *A Speedie Post With certaine New Letters*. 2nd ed. London, 1629.

Wallerstein, Ruth. *Studies in Seventeenth-Century Poetic*. Madison, 1950.

Wankel, Hermann. '"Alle Menschen Müssen Sterben": Variationen eines Topos der griechischen Literatur'. *Hermes* 111 (1983) 129–54.

Weitzmann, Francis White. 'Notes on the Elizabethan *Elegie*'. *PMLA* 50 (1935) 435–43.

Werdmüller, Otto. *A moste fruitefull, pithie, and learned treatise, how a Christian man ought to behaue himselfe in the daunger of death*. Trans. Miles Coverdale. London, [1574].

West, M. L., ed. *Iambi et Elegi Graeci*. Vol. 1. Oxford, 1971.

West, Michael. 'The *Consolatio* in Milton's Funeral Elegies'. *Huntington Library Quarterly* 34 (1971) 233–49.

Whetstone, George. *Sir Phillip Sidney, his honorable life, his valiant death, and true vertues*. London, [1587]. Facsimile in Colaianne and Godshalk.

White, Helen C. *English Devotional Literature [Prose] 1600–1640*. Madison, 1931.

Whitgift, John. *The Defense of the Aunswere to the Admonition, against the Replie of T. C.* London, 1574.

Wilson, Elkin Calhoun. *Prince Henry and English Literature*. Ithaca, 1946.

Wilson, Thomas, ed. *Vita et obitus duorum fratrum Suffolciensium, Henrici et Caroli Brandoni*. London, 1551.

   The Arte of Rhetorique (1553). Facsimile ed. Robert Hood Bowers. Gainesville, 1962.

Wimmel, Walter. *Kallimachos im Rom: Die Nachfolge seines apologetischen Dichtens in der Augusteerzeit*. Wiesbaden, 1960.

Bibliography

Wittreich, Joseph Anthony, Jr. *Visionary Poetics: Milton's Tradition and His Legacy.* San Marino, 1979.

Wolfenstein, Martha. 'How Is Mourning Possible?' *The Psychoanalytic Study of the Child* 21 (1966) 93–123.

'Loss, Rage, and Repetition'. *The Psychoanalytic Study of the Child* 24 (1969) 432–60.

Woodhouse, A. S. P., and Douglas Bush, eds. *A Variorum Commentary on The Poems of John Milton.* Vol. 2. New York, 1972.

Wright, Louis B. *Middle-Class Culture in Elizabethan England.* Chapel Hill, 1935.

Wrigley, E. A., and R. S. Schofield. *The Population History of England 1541–1871.* Cambridge, 1981.

INDEX

179

Index

Index